ART OF THE WORLD

NON-EUROPEAN CULTURES

THE HISTORICAL, SOCIOLOGICAL

AND RELIGIOUS BACKGROUNDS

China boasts a proud and ancient tradition of art and civilisation, a tradition which has never been interrupted or lost its vitality. Her gifts to the world are many; porcelain and silk, lacquer, paper and tea, wisdom, poetry and enlightenment. We all marvel at her and praise her, and many of us love her, but hardly anyone realises how little we actually know about her, or how one-sided what little knowledge we have still is. There are still immense reserves of works of art and of books to be revealed. Excavations in the last few years have greatly deepened our knowledge, but the earth yet holds great hoards of treasures. There are many blank areas on our maps of Chinese art history, and many gaps in our tables of historical development. For hundreds of years, hundreds of learned men have been working on the art history of Europe and the Mediterranean lands, but such studies are only just beginning in the lands outside Europe. There are indeed introductions to the study of Chinese art, and books providing a general survey of the subject; and it is an ever fascinating task to sketch the general picure again and help to fill it out. But there are very few really reliable fundamental publications, from which to establish a solid basis of knowledge as a foundation on which further work can be based. Even museum catalogues are inadequate. The great number of special studies of matters that are clearly of subsidiary importance, give the false impression that the main facts are often astray in a wide open sea. That is the joy and grief for all who try to make progress in the study of art outside Europe. One is continually faced with the unknown waiting for some discoverer to bring it to life. So this book cannot and does not attempt to give a final picture, or even a systematic account, of Chinese art. My endeavour is to make the best out of what is now possible, to avoid what has often been reproduced before, and to take advantage of coloured illustrations to call attention to things less well-known. Such illustrations, it is hoped, will make the beholder long to see the things themselves and handle them. I take this opportunity to offer my sincerest thanks to all those experts, collectors, men of learning and institutions whose friendly help has lightened my task. They will all agree — museums were indeed founded because of this belief and live by it — that only the original itself can reveal the full value of a work of art.

If an account of three millenia of high aesthetic achievement is to be compressed into a few pages with a small number of illustrations, obviously one must stick to restricted basic themes. Here my first care has been to try to grasp the spirit of each successive epoch. An epoch is not quite the same thing as a period. Its boundaries may spread over a wide expanse of time. It begins with a genius, a thought, or an event which gives a new turn to creative activity, and it lasts until a new epoch begins. There are no hard and fast boundaries in the matter. Old ideas may linger on, and there may have been anticipations of the new before their time. But each epoch has its own peculiar conception of reality and of tradition, and creates its individual spirit. It can be most easily and surely understood by looking to the state of society. Statistics, which can say nothing about individuals, are useful in measuring the state of society. Society carries art along with it, and often destroys the artist who will not abide by the rules of the game; afterwards it is sorry for him. This is not the place to enter into the question of the relationship between society and the individual, or the question whether society creates consciousness, or consciousness society. Consciousness by itself is not spirit, certainly not in the field of art. But there are hierarchies of rank in the domain of the spirit, and many who have given their attention to this question, have come to the conclusion that the Chinese spirit and Chinese art are the most cultivated to which humanity has yet attained. One can only touch on that question here. But there is one undoubted lesson to be learnt from the history of China and Chinese art; that there are not, and need never be, predestined periods in the life of the spirit and of history. In China the spirit has been alive for three thousand years without interruption; it has never gone under, and does not intend to do so now. If we listen to those who, basing their arguments on mathematical periods, would prove that degeneration is due now, we blur our view of the future and spoil our joy in the art of tomorrow.

WERNER SPEISER

LIST OF ILLUSTRATIONS

ACKNOWLEDGMENTS

We take this opportunity of expressing our sincere thanks to all the people, museums and institutions listed below for their kindness in allowing us to reproduce the works of art mentioned, and more especially for their valuable assistance in correcting the proofs of the plates:

Museum of Asiatic Art		Mr. S. Kawai, Kyoto	44
(loaned by Dr. R. Flaes)	130	British Museum, London	60, 99, 183
Berlin Museum	172	Institute of Arts, Minneapolis	39, 70
Museum of Fine Arts, Boston		Museum of Ethnography, Munich	85
74, 107, 150, 157, 177, 202		Central Asian Antiquities Museum,	
City Art Gallery, Bristol	133, 152	New Delhi	92, 123
The Art Institute (Kate S. Buckingham		Yamato Bunka Museum, Osaka	179
Fund Purchase), Chicago	164/5, 197	Musée Cernuschi, Paris	34, 52
The Art Institute (Lily Maud Buckingham		Musée Guimet, Paris	47, 88, 118, 142, 189
Collection), Chicago	186	National Museum, Peking	68
Museum of Arts and Crafts, Hamburg		University Museum, Philadelphia	66, 115, 160
192, 214, 222		Marquis Maeda, Tokyo	110
Atkins Museum (Nelson Fund),		Freer Gallery of Art, Washington	3, 49
Kansas City	57, 73, 76, 83	Dr. Kurt Herberts, Wuppertal	207
Museum of Far Eastern Art, Cologne	29, 63,	Rietberg Museum, Zürich	137, 163
108, 139, 200/01, 204, 210/11, 216, 218, 222, 225			

PHOTOGRAPHERS

The coloured illustrations listed below were kindly supplied by:

W. Bruggmann, Winterthur	137, 163	J. A. Lavaud, Paris	34, 47, 52, 88, 118, 142, 189
Dr. F. W. Funke, Cologne	195	R. L. Mellema, Amsterdam	130
R. Goldberg, Philadelphia	66, 115, 160	Dr. W. Salchow, Cologne	139, 204
R. Kleinhempel, Hamburg	192, 214, 222	J. Skeel, Orpington	60, 99, 183
Dr. W. Krieger, Cologne		Professor Dr. W. Speiser	44, 92, 123
29, 63, 108, 216, 218, 225, 227			

CONTENTS

(136). Rebellion (138). T'ang architecture (140). Silver and gold work (141). Pottery (144). Tomb figures (145). Sculpture (146). Painting (147). Wu Tao-tse (149). Chung K'uei (151). Lacquer painting (153).

I. INTRODUCTION

The land mass of China between the Pacific and the high mountains of *Geography* Tibet is almost a continent on its own. Peking is over 1200 miles from Canton, that is about the distance from Copenhagen to Palermo, and it is 1100 miles from Shanghai westward to Ch'engtu in the border province of Ssech'uan, roughly the distance from Vienna to Madrid, so the area in which Chinese culture developed is no smaller than Europe, and her civilisation is at least as rich and as varied. This land mass, the domain of the long-established 18 provinces, is divided up by three vast rivers with their tributaries; the Huangho in the north, the Yangtsekiang in the centre, and the Hsikiang in the south. Northern and central China have a more precise boundary in the Huai river which flows parallel to the Yangtse some 100 miles to the north of it, on the same latitude as Baghdad and Tunis. North China is a land of wheat and millet, which flourish in the great dry loess plains. Central China is a rice country with many lakes and streams and flooded fields. South China is a land of mountains and mineral deposits, with inaccessible valleys and places of beauty, stretching into sub-tropical regions.

But this land mass lacks natural boundaries, either external or internal. *Neighbours* Even today there are many great areas of impassable country that have never been opened up and made to form part of a unified system. A great variety of cultures, peoples and languages have never been shaped into uniformity. If one considers the analogous position of Germany in the middle of the continent of Europe, which Tacitus described so accurately in terms that are still relevant, one finds both likenesses to and differences from the Chinese situation. China was never surrounded by powerful peoples whose strong armies tried to add her lands to their own, peoples against whom fear supplied the only boundary. For thousands of years China has been the land of a dominating culture and of a great people who drew other nations to themselves and assimilated all conquerors. Foreign peoples have many times gained dominion over China, but they were never numerous enough to dominate or change the Chinese people, and none of them could think of anything better to do than to become Chinese as quickly as possible. China had nothing to fear in the south. The climate was hot and sultry and the land impassable. But an even greater protection for China lay in the kindly, friendly and undemanding nature of her neighbours. There were times when the Chinese made conquests in

13

the south. Two thousand years ago what is now Vietnam formed part of the Chinese empire. The excavations of the Dong-son culture prove that. But the Chinese did not press these conquests with any great energy. For the most part they found it more convenient to live in friendship with their neighbours, rather than to spend their blood in winning a reputation for martial glory. Occasionally they conquered and ruled their neighbours in the tableland of Tibet. But they left them in peace, and China gave more, in the way of works of art certainly, than she received. It is only now that considerations of power and strategy on the part of a new regime with worldwide ambitions have made life hard for this happy and friendly people.

Dangers Only in the north did serious danger threaten. The wastes and steppes of Mongolia were no more protection to the Chinese than they were to the peoples of the Near East. The steppes are like a sea, but easier and quicker to cross than the ocean, when its peoples are minded to turn against the richer lands of the south. Until quite recent times the changeable climate of the Mongolian and Siberian steppes has made any way of life other than a half-nomadic existence impossible. The herdsmen and hunters of the steppe were always bound to be attracted by the advantages of lands of settled cultivation, even though they had in their own country great store of gold, copper and other riches. And since the nomadic way of life is of its very nature close to the military one and makes a training ground for martial virtues, there was always the possibility, before as well as after Jenghis Khan, than many tribes would come together in greater or smaller bands in order to break into the lands where life was more secure. Now it is certainly easy to depopulate and waste settled land, but the results of doing so are just the opposite of what is wanted. So all the conquerors and conquering peoples who have come from the steppe have quickly allowed themselves to be convinced that it is better to give up their nomadic life than to turn cultivated land into steppe. Therefore everyone who has invaded China, whether Tartar, Tangut, Tangus, Mongol or Turco-mongol, has been at such pains to turn into a Chinese that it now hardly seems worth while to try to sort out the ancient origins of separate peoples by paying attention to linguistic survivals, literary evidence (in which the names are anyhow used very casually), or excavations and skull measurements. The great steppe land from the Amur to the Danube certainly does have much importance for the history of art, but, as far as we are able to get the picture clear, the nomads seem to have been middlemen and patrons (though often patrons with marked tastes of their own), rather than the creators of any new or great art. The Chinese learnt much

14

and took over much from and through them, but not nearly so much as they gave in return.

At present we do not know very much about the state of affairs in old days in Manchuria and East Turkestan, though there must have been times when these provinces were important for Chinese art and the exchange of artistic ideas. But it would not seem that they ever rivalled Korea in independence and creative originality. At times parts of Korea belonged to the Chinese empire, and she was consciously grateful for her ties with China, but she developed so much that was original that one cannot just simply include Korean art as a branch of Chinese. The same is even more true of the Japanese whose art was more independent of China than ever Rome was of Greece.

But who are the Chinese themselves? Certainly they are not a single people. Since the dawn of history they have lived in the land where they now are, and they have grown together and been moulded by the influence of a common language and writing. The Chinese language is composed of monosyllabic words to which a different tone-accent can give entirely different meanings. Mandarin Chinese can be understood throughout the whole land, in spite of many different dialects, at least by the literate. The language is related to those of the Tai group in Siam and Indo-china, but has nothing to do with the Mongolian, Korean or Japanese families of language. These three advantages at least can be claimed for Chinese; it is simple and, for what is worth, is always written the same; it is a witty language lending itself to play on words; aesthetically rhythm counts for most, and it has a peculiar melody of speech that depends much more on rhythm than on sound. Play on words is a constant enrichment of Chinese art. For instance *fu* means a bat, but also, with a different ideogram, luck or a peony; *mao* means a cat but also old age, *lu* means a deer but also riches; *ho* means a quail but also harmony; *p'ing* a vase but also peace and so on. A great many pictures and decorations that illustrate such things either in their immediate beauty or in stylised form, have a meaning that has been obvious to any Chinese since his childhood. Such pictures with their symbolism should bring luck unaided by any hidden magic; their choice and repetition may often strike us as strange and pointless, but they have a deeper meaning. The taste for the ugly, which plays such a part in our accepted tradition, does not exist in China; there, everything unpleasant and annoying is avoided. Even their way of speaking at first rings strange on our ears, until we come to some understanding of the pitch of their words and sentences and their frequent changes of rhythm. Our music, whether in three four time or four four time, strikes a Chinese ear

Language

15

as equally monotonous, and we on our side need some experience before we can tell whether a Chinese poem, which is always sung and never simply recited, is gay or sad.

Writing But the greatest unifying force in China is the writing. Originally the thing intended was drawn with a few lines; two legs meant a man, a triangle the mouth, and a triangle with four lines added, meant speech; a trunk with two branches and roots meant a tree, and so on. 160 basic signs with their various combinations were sufficient to express all that required to be expressed. The ideogram for man combined with that for speech signified "he who keeps to his word", hence truth and faith; the ideograms for mother and child together signified love. Heart and middle together signified the right-acting man, for he "keeps his heart in the right place"; an altar with two men below, three mouths above and rain at the very top, meant spirit or spirits. How clear a picture that gives of prayer for rain, and a thousand other ideograms are just the same today. Chinese, whether written or spoken, is easiest understood if we first consider what picture it is intended to represent. By the same token this picture-writing generally gives no indication of pronunciation. Like Arabic numerals, each sign can be pronounced differently in different languages. The "two legs" may be called *man, l'homme, jen* or *hito* and there will never be any doubt that it is a human being that is intended. And if the sign for man and that for two are put together, then a neighbour or humanity are in question. Chinese would make the best world-script; everyone could read it in his own language, and indeed anyone who knew what the signs meant could understand it without needing to read it. The Japanese have completely taken over this writing with all its beauty; the Koreans and other peoples have evolved their own writing from that basis. There have been changes of pronunciation as well as varieties of dialect in China, but it is still reasonably easy to understand what was written down a thousand or two thousand years ago.

Unlike the Sumerian hieroglyphics which were soon employed in the Middle East for practical economic purposes, Chinese writing was, for eight hundred years, almost exclusively limited to religious uses, the concerns of yesterday and of ancestors. So it kept a strong link with magic for a long time, indeed almost up to the beginning of this century. The oldest inscriptions are short sacred texts that tell us a great deal that is still valid today about Chinese religious conceptions. To put the matter in simple terms, they have no conception of God as creator, almighty and merciful. There are indeed hundreds of gods and demons incorporating every variety of things good or bad, but they are all subject to the same law of cause and

16

effect. They may try to get round this law or to forget about it, but they can never break through it or wilfully alter it. The Chinese call this law *tao,* a word which signifies the way along which all must go, whether gods or men, and from which there is no escape. This conception is very close to the Neoplatonic demiurge, the creator and ruler of the world who is just as subject to the One as the gods of China are to the *tao.* It would be interesting to know for certain whether there really were Neoplatonists in India, who could have introduced this Asiatic idea to the West where no less a man than Goethe held it as true. Nor is this basic conception in any way diluted by ideas concerning the hierarchy of heaven, about the highest god *(shang-ti)* and about Heaven itself *(t'ien)* which, for instance, entrusts the good ruler with his mandate and withdraws it from the bad. Heaven judges and decides, distributes gifts and fates, but its judgement cannot be arbitrary, it cannot prefer mercy to justice. But, in this unlike the Old Testament, it is in no hurry to interfere in small matters and does not threaten terrible dooms: it does distinguish sin from stupidity, sets the balance right again and brings all things, albeit sometimes painfully, back to the right way.

Neither now nor ever before has China known of God's mercy. The ruler indeed bears the mandate of heaven and is called the son of heaven. But in that title there is less of prerogative than of duty and responsibility for all that happens in his empire. His subjects have not only the right, but also the duty, to turn out a ruler who misuses his mandate. And so it came about that there was no priesthood claiming an ex officio sanctity. Priests and their assistants were respectable experts in religious usages, held in regard when their station so warranted, but of little repute if their employment was menial. The emperors too, the heads of families, and later on officials, all, in fact basically everyone, had priestly functions. The Chinese have a very strong feeling for the interrelation of rights and duties, but a very slight sense for any legitimate prerogatives of birth, official position or property. Any prerogative, whether gained by a man or pressed on him, brings with it the corresponding responsibility, be it only the obligation of modesty. Two actual illustrations will perhaps make these conceptions clearer than any abstract generalisations.

At the beginning of the 'Sayings' of Confucius (Lun-yü XX.[1]) there is a prayer attributed, with little historical reason, to T'ang Li the founder of the Shang dynasty. As often happened in China in later days, he had set aside the last unworthy ruler of a degenerate race and founded a new dynasty. He confirmed this act by a sacrifice at which he uttered this prayer: "I, thy little son Li, venture to sacrifice a black bull and to announce to

Religion

17

thee, high and mighty god, that I did not dare to pardon the guilty and did no violence to the rights of thy servant; thy heart must judge. If I have done wrong let not the guilt rest on the lands; if there is wrong in the lands, let the guilt rest on me".

Art From quite a different age comes this short poem of Su Tung-p'o, which shews very clearly how the Chinese conceive of art as the work of heaven and an inspiration which cannot be learnt:

> *He who judges pictures by the likeness of shapes,*
> *Must be thought of as a child;*
> *He who hammers out verse by rule,*
> *Shews that he is not yet a poet.*
> *Poetry and painting are rooted in the same law,*
> *The work of heaven and of the first cause.*

China cannot claim, as India can, to be the classic birthplace of religion, or as Greece, that of philosophy, or as Rome, that of law, but it is certainly, and perhaps in the highest degree, a classic land of morality. Moreover our philosophers are quite right in regarding Chinese "philosophers" as something different from themselves; most of them in fact could be better described as moralists. With all respect to Kant, those who do not know their thoughts and arguments, can hardly have any idea of what morality is and can be. This is not the place to enter on a dissertation about the three fundamentals of Chinese morality, reverence *(hsiao),* responsibility *(hsin)* and humanity *(jen),* but one should briefly indicate how they came to have such great significance in China and what they stand for.

Confucius There were no hard and fast boundaries to the great area in which Chinese civilisation developed. There were no constant external threats, and internally compliance with the orders of feebly evolved political and religious establishments could usually be avoided. So each man needed an inner law to direct his life and behaviour in society. The moral lawgivers of China, Confucius especially, were concerned the whole time to find the right mean between the ideal and the practical, to require what was possible and avoid excessive tension. They knew that every day demanded decisions for which there were no one-sided patent solutions; that it is very easy to demand justice from others, but hard to perform it oneself. So they recommend, when possible, not to want to control and alter everything oneself, not to force one's way *(wu wei),* but to let things grow naturally and yet, when necessary, to make firm decisions and stand by them. They advised against desiring to do everything anew and better, but rather to test and learn why the ancients had not done things differently. "The truth was

18

found out long ago... stick to the ancient truth". That is as much a maxim of China as of Goethe. However the *wu wei*, the "do nothing", is completely different from quietism or fatalism: Chinese conservatism has no immobility or stubborness about it. The symbol of the perfect Chinese is the bamboo, which is elastic and strong, bends in no slavish way, but bears the strength of any storm and the weight of any burden, at once springs back straight again and is as it was before. That which is stubborn, forceful and brutal does not attract the Chinese, but rather that which is enduring, patient and diplomatic. For this reason the Chinese do not esteem soldiers, and regard wars as natural catastrophies, the only good result of which can be the peace that follows them. One wonders what Li Hung-chang thought when he sought out the great statesman Bismarck at Friedrichsruh, asked his advice, and was told that this was the most essential: as China was a continental power, she must before everything else have a strong army to ensure order within and peace without.

It took half a century before the Chinese became convinced that, in the context of our own day, Bismarck was right. Confucius thought otherwise. Once two of his former pupils came to him for advice. They had become the advisers of a prince who wanted to annex a small country on the pretext that that would avoid threatened unrest. The master answered by quoting and commenting upon this folksong about a prince:

> *It does not matter that his people are poor,*
> *It only matters that there is no inequality;*
> *It does not matter that they are but few,*
> *It only matters that they live in peace.*

"And in fact, when everything is divided evenly, no one is poor: where harmony prevails, numbers are not short. So if distant people do not wish to join up with us, we must induce them by education and virtue to wish to come, and, if they do so, we must give them peace, and where peace is, there is no rebellion". These sentences are exemplary of the Chinese moral and cultural approach; not to seek for the guilt in others, but first of all in oneself; not to want to improve others and make them happy, but to persuade them that one has something to give oneself; not to suppress and rob them, but to offer and educate; not to talk about virtues, but to show them in act. Moreover Confucius who is so often misrepresented as a moral prig and pedantic master of ceremonies, was among other things a man of aesthetic perception who knew what art was and what was its function in society. He loved and practised music; he loved songs and felt their power and seduction. One of his maxims contains all that China

19

has to say about the True, the Good and the Beautiful (Lun-yü VII. 6):

Fix your mind on the way,
Prove yourself in virtue,
Direct your attention to humanity,
Raise yourself to the beautiful.

Practice One can praise or be critical of Chinese theories of morality, religion and aesthetics, but when one looks at the fruits of their teaching, no defence is needed. They have preserved and sustained a society of hundreds of millions of men throughout three thousand years. They have shaped a culture which until the 13th century A.D. was superior to all others, and which may have been equalled, but has never been surpassed by others since then. Finally it was China which in the 17th century, after the frightful waste and carnage of the Thirty Years war, was the first influence towards our age of enlightenment; she gave Europe the conception of rationalism, of which the latter made such doubtful use. Meanwhile China went on her way with quiet spring and life. There is no doubt that in the future too China will be one of the most fruitful motherlands of culture, and the only one in the world with an unbroken continuity of development.

China is not among the very oldest civilisations in the world. Egypt and Mesopotamia came before her; the Mediterranean lands and Persia have at times outshone her: but none of those peoples has enjoyed such a steady and lively growth as China. There have indeed been wars, murders and atrocities in Chinese history too, but none of the full-scale catastrophes that overwhelmed other civilisations either completely or for hundreds of years on end. Many reasons have been given to explain this fact. The conservatism of the Chinese, their respect for old people and for ancestors has been seen as a perpetual guarantee of the dignity and antiquity of their civilisation, while conversely, their practical, pragmatic sense has been criticised as materialistic. But this argument overlooks the fact that the Chinese are much less concerned than we are with the preservation of the evidences of permanence and antiquity, for with all their respect for the ancients they love life and are more at pains to serve the living than the dead. There are no pyramids or towers of Babel in China, no Acropolis, no Parthenon and no massive castles. The oldest building above ground is the pagoda at Sung-shan which only dates from 530 A.D. How does this phenomenon fit in with the general conservatism of the Chinese? Two thousand years ago there were splendid palaces; we have descriptions of them. They were not just built of wood and tiles with frescoes and sculpture and painted carvings, but buildings in which marble and gold and other enduring materials were used. But its antiquity was never regarded as a reason for looking after a building. The Chinese have no respect for buildings. When they fell down or were destroyed, the local inhabitants came like ants and carried off any material that could be turned to use for the needs of the living. It is almost impossible to believe how quickly and completely a building in China is pulled down, when no one takes care of it. Even now one can hardly attempt to write a satisfactory history of Chinese architecture, in spite of all the painstaking reconstructions based on illustrations, descriptions and the evidence of richly provided subterranean grave chambers. We know that there was great architecture, and fragments from the less ancient periods are preserved. But this branch of art, which is so important in the West, does not attract much attention in China, since there are too few originals preserved to entice one to prolonged study, whereas the supply of other things of beauty and works of art is so vast. This is characteristic of China and provides a key to the understanding of the Chinese approach to such matters and their subtle adaptable ways of thought.

There are important differences between the Chinese and the European approach to aesthetic questions and works of art. Obviously it would be simplifying things down much too much to attempt to generalise in a few lines about the fundamental principles that have been in force for three thousand years, and no one will need to be told that these rules were not ready made at the beginning of history. Of course they developed and became confirmed as time passed, and naturally there are exceptions. Nonetheless one is surprised to observe how firmly these rules, subsequently discovered, have been kept, and how strongly they are rooted in conceptions which are older and more potent than their manifestations in works of art, and are more enduring than the works themselves. Perhaps it is easiest to illustrate this point by imagining that we have undertaken to write an account, not of Chinese art, but of Chinese artists. How different that would be from a history of European or Japanese artists. In Europe we should have to begin with hundreds of sculptors, architects, painters, engravers, goldsmiths etc: in Japan there would also be hundreds of swordsmiths, lacquer masters, netsuke-carvers and others besides. Whereas in China it would be easy to find thousands of biographies of painters, numbering among them emperors, princes, ministers and generals; the handbook or Sun T'o-kung, the first to be used, includes about 25.000 painters alone. Then one would have no trouble in finding out about hundreds of calligraphers, who are not just practitioners of fine writing, but gifted people whose spirit so expressed itself in their writing that they became famous

Aesthetic approach

21

and were accepted as models. But it would be difficult to collect the names of a couple of dozen architects or even a couple of sculptors. Inscriptions and local chronicles do mention architects and workers in the plastic arts, but Chinese art history records no names of men of originality who have created styles or architectural orders which have set a standard for others. There are of course the mythical discoverers of each craft, but no Vitruvius or Palladio, no Phidias or Michelangelo, no outstanding architect, sculptor, goldsmith etc, and hardly a designer as an individual artist; a few lacquer masters, especially if they count as lacquer-painters, a few official heads of the imperial porcelain factories, no textile designers, and incidentally only a few musicians as composers. By our standards the art history of China would seem jejune, but where painters and calligraphers are concerned it is immeasurably rich.

Artists But calligraphy is one great category of art that remains almost a closed book for us. There is hardly anyone in Europe so well informed or so perceptive that he can say for certain whether a given specimen of writing is, or clearly is not, by, say, Chao Meng-fu or Tung Ch'i-ch'ang and done with his own hand. All this shows that the Chinese, though they have no word for it, make a clear distinction between the "free" arts, of which the chief are calligraphy, painting, poetry and music, and the ancillary arts which are bound by workshops, commissions, quantities of material and costs of labour. The practitionens of these are regarded as worthy craftsmen who profit by knowledge that can be taught and have skill and ability to make useful and beautiful things. That is so even though the Chinese potters, for example, not only discovered porcelain, but were the greatest anonymous artists in this medium in all the world. The fine arts were the learned and cultivated amusements of noble spirits, and the high sensitivity of their spiritual nobility was expected to show in every stroke of the brush. It is therefore no chance that portraits and religious pictures, that is to say mostly Buddhist ones, have for many centuries in China not counted as categories of art, for they were too much tied to commissions and to the subject required.

Writing and Painting These conceptions have ancient roots. The links between writing and painting are abundantly clear, for the writing is nothing but a special strictly stylised formula of painting. The select band of those who could write ideograms was very small to begin with, and remained extremely limited until the invention of printing in the 10th century and even right up to the beginning of the modern age. One result of this was that the themes that were considered worthy of pictorial representation remained remarkably few, and indeed until the 5th century B.C. were almost entirely restricted to sacred or semisacred subjects. It was not until the 4th century B.C. that prose and poetry began to come into their own as art forms, and not until the 2nd century B.C. was writing in such general use for mundane purposes that literacy became obligatory for officials. Even now painting and writing remain linked by the fact that they use the same materials, brush, paper and ink. Anyone who learns to write acquires at the same time the fundamental skill with this hands that is required in painting, and must master it even though he has neither gift nor inclination for painting. Not only was writing sacred and full of magic power in Chinese eyes, it was also symbolic of their civilisation. Their most inspired spirits were expected to write not just beautifully but "well" in both senses of the word, both the external form and the inner content and choice of words being alike inspired. This accounts for the great importance attached by Confucius to the learning of songs, so that, in an age when literacy was not widespread, men could learn how to think as well as how to express themselves. Poems that are sung make a deeper impression, and the question how far music shapes speech and ways of thought was clearly present to Confucius in a very practical form, even if he did not consider it from the theoretical angle. With us since Nietzsche and Hofmannsthal the question seems to have been worked to death. If a Chinese were to conceive of an universal work of art, for him it could only mean a picture with an original poem, a poem to be sung, written on the picture in inspired writing. A work therefore that combines writing, painting, poetry and *Poetry* music. A knowledge of poetry and music is still essential for any deeper understanding of Chinese art. To mention only T'ao Yüan-ming's short SEE P. 109 poem about his garden's eastern fence. For fifteen hundred years this poem has provided artists and craftsmen of the whole of Eastern Asia with an inexhaustible theme. It is fair to say that, since the poem was written, no chrysanthemum could be painted, carved, woven or used to decorate porcelain or lacquer, without its evoking an overtone of T'ao Yüan-ming's poem.

We must also remember that there are many things we do not know, which are important for the content of Chinese culture. There is a generally accepted symbolism, so obvious to artist and beholder, and so deep a part of their natural response, that even now no one has yet consciously put it into words. For us the colour white, especially for clothes, is fresh and young and festive. In China, simple and undecorated, it is the colour of mourning. With us a "red rag" excites men as well as bulls to anger, whereas in China it is the colour of happiness and festival. For the Chinese a rose with its thorns is something unfriendly and coarse, and its scent is

23

overpowering. However one cannot say that their art is more dependent on literature than is our own, and one can get a great deal of pleasure out of their works of art without fully understanding them. If one wants to think and feel in Chinese fashion, one must realise that they have from the beginning grasped and developed a form of thinking, speaking and feeling which has long been unfamiliar to us. They think in terms of correlation or polarity. And they do not think in terms of contrasts, "either-or" alternatives, or higher and lower categories. Indeed there are a fair number of Sinologues who assert that the Chinese language is without logic, without grammar, and without words limited to a single meaning. Chinese loves analogies, parallels, modified echoes and symmetrical completion. But it goes further than that. Many ideograms contain in themselves just the opposite of their simple meaning; indeed in China everything holds its own opposite within itself. Thus the ideogram for civilisation, a combination of those for "man" and "do", can either mean high rank, or the falsification of nature, or even simply hypocrisy. A Chinese would see no objection to calling darkness minimum light, and light minimum darkness, nor to calling rest, suspended movement and vice versa. Everything contains some accent of its correlative within itself; a man has a more or less great element of femininity, and a woman of manliness; there is something of death in life, and of life in death. It was in the 4th century B.C. that the Chinese first thought out in a conscious, if speculative, way the nation-wide theory known as *"Ying-yang"*, which depends on the polarities light-dark, earth-heaven, man-woman etc, with their actual and their symbolical associations. This thinking in terms of polarities is fundamentally different from the conception of antithesis in the thought and art of the Near East. There light and dark are at war with one another, whereas in China there is a friendly exchange. There, as A. Moortgat has so clearly explained, life is the wonderful thing, and it is symbolised in plants, in cattle and in domestic animals useful to and protected by man whose life depends on them; death is the enemy, the wild carnivorous animal, the perpetual opponent. In China they are both no more than changing appearances of the same thing, and are subject to the *tao* of becoming and perishing. Su Tung P'o answers the question what is life and what is death thus: "A thousand changes and ten thousand transformations underlie everything and nothing has been assimilated to anything else, but everything that stays in its right place is in harmony with the creative activity of heaven . . ."

Chinese artists have found various symbols for this changefulness which also means eternity for them, and these symbols are frequently used as decoration. The chief of them is a circle divided into light and dark sections, often by an S-curve, which symbolises the Ying-Yang. Besides this the Chinese are fond of inscriptions written on matched pairs of tablets or rolls, pairs of vases, pictures — dyptichs — incense burners etc. The European amateur or collector who separates such a pair, and is content with, or even actually prefers, the single specimen, only shows thereby how little of the Chinese there is in his thought and feeling. But there is a deeper meaning in this thinking in terms of polarities, which has so many outward manifestations. This meaning gives Chinese art its peculiar value. Three thousand years of existence in a boundless continent have driven the Chinese to the conclusion that everything under the sky would be without exception happier, if the Chinese emperor could speak for it all as a sort of Pontifex Maximus in the face of heaven. In this Middle Land people did not worry about boundaries or, in theory, admit that there were any. What they were concerned with was that every thing and every being, and its partner and neighbour should be in its proper place. Now this place depends not on external compulsion, but on inner feeling. How else then can it be found except by measure, the right mean and a polarity that both stretches out beyond itself and comes back into itself? Value is not a question of "having" or "doing" but of "being". Without conscious intention, the greatness of Chinese art lies in the expression of this value.

II. ANTIQUITY

The first glimmerings of our historical knowledge about China at present begin about 1,500 B.C. and the fully historical period about 1,300 B.C. Chinese historians record that the 10th King of the Shang dynasty, Chung-ting who, according to the old chronology, reigned from 1,562—1,549 B.C. but probably in fact about 100 years later, founded a capital at Ao. The site has been identified near the present town of Cheng-chou in Honan, half way between K'ai-feng and Loyang, and excavations started in 1952 are still continuing. It has been possible to trace the line of the rampart of beaten earth twenty yards wide which surrounded the town, a regular oblong a mile and a quarter from north to south, and 1 mile east to west. The area of the town was about 750 acres, so there was room for 10,000 inhabitants or more. Within and without this rampart, remains were found of many different sorts of workshop, bronze foundries with moulds, potter's kilns, places where bones and horn were carved etc. There were also found a few specimens of bronze vessels of similar types to those found in greater numbers and more magnificent examples at Anyang and elsewhere. It was in about the year 1,300 B.C. that P'an-keng, the 17th king of the Shang dynasty, moved the capital nearly 100 miles further to the north-east, and it was this site, close to the modern Anyang, which has been discovered and excavated with such splendid results. Besides the superb bronzes and other works of art, some of them from royal tombs, there were tens of thousands of oracular inscriptions on bone and tortoiseshell. As there are frequent mentions of the names of the kings who ruled there, there can be no doubt that the Shang dynasty really existed, especially the last three hundred years of it at Anyang, though there may be a marginal doubt, of about a hundred years or so, in our calculation of the dates of the reigns of P'an-keng and his successors. The three primary necessities for high civilisation were already there, a city, writing and metal (in this case bronze), and the forms of all these have persisted without fundamental alteration from that day to this. Further excavations may show that they can be traced back longer into prehistory.

Pan-po

Since 1954 excavations have been going on at Pan-po, a place nearly five miles to the east of Hsian-fu in the Wei valley, a town on the site of the famous ancient capital of Ch'ang-an. It is the largest settlement known, older than Ao / Cheng-chou. The settlement covers about 5 acres and dates from neolithic times (probably the third millenium B.C.) no bronze

26

being found there. It provides a broad picture of civilisation in those days. Here too there was a rampart of beaten earth, but whether it was a regular shaped town and how it was laid out, still remains uncertain. It was possible to trace the ground plans of two different types of building close to each other; there were round houses about 16 feet in diameter, and oblong houses measuring 27 by 42 feet. All of them were built of beaten earth and traces of holes for wooden pillars to support the roof were found. The variation in size shows that even then there were rich and poor, and that the chief people in the community liked or needed to have large houses. Their way of life was in general not very demanding; one can guess this from the well-shaped pots, including some larger vessels with bodies running down into a point, which would be good to stick into the bare earth but hard to place on a smooth floor. For decoration there are strange heads and fishes placed singly and unsymmetrically on the pots.

There is no great difference between the houses at Ao and those at Pan-po. *Houses* At Ao too there are moderate sized pit-dwellings which are round, oval or of long irregular shape, which probably were roofed over and which cannot all have served as storehouses. Close to them one finds oblong houses of some 26 by 55 feet, on raised foundations of pressed clay with wooden pillars supporting thatched roofs. The same type is found again a hundred years later at Anyang. There were also fine halls 33 feet by 100 with places for pillars along the length of the walls. The inscriptions found at Anyang, more especially the ideogram for "great", show that there must have been, on the ramparts even if nowhere else, towers of two or more stories with hipped roofs. The exceptionally fine buildings at Anyang and Ao presumably were for the kings and their great ones. There must have been families of property, who were in a position to use the horse drawn warchariots, the most formidable weapon of that day, whose acquisition and support required considerable resources. The great halls may have been used at times both for wordly ceremonies and for religious ones, especially reverence of ancestors, for the oracle inscriptions give evidence of this. No other religious buildings or temples have been found, and it seems unlikely that they will be found.

These are some of the more important facts from which we can start to build a picture of early Chinese civilisation. Excavation only began 35 years ago and the network of uncovered sites is still too thin to provide convincing data; too many of the learned and brilliant hypotheses that have been put forward, may be proved right or wrong by one lucky dig of a spade, and nothing is so thankless as to make a negative assertion which is proved incorrect at the very moment it is made. Conditions at Pan-po

27

must, or may, have been different from those of Shang times; for it is probable that the war-chariot, whose effect in binding society together must have been considerable, was not then known. It is true that bones of horses have been found, but outside the settlement and not in the pits which, it was thought, might have been used as stalls. So it seems too soon to assert that high civilisation in China came to birth on the middle reaches of the Huangho or in the Wei valley. Fine raised houses in rectangular towns protected by ramparts are found for instance in Shantung at Cheng-tz'u-yai. This town measuring 500 by 430 yards belonged to the Lung-shan culture, but it is not quite certain that it is older than Ao or Anyang. As to how things were in the south, in the rich lands of middle China, we know nothing. Excavations have indeed proved the existence and, in part, the location of the Shang dynasty whose name is so famous in the history books. We can make out that there was a king, some sort of aristocracy with war-chariots, and numerous craftsmen in the towns, while the great majority of the population were occupied cultivating the land with plough

Shang dynasty   and hoe. But the Shang kingdom was not the whole of China; it may have been some 280 by 180 miles in extent, and it surely did not exist in a vacuum. It is likely enough that their neighbours too had small agricultural kingdoms with similar organisation, although the historical tradition says nothing about them, and Shang art-forms, especially bronzes, are found beyond the limits of Shang power. That the Shang kings won the reputation of founding the first dynasty of China, after the purely legendary Hsia, seems due to two reasons. They may well have been the first to discover writing and so gain command of a workable means of handing down a tradition. Secondly, later Chinese historians, pledged to a theory of the state which postulated that China had existed as an undivided unity since primaeval times, may have allowed all other traditions to be forgotten, if they did not actually obliterate them. As late as the 3rd century B.C. one finds references to the neighbouring peoples of north-west and central China as "barbarians" who spoke a strange language that could hardly be understood, even when, as in the case of the Ch'u in the Yangtse valley, they were enviably rich. But excavations show that comparatively similar, though not exactly the same, conditions of life and art-forms flourished throughout the country. Some pottery, naturally much more in some places than in others, has been found in all the provinces, and that is the category of art in which the Chinese have always achieved their most individual and exceptional successes, and on which their fame rests.

The extent and quality of Chinese art as early as about 2,000 B.C., more especially pottery, puts it in a class apart from prehistoric cultures anywhere

Two-handled vase handmade without the use of a potter's wheel and painted with unfired colours. The concentric spiral on the body is typical of a neolithic style called after Hsin-tien, the place in Kansu where it was first unearthed. Probably 2nd half of the 2nd millenium B.C. *Museum of Far Eastern Art, Cologne (5 inches high)* else in the world. Apart from some things made of jade, the other objects found need not be mentioned in a history of art. The chipped and polished axes, whorls and weights are much the same as those of any other people learning to control its surroundings, things which are more important for the statistical conclusions to be drawn from thousands of finds, than for any individual worth. They prove that for half a million years, down into the old and the new stone age, China was inhabited and cultivated continuously by one or more autochthonous people. We already have a pretty good picture of how things were in the new stone age, about 2,000 B.C. Of course there was no uniformity of type over the whole land, and we cannot yet make confident assertions about the changing relationships between the various local cultures, identified by their use of different sorts of pottery, black, grey, red, painted and matt, so long as central China, the middle bend of the Yangtse, remains comparatively unexplored. But neolithic pottery is found everywhere in China and it would seem that it was made by an agricultural population. We get the best insight into their art-forms in north China, and they reach a high level. Refined, thin-skinned vessels mostly of black pottery turned on the wheel, excel all others in the purity of their shapes. There are tripods and jugs abstaining from the addition of ornament, which prove that these prehistoric potters had a fine sense of form and that they could be great artists.

The domain of this culture whose homeland is at Lung-shan in Shantung, stretches, with only slight differences in shapes, across the lower Yangtse in the south. To the west the Lung-shan culture borders on that of Hsiao-t'un, so called after the place near Anyang where finds were made. Here the the pottery was usually grey and ornamented with impressions of mats and ropes, often in complicated patterns. The area sprang into importance because the Shang capital was established there about 1,300 B.C., so there is a chance of comparing the potter's forms with those of the bronze vessels. The earlier pottery of this area, though there was no cultural uniformity about it or shame at borrowing from the Lung-shan culture to the east, does actually bear some relationship to bronze forms, especially in the case of tripods, the shape which even today takes central position among vessels for sacred use.

Yang-shao The neolithic "Yang-shao" culture is archaeology's problem child. Yang-shao is to the south of the great bend in the Huangho where the Wei river joins it, about 125 miles west of Anyang. There in 1922 the Swedish geologist Andersson was the first to find evidence of neolithic culture in China, and "Yang-shao" came to be used as a general term for the art of about 2,000 B.C. As it came to be seen that this name was used too generally to cover a diversity of phenomena, some authorities wanted to drop it altogether. But the Chinese cling proudly to the term, and mean by it especially a type of pottery with bright red body and impressed mat patterns and shapes resembling some of those found at Hsiao-t'un. This red pottery is found far to the north throughout Shensi and beyond. But the Chinese also use the term to cover a type of pottery differently decorated from that found in the east. Both around Yang-shao and at Pan-po there are examples of designs asymmetrically placed. These differ so substantially from the pottery painted in many colours that is found in Kansu, that one must make a distinction between the Yang-shao culture near the bend of the Yangtse and that in the northwestern province of Kansu.

Both art-lovers and historians were immediately attracted to the pottery found in Kansu on the upper reaches of the Huangho, and especially in *Many-coloured pottery* the area where its tributary, the T'ao-ho, joins it. There are magnificent bands of decoration and ornamental spirals. Because foreign collectors paid high prices, the poor peasants dug these beautiful pots out of the graves, so that hundreds of them are now scattered and have lost their value for the scientific study of neolithic Chinese art. The clay is leather-brown, and the pots are hand shaped. The surface is smooth and burnished, looking like enamel, with its rich variety of ornament applied with a sure touch in black and red. Huge spirals and interlocking circles are the dominant motifs, but chess-board, 'bottle' patterns and others are used too, either directly and boldly painted on or reserved in the ground between the main designs. Animals and men feature but seldom, and when they do they are painted with less assurance. The most important sub-divisions take their names from excavations at Pan-shan and Ma-ch'ang. Pan-shan covers the jugs, bottles, amphorae and cups of simple and strong shapes that may well date back to the 3rd millenium B.C. From Ma-ch'ang come the later, more elongated and elegant shapes which have obviously been developed from the earlier ones. Now both the outlines of these pots and their ornament show striking similarities with a type of pottery, ornamented with bands of painted or engraved ornament, found throughout the Eurasian continent. It has been found at Anau in western Turkestan, at Tripolje in the Ukraine, at Cucuteni in Rumania, in Bohemia and in Silesia, on the Rhine and on the Maas, to mention only the better known excavations. The similarity is such that a pre-historian, familiar with Europe only, would never guess that they were Chinese. So naturally enough there is talk of migrations of peoples, of cultural exchanges and world-embracing relationships back in the stone age. The Chinese on the other hand argue that it has been proved that these great vessels were used by a settled agricultural society, and could not have been carried by animals wandering with nomads from land to land. They also point out that there is no conclusive evidence that the comparable types in Europe and in Asia date from the same time, that there were differences in the structure of society, and finally that the Kansu pottery apparently remained in use much longer than the other types of pottery with bands of decoration, probably, with some changes, down to the end of the 2nd millenium B.C. I only mention these resemblances and differences to show that it is an important but difficult problem in the history of art. From the Maas to the T'ao-ho band-decoration is always associated with settled agricultural societies; if they were clever enough to seek out the best bits of land and the rich loess soil, why should it not be possible for peasants to learn and take things over one from another, for pleasure as well as use, without a thought about racial origin or language? There is no need every time to invent hypotheses involving migrations and conquests, at least not on a great scale. Moreover in Kansu as in the rest of China, apart from a few exceptions of which Buddhist monks in later ages are the most notable, the dead were buried and not burnt, as was the rule at Tripolje, for instance, and at other places. Anyone with an ear for the niceties of technical language will notice at once the hasty misunderstanding that is involved when collectors or men of learning refer to the beautiful vases of Pan-shan or Ma-ch'ang type as "urns". Certainly vases of similar forms were used in Europe as urns for the ashes of the dead. But the conclusion does not follow that they had the same use in China. They were indeed put in graves with the dead and the bands of saw-tooth decoration, that surround the spiral ornaments, seem to be connected with the cult of the dead, for they are not found on the vases discovered in dwelling quarters; but they held food and drink for the last journey and never ashes. That was the naive and obvious way in which the peasants of Kansu expressed their belief in immortality. So it would seem that, within the context of a material culture widespread over many peoples, the peculiar spiritual conceptions of separate entities could survive, and nothing excludes the possibility that the peasants of the Kansu culture were just settled Chinese with enough intelligence to learn something from their neighbours. In any case it is clear that even in the stone age there were cultural relations between mankind, and that there was give and take over the whole continent of Europe and Asia in which China took part, so that one will never have the whole picture, if China is left out of account.

Hsin-tien
PLATE ON PAGE 29 The art of painting pottery in many colours was long preserved in Kansu, indeed right down into historical times, probably the end of the 2nd millen-

ium B.C. The bowl with two large handles illustrated here belongs to the Hsin-tien type and was doubtless obtained by dealers from Kansu. It can be dated to that period. It shows the typical strong shape characteristic of that culture, the pinkish hand-moulded pottery, and for painting, on either side, a great simple spiral which almost looks like a tight, oft-repeated concentric circle. The neck is decorated with short double lines of waves above a thick black band. The ornament on the handles resembles a series of W's one above the other, connected by a vertical line running through the middle of them. We are not as yet able to say for certain whether the decoration is there simply for fun, or whether it represents something with a deeper inner meaning.

While these inheritors of a stone age agricultural tradition had shown a definite capacity for ennobling the necessary utensils of their simple life, in the Shang kingdom, and beyond, a civilisation with towns, bronze and writing, had made a great step forward. It was at Anyang that, for the first time, a truly overwhelming number of magnificent bronzes were found. So this name is taken to represent the first high peak in Chinese art. Bronze was not merely known, but moulded into superb vessels for sacred use, which have never been excelled in all the world. Their forms are strong and monumental; they seem to express themselves in some primaeval, universally understood language; their religious content is immediately and directly apprehended; the modelling of men and beasts is powerful and sure; all that together with wonderful technical accomplishment and, frequently, splendid patina raises these bronzes to a level where there are no rivals in all the world, and everyone who sees them is struck by them. There may be much that is strange and mysterious to us in the formal world of the late Shang period, which is the zenith of Chinese antiquity, and we may not understand or interpret every detail correctly. But the achievement stands out calm and clear in its integrity as the original and underived expression of a rare spirit with its own peculiar way of understanding the nature of the divine, for which it discovered symbols of deep meaning expressed with sublime art.

Anyang

There is a particular vessel of the type called *yu* by the Chinese, a portable vessel probably intended for sacrificial wine, which has always provoked fascinated speculation. There are two completely similar examples known, so it presumably gives classical shape to a once current motive. One of the examples is in the Sumitomo collection and the other in the Musée Cernuschi in Paris. The vessel is shaped in the form of a wild animal whose hindlegs and tail provide its three feet; it has a lid and a movable handle. Its teeth and claws prove the animal to be a tiger. It squats on its hindlegs,

Sacred bronzes

PLATE ON PAGE 34

33

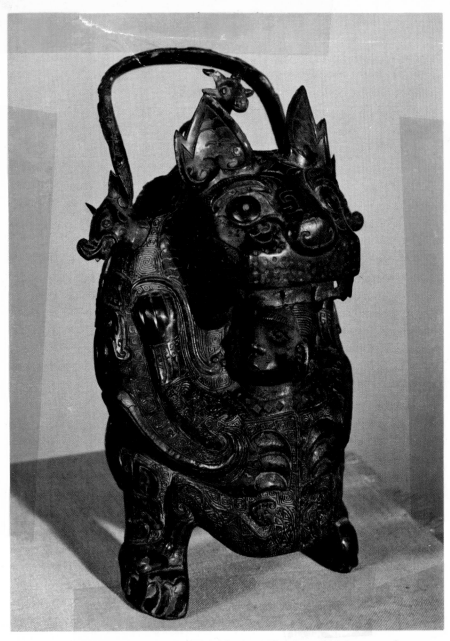

Vessel with handle, probably for sacrificial wine, in the form of a tiger which has spewed up a man and is clasping him. The symbolic meanings of the filling ornament of snakes, deer, rams' horns etc. indicate that the vessel represents the fruitful earth. End of the 2nd millenium B.C. *Musée Cernuschi, Paris.*
(Bronze, 12 inches high)

34

while its forelegs clasp a man under its wide-open jaws, the lower jaw not being fully represented. The tiger's body is moreover covered with other animals, ordinary snakes and others with magnified heads. On the back is a mask very like the tiger's head, with buffalo's and ram's horns above. On the lid, a deer is modelled in the round, and on the body too there are animals resembling a salamander and fish. No surface is left empty. Spirals fill in the gaps between the animals' bodies; there are triangles on many of the snakes' bodies; even the man has a border decorated with rhomboids between his shoulders. When the vessel first became known in Europe men of learning, familiar with the Phoenician Baal, took it as a representation of Moloch to whom human sacrifices were made, and even in 1926 a worthy Parisian authority described it as a terrible monster dragging a man towards itself with the clear intention of swallowing him. Then many clever heads got busy seeking out the meaning of this vessel whose religious significance was clearly great, and which might hold an important key to the understanding of beliefs in the Han period. But in this, as in many other cases, it is best to trust one's feelings first of all. If, without prejudice, one lets the impression soak in, this longhaired and presumably clothed man expresses nothing terrifying or shocking. He actually snuggles trustfully up against the tiger. His hands stretch up and rest on its shoulder, but they are not straining themselves to defend him against its violence. There is nothing of terror, struggle or tragic sacrifice; only a friendly interplay of different natures and it is only to us now that, in common with the tiger and the snake, they appear evil and bloodthirsty.

But first of all one should get rid of one's own atavistic preconceptions, *Meaning* and then ask what this being meant to another people in another time. We must here note a stumbling block in the way of the realistic interpretation of the religious conceptions of antiquity. It goes without saying that like symbols do not always mean the same to different peoples. Indeed the opposite is often true. We turn next for information to the immensely voluminous religious literature of China. But the vast majority of this was only written down later, when Shang traditions had been altered in important respects, or even obliterated by the Chou. Speculation too, especially the teaching about the five elements in the 4th century B.C., had forced these things into a theological system that did violence to the primitive conceptions. There is nothing in Chinese literature just like Hesiod, but to interpret Shang conceptions in the light of later literature, would be much as if one used Hesiod's rationalisations as a key to the understanding of the ideas of the Myceneans. The comparative method too in the study of folklore, though it has shown fine results, has its limits, for though a great

35

number of external resemblances can be collected together, the inner meaning of them often has to be left in the dark. It would seem that we must rediscover the trusted methods of classical archaeology, and apply them to the solution of our problems. The only reliable forms of evidence are contemporary inscriptions which do exist on the oracle bones from Anyang, though their meaning is often hard to grasp and uncertain, and also the methodical study of the development of each separate theme in the archaeological material of China herself. The present day practices of the common people in China can help to fill in the picture, especially when there is no ancient literary account of them; for no one writes about what everyone takes for granted, and it is always just that which proves hardest for historical research to discover.

Earth-symbol We learn from the Anyang oracle inscriptions that the tiger is conceived as being in close connection with the earth, and that the earth is the central point in all religious conceptions and sacrifices. So enduring was the vitality of these conceptions that they come forward again in the teaching about the five elements, according to which all animals with long haired fur, such as tigers and bears etc., count as symbols of the feminine *yin* and of the earth. Even in the much later Japanese Zen painting, the tiger appears as the symbol of the feminine *yin,* whereas the dragon stands for the male *yang.* In folklore even now the tiger is a good friend and protecting spirit, for he never needlessly attacks human beings, but destroys many pests to their fields. One of the oldest of Chinese marble statues in the round represents a squatting tiger, without a man this time. It was found in a king's tomb at Hou-chia-chuang near Anyang together with an equally large representation of an owl with a snake on its wings. We cannot be sure of the original arrangement of the figures, since the grave had been disturbed by robbers, but it is probable that they were counterparts. There has also been found in an excellently preserved grave in central China, admittedly dating from the 4th century B.C., a squatting tigerlike figure made of wood covered with lacquer and placed in a special niche. Horns placed on its head, round eyes and a long tongue hanging out, all spoil the first impression of a tiger. But it seems safe to say that we find figures whose fundamental shape is based on a tiger's body, standing by the dead. Their significance is extended and made more intense by a host of other reprentations with the same or analogous symbolical meanings, but in any case it is certainly no monster but a helpful, good spirit that is intended.

Eternal life The argument that the *yu* in the Musée Cernuschi is concerned with the symbolical representation of the earth-spirit, is reinforced by the many snakes that lie along the man's body, stretch out towards the tiger's jaws

36

or spread over its back. For the snake is a symbol of the earth and of all the new life to which she ever gives birth. Every time it changes its skin, a new being slides out of the old. So the snake is a natural symbol of continual renewing and rebirth, the same force that man recognises in every plant that springs from the earth. Thus in China the snake is generally a good creature, very close to mother-earth and her perpetual renewal. There are places in China that make a regular cult of snakes, and nowhere are they wantonly killed, indeed in some parts of the country they are accepted as domestic animals, for whom food is provided and who on festive evenings creep on to the laps of the old people to warm themselves. Although the Chinese are not reckoned to be particularly fond of animals, they have a very precise knowledge of them, and they think of them as enjoying a way of life similar to their own, or rather half way between them and the plants, a life that is like that of humanity but often more unaccountable. Hence animals can easily be taken as symbols of that domain which men feel is ruled by demons. The Chinese tried to gain knowledge about the demons. But they did not set about this by raising animals to the level of things sacred and therefore beyond discussion. So their representations of them are not idols. There is no Horus-falcon in China nor any temple of monkeys. It was not until the 4th century A.D. that the Buddhists, though themselves in theory without gods, insinuated representations of the deity into China. So when a symbol of the earth-demon was put in the tomb at Hou-chia-chuang it must be understood not simply as an offering to the earth, but also as a sign that her power was understood, and a reminder to use it for the good of the dead man, to receive him as a seed and bring him to new life again in the sun. When sacrifices were made to the earth over the ground — and no doubt sacrificial vessels such as our *yu* were not originally made to be buried — the ritual utensil bore the marks of its purpose, showing to whom and why sacrifice was made. So this is the symbolic meaning of the *yu* in the Cernuschi museum: each and every man is spewed up, or born, from the tiger-earth, and clasped by it; all creatures of like meaning come together to accompany this birth and the resurrection that is bound up with death, and lend it their support. This is no terrible and cruel Moloch, but a friendly harmony of beings who unite to serve the good and everlasting life. There is nothing cruel, not even anything apotropaic (defensive), about the *t'ao-t'ieh* masks which have so long been found puzzling as they appear, for instance, on the back of the Cernuschi *yu* and, in various forms, on thousands of other bronzes. They are, from one point of view, just formalised and simplified face-masks, and, from another, they stand for the

37

mythical earth-demon, enriched by a varied crowd of symbols in the form of rams' horns, ox horns, snakes etc. As one would expect among a settled, agricultural people, this symbol of mother-earth is the most important to them, and the one nearest their hearts, a symbol which in Shang times not only had vitality, but found its most impressive formal expression. This tradition was snapped in the warlike times of the Chou. By the time of the feudal age the meaning of this formula was entirely forgotten. As often happens when things cannot be explained, a word was found, the strange foreign word *t'ao-t'ieh,* whose meaning and etymology have still not been unravelled, and which perhaps once designated something entirely different. The two places in which the word is first found, in the Tso-chuan VI. 18 and in the Lü-shih ch'un-ch'iu V.I, only let us know that, at that time, no one knew the meaning of the *t'ao-t'ieh.* But what was the meaning of the counterpart to the tiger or t'ao-t'ieh or earth spirit, the owl which balances the tiger in the royal tomb at Hou-chia-chuang, and figures so often on Chinese sacred bronzes? Here the meaning lies very near to our own conceptions, so near, perhaps, that we are not prepared for it. The owl, and indeed all others birds represented in Shang times, stands for the air and the spirit, the spirit that cannot be seen, but which moves itself and moves others, as do breath and the wind. Christian artists are at one with those of Shang times when they represent the Holy Spirit as a bird.

Spirit Metaphors from wind, aether or breath enter into all our words for spiritual things, for that which distinguishes all living beings and man in particular. It is and always has been just the same with the Chinese. But the Shang bronzes prove that this earthy people who think in pictorial terms, gave first place to the earth, the earth which gives out, bears, sustains and again receives the spirit as well as humanity. If one looks at bronzes some of which have only been published quite recently, this conception stands out clear beyond all doubt.

PLATE ON PAGE 39 On the lid of a finely shaped portable vessel in the Museum of Minneapolis, a bird stands on the wide open mouth of a snake. Perhaps some materialist will suggest that the snake is going to swallow the bird. But as we remarked about the tiger-*yu* in the Cernuschi museum, the Shang artist knew how to express the trusting attitude of the man, so again the unprejudiced eye can see that there is no suggestion of tragedy or deadly fight in this representation. The bird here stands upright, happy and ready to fly away. It is not anxious or struggling on the defensive, still less is it trying to attack the snake with its beak. The implication is much more that the snake, that is the earth, has spewed up, or given birth, to the bird, and is letting it go into the air and light. This interpretation is made more con-

38

Portable vessel, presumably for sacrificial wine. The lid is joined to the handle by a snake, the symbol of the earth, which spews out a bird, the symbol of air and of the sun, of the spirit and of resurrection. On the rectangular body are typical *T'ao-t'ieh* masks. About 1000 B.C. *The Minneapolis Institute of Arts (Bronze, 13 inches high)*

vincing by bronzes of the 5th century B.C. in which this motif is unmistakably further elaborated, where the bird, with its head forward and its wings outspread, is flying out of the snake's jaws. A similar conception must be at the bottom of the very numerous representations of the owl, though it is just this bird that tends to give research workers a headache. For clearly the owl is a bird of night, of darkness and therefore logically of the *yin*, so that the polarity of earth and air, darkness and light, seems to be broken. Some have raised unconvincing doubts as to whether the birds really are owls, as for instance recently Li Chi who speaks of some nobler form of bird. Others point out that in folklore the pheasant is the symbol of the sun, of light and of the male *yang* principle in general, but the hen pheasant, as being a female animal, does stand for the *yin*. So, if the logical principle is to be preserved, the owls must always be male birds. But there

Correlation are other paths known to Chinese logic. It avoids antithesis and loves correlation. It is possible to suppose that the owl of all birds was chosen as a symbol just because it clearly stood for the opposite, darkness, so that the completeness of the complementary relationship could be emphasised. This may appear, and be, too subtle an interpretation, but it serves to remind one of the ways of thought to which one must become accustomed, if one wants to obtain even logical understanding of Chinese art and, therewith, forms of speech. There can be no doubt that Shang artists possessed a vivid and developed consciousnes of polarity. The way in which they place together tigers and men, snakes and birds etc., as complementary one to the other, make that plain. Their love too for cicadas which often appear on Shang bronzes, is a perfect example. The cricket which passes much of its life as a snakelike larva in the earth, works its way up to the light, breaks out from its crust, and turns into a winged insect that flies up like a bird into the sky, is a living parable of the complementary polarity of changing forms, of the alternation from *yin* to *yang*, material to spirit. There is no more compelling and convincing emblem of the power and continuity of this fundamental conception. Cicadas of jade or glass are found in the mouth or on the eyes of the dead in Han tombs as simple testimony of faith and hope for resurrection, and even now cicadas are worn as ornaments or charms. In Shang times we find crowds of symbols that, at first sight, appear contradictory, but the juxtaposition of which, understood as correlatives, is full of meaning, and generally based on clear and simple fundamental ideas, even though we may not now be able to unravel the meaning of all their variations. At that time the earth, the dark and fruitful *yin*, was felt to hold prime place. That, perhaps, is why, the *yin* emblems, tiger, snake, elephant etc. can stand either alone or

40

enhanced and crowded over by a mass of symbols of the same or similar meaning, whereas the indication of the other complementary pole may, but need not, appear. On the other hand the symbols of air and spirit never stand without an indication of that which completes them, such as the snake on the wings or at the feet of the bird.

Mr Kawai in Kyoto had, in 1958, a magnificent bronze with a cover, PLATE ON PAGE 44 standing out in the round down the middle edge, are common to both birds were rendered in profile and in perfect symmetry; only the beaks, standing out in the round down the middle edge, are common to both sides; the feather-encircled eyes look straight forward, and the crown of feathers above and the wings are in full profile; above the wings, as always, there is a snake, this time without a head. But lest the earthy side of the complete story should be left too little emphasised, there are dragons with snakelike bodies and huge wide-open mouths and eyes close to the owl. The illustration shows, better than any description, the clear, sure modelling of the forms, and the firm yet gentle outline of the vessel, which attest the maturity and confidence both of conception and of execution attained by the artists of this time.

The cover, which is all that is left, of a bronze in the Musée Guimet, is an- PLATE ON PAGE 47 other masterly monument of faith from Shang times. On its summit stands a bird with fine head-feathers and a long tail. It is usually called a pheasant or, perhaps better, a hoopoo, which was later the classical emblem of the sun, the *yang*. The origin of this bird and its flight up out from the earth are here very clearly represented by the four *t'ao-t'ieh* masks which, separated by a raised ridge, decorate the arch of the cover. But "decorate" is not the right word; if they were there merely as decoration, they would not be upside down with their horns pointing downwards and their jaws and wide nostrils on top. The symbolical meaning is clear; the earth-demon which lets the bird rise from its jaws, which spews it out, is letting the spirit loose into its element, the air. Perhaps it would be carrying the interpretation of details too far to suggest that there is meaning in the ring with a running row of volutelike twirls, which lies between the bird' claws and the *t'ao-t'ieh* masks. Just the same twirls appear in the oldest ideograms for the sun, so one might suppose that the pictorial symbolism would read as follows: — light, sun and spirit rise from the darkness, from the beneficent dark chasms of the earth according to the Chinese conception. Perhaps it is straying too far to note a similarity with well-known and admired representations of birds from the art of the rest of the world, from the tombstone of an Ionian girl to Picasso, from Cranach to Mansur, and from Hui-tsung to Niten. Was ever bird formed with more spirit? Can we

41

conceive of a bird, intended as the emblem of spirituality, more tellingly shaped than that on this cover, the work of a nameless master 3,000 years ago? Is it not the very embodiment of everything that the Chinese, when they formulated aesthetic theories in the 5th century A.D. meant by the term *ch'i-yün,* which they regarded as the most precious quality of all? *Ch'i-yün* can be translated, very literally, as "conformity with the spiritual", a word which in China too carries a double meaning of air and of spirit. But this masterpiece has a special importance for another reason. It is said to have been discovered at Ch'ang-sha in central China, 600 miles from Anyang and certainly outside the Shang domain. It may therefore lend support to the suggestion that bronze working flourished in central China earlier than it did in the north. There is much more copper there than in the north; moreover the animals that play so prominent a part in Shang bronzes, the tiger, water-buffalo, elephant, rhinoceros, scorpion etc. are, today at least, the fauna of central and southern China, and can no more be found in the north.

Climate The art history of early times would be assisted if there were more general studies of changes in climate and fauna throughout the world. Such researches are possible, and when it comes to the iron age we are thoroughly well informed: so prehistorians and historians of art must be at pains to supply the geographers and meteorologists with the material they need. In the excavations at Pan-po and Anyang there was evidence that rice was used, and it is improbable that this would have been transported over some 300 miles from the south. At Anyang there were also bones of elephants, tapirs, rhinoceros etc., all animals that have now left those parts, so that one can be sure that, at any rate in the second half of the second millenium B.C. in north China the climate was warmer than it is now, and presumably like the sub-tropical climate now found in central and southern China. There must also have been wide extents of primeval forest. So there is no need to look southwards, that is to say to central China, where there has been as yet little archaeological investigation, for the roots of this art. But on the other hand there is no evidence against the possibility that in early times there was similar, even if not homogeneous, art there. As the history of art is always based on actual works, and not on deeds and tales that are often embroidered by legend, it is able not only to illustrate historical traditions, but also often to provide the first conclusive evidence of developments of which historians of religion and politics and sociologists have to take notice. That is so at least in China. Here are two examples. We have more than ten thousand bronzes and tens of thousands of pots from Chinese antiquity to examine, and we find practically no trace of a

42

plant or plantlike motif. It is safe to venture that negative statement, as any instances that might be discovered could only count as exceptions to the general rule. It is also true that among the many and various representations of animals in Chinese antiquity no animal-fight is found, whereas in the older or contemporary art of the Near East animals are continually struggling with one another, fighting and killing each other. Moreover in the Near East plants play so great a part that rosettes and palmettes could be taken as emblems of the art of Hither Asia. These are prima facie indications that the Chinese culture often called "Huangho" is clearly differentiated from the other river civilisations, of the Euphrates, Nile and Indus, though one would gladly place them in one line of development. All these rivers flow through deserts. The land along the banks, often only a few miles wide, is under constant threat and must be carefully watered. Life there is a continual struggle for the inhabitants, with the additional danger of attacks from wild beasts forced by thirst down to the water, and this sense of danger has left its indelible mark on Near Eastern art. This sense was a perpetual school for antithetical thought, and the Near East taught Greece and Europe. In China the opposite is the case. The Huangho is even today a source of anxiety for China, but because it has too much, not too little, water. The legend of the Emperor Yü, who dealt with an obstruction or flood of the Huangho, may contain an element of truth since the task which he performed has had to be repeated again and again. In China there was no threat from deserts; boundless land encompassed her, and the very numerous little agricultural communities of Chinese in antiquity knew nothing of land hunger. That is why there are no legends of the creation of the earth and of man. There had been so much of both for so long that it was taken for granted. The only sensible but not unmanageable threat must have come from the forests. Fire and axe could be used to combat them. Fear of the forest was as great in ancient China as in North America today, and it continued to *Distaste for plants* be a menace down to times when the climate had changed and the population increased. So this may have had its effect on the Chinese way of feeling, and prevented any inclination to portray plants, although there as elsewhere the fruitfulness of the earth and of man formed the basis of their religion and their observances.

Our understanding of Chinese religion in antiquity would remain very *Ancestors* defective without a sense of the importance of ancestors in their faith. The oracle inscriptions from Anyang give us varied information about this, though they do not mention what was obvious to contemporaries, namely the details of their rites and ceremonies of sacrifice. Whether

43

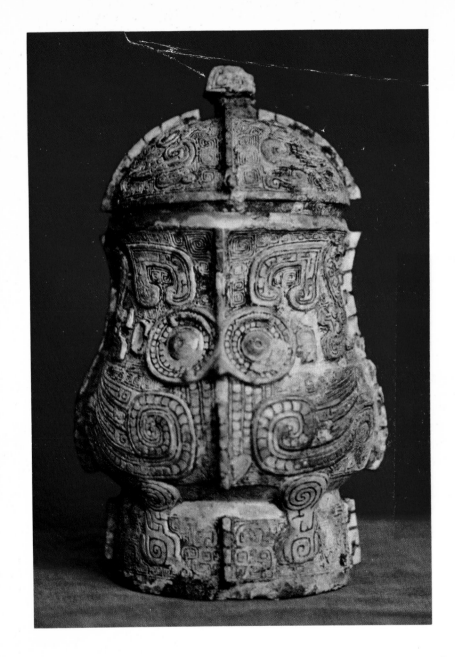

Bronze sacrificial vessel, presumably from Anyang, the capital of the later Shang dynasty. The body shows two perfectly symmetrical owls, the symbol of the sun, air and spirit, side by side, with the snake, symbol of the earth-demon, close by. End of the 2nd millenium B.C. *In the possession of Mr S. Kawai, Kyoto (7 inches high)*

44

for instance there were special temples for the ancestors in Shang times, as there were under the Chou, is a question still needing thorough research. Meanwhile, it seems reasonable to suppose that the spirits of the dead rose again from their graves, went on living immortally as individuals and took an active part in the fate of the family and of the country. Thus we learn from the inscriptions that offerings of wine and food were brought to ancestors of both sexes, that their advice was asked by means of oracles and their help implored. Thus there is an inscription imploring Grandmother I to send rain. Belief in resurrection is a matter of course to the Chinese and their relationship to past members of the family is very trustful and only demands that they should not anger them by neglect. That does not mean that the Chinese worship their ancestors every hour of the day, but that they live a life that is respectable in their eyes, express their reverence for them from time to time, and are careful to bring forth numerous progeny to ensure the continuity of this reverence. Such ideas are intertwined with all the efforts of this basically agricultural community to preserve and increase the fruitfulness of the soil. Concrete evidence, as usual for early times, gives the best proof that this was so. None but farmers and the kings of farmers would put so much valuable furniture into graves. *Grave furniture* In the royal tombs of Hou-chia-chuang dozens of the most magnificent ritual bronzes were found, which must then have been of substantial worth; besides these there were helmets and weapons, carvings in jade and bone, sculpture, pottery, and also lacquer and silk, of which slight traces remained and, before the robbers came, objects of gold; finally there were dozens of human skeleton, (though men may not have been particularly valuable in those days in the East) and horses and chariots. All these were things of use and value to the living, the labour of patient craftsmen. The perfection of the craftsmanship is particularly striking in the bronze work, and hardly a single defective or incomplete object has been found. Excavations of workshops have shown that stamps and moulds were used to impress repetitive ornament on the soft model, but they must have worked over the wax carefully before casting, for no rough or irregular casts are found.

Shang taste favoured inlay, especially turquoise and gold on bronze, the juxtaposition of bronze and jade, and all the polychromy of varied colours and materials. A magnificent example is the ceremonial axe from Anyang, PLATE ON PAGE 49 whose blade is of jade and whose long shaft is inlaid with turquoise. It is not strong enough and too costly for actual use. So it must have been intended for ritual purposes, but it would seem that it was buried almost as soon as it was made. Its ritual nature is further proved by the simple

45

and impressive designs of the inlays which show the *yin* and *yang* in their full circle of change. At the foot of the shaft a *t'ao-t'ieh* with curled up snake's body, tiger head and horns, stands for the earth. It spews up the larva of a cricket, triangular and pointing upwards; above that is a snake which must in turn spew up a bird. This bird is attached to the shaft on the right, and above there is another *t'ao-t'ieh* like the one at the bottom.

There is yet another, this time uncurled, on the jade blade. One can judge the maturity and the high attainment of these Shang artists in bronze, an attainment equalled perhaps but never surpassed anywhere in the world, by the quantity of these expensive furnishings and the great number of perfect specimens. All casts that did not come out quite perfectly, must have been melted down again at once, for a ritual utensil had to be free from the slightest blemish.

Chou dynasty In the year 1027 B.C. (adopting the more up-to-date Chinese chronology) the Chou broke out from the Wei valley with their infantry and their war-chariots, attacked Anyang, overthrew the last emperor of the Shang dynasty, who committed suicide, and founded the Chou dynasty. The Chou reigned for 777 years down to 250 B.C. generally from P'ang, near the later Ch'ang-an, in the Wei valley. The first six Chou kings were great soldiers who substantially extended the former domain of the Shang, and ruled it more firmly. This was done by entrusting great feudal districts to members of their family and their chief supporters. These new feudal lords settled with their garrisons in the existing towns and founded new ones. The dependents of the Shang house were spared and allowed to become the priests of country districts. The craftsmen worked for their new, as for their old, lords. Chou civilisation shows a number of new features, though in some respects it is uncertain how far old tendencies were merely accentuated and developed. It may well be that the contrasts between Shang and Chou are often exaggerated by those who suppose the Chou to have been largely nomadic, patriarchal people of Turkish stock, as opposed to the settled, agricultural and matriarchal Chinese. Certainly succession from father to son, which was the rule with the Chou, is more patriarchal than the inheritance by brothers among the Shang, but the latter no longer maintained strict principles of matriarchy. It is certain that in their religious ideas the Chou attached more importance to the sun and stars, but such conceptions were not entirely foreign to the Shang. The conception of the ruler as "son of heaven", which appears in the earliest Chou inscriptions, is certainly new. But there is more doubt about the conception of Shang-ti, the first ancestor and the ruler of the gods, which

46

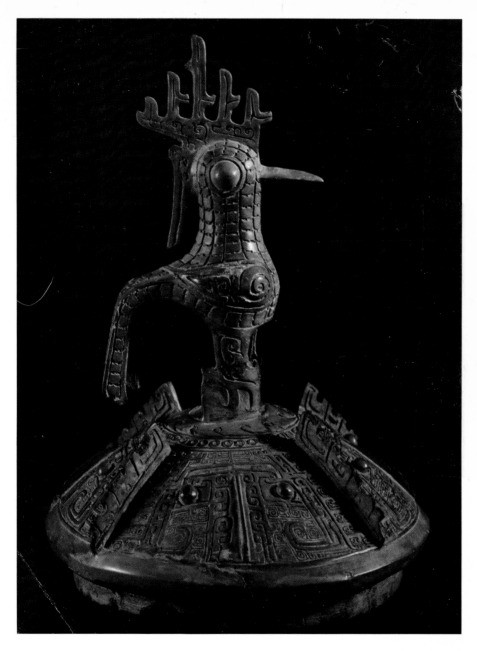

Lid of a ritual vessel, said to be have been round at Ch'ang-sha in central China. A bird, emblem of air and spirit, surmounts upward pointing *T'ao-t'ieh* masks, the emblem of the earth. End of the second millenium B.C. *Musée Guimet, Paris (Bronze, 11 inches high)*

47

existed in Shang times, in a vague form perhaps; he now apparently takes on greater importance and is transferred to heaven.

Ancestor worship The Chou did everything they could to support ancestor worship. Temples of ancestors certainly have a new and great importance among their buildings, and perhaps they were the first to erect actual temples for them. But we have not the least idea of the external aspect of these two innovations. The texts about the *"Ming-t'ang"* or "Hall of Light", on which we are forced to rely, still puzzle both philologists and art historians. Nor are we able to venture hypotheses as to how far the Chou introduced their own conceptions of ancestor worship, and how far they developed what was already to hand. Anyhow they must have seen that it was useful to them, in establishing their claim to rule as the guardians and successors of an ancient tradition, to base their rights on a deep-rooted and well established religious institution. This was later to result in a lot of genealogical nonsense, when all the great feudal lords were determined to trace their descent from the mythical emperors of primeval times, and one must be very careful not to mistake these ad hoc invented stories for real myths, though this or that fragment of genuine mythology may be imbedded in them. However the new style of tomb architecture is plain to see. The royal tombs at Anyang are large underground structures contrived, as far as possible, so that they do not appear above ground. But the Chou built high grave mounds which often stand out as landmarks in the plain. Moreover human sacrifice ceases under the Chou. Men seem more valuable to military minded people than they did to peaceful cultivators, and they can be better used to protect their fellow men than as symbolical offerings to increase fertility. We must add that questions about the calendar come into striking prominence in Chou times. Naturally the Shang people, as one would expect of agriculturalists, were much concerned with such questions and they are found on the oracle inscriptions. But there is hardly a single Chou bronze inscription that omits to begin with the day, the month, and the quarter of the moon. A change of spirit has been at work prompting this new interest in the sun, moon and stars, and the most essential element in the old time religion has been changing into its exact opposite. The earth

Heaven loses its primacy. Heaven which had been a secondary and feebler element, is exalted and takes first place. In Shang times it is, "earth and heaven", in Chou times "heaven and earth". Admittedly the Chinese now say *yin-yang*. In Shang oracle inscriptions that phrase generally means darkness and light, and now female and male. It is just the old way of speaking that has survived from times before the Chou, with perhaps an overtone of the ancient accent, but the meaning has changed as the new order of

48

Axe for ceremonial sacrifices, probably excavated at Anyang. The turquoise inlay on the shaft and the jade blade show *T'ao-t'ieh* snakes as symbols of the earth. Above that comes a cricket downside up. Above that again is a snake which spews up a bird. On top and on the blade are more *T'ao-t'ieh* snakes. End of the 11 millenium B.C. *Freer Gallery of Art, Washington (13½ inches long)*

49

precedence became accepted. Or is there some ambivalence and difference of stress?

Contemporary inscriptions which are more numerous and lengthy especially from the 10th century onwards, teach us a great deal about the new ideas of Chou times. Sacrificial bronzes now often have inscriptions moulded in with them, a technique which had been used in Shang times, but only for conventional phrases of two or three ideograms. Externally the ritual bronzes look just the same as those of Shang times; some shapes were given up and a few new ones made their appearance, but there is little change either in their outlines or in the subject matter of their decoration. So it is quite clear that the same craftsmen continued to make the same things for new masters. There is no faltering in their high technical standards. Only the inscriptions, on or under the body and on the lids, are new. They generally give very precise reasons why the bronze was made, and often record an investiture or appointment. Very probably most of them were intended for display in the temples of ancestor worship. They are therefore most important sources for history, whose value has not yet been fully exploited.

Change of style In the reign of the 6th Chou king, Kung-wang (927-912), there is, without any warning, a complete change of style, for which no sufficient reason has yet been discovered. The tradition of symbolical representation seems to have been swept away at one blow, and at the same time there is a very marked falling off in technique. All the numerous bronzes with inscriptions of king Kung-wang and his successors down to about 600 B.C., and contemporary feudal chiefs and great men, are all in a new style which has come to be called "Middle Chou". There are no fundamental changes of shape, but profiles have lost much of the power, tautness and tension of Shang and early Chou bronzes. One can recognise a middle Chou bronze, even in the distance, by its weak and flabby outline, the product of no sense or feeling for form beyond a memory of the strong and boldly conceived inventions of Shang times.

There is a great change too in the subjects represented, which have become nothing more than decoration. The parallel rings and bands of the middle Chou style, often no more than intertwining patterns, are just ornaments, not emblems heavy with meaning. In the case of a Shang bronze one can never dismiss the slightest line or curl as simple decoration; even when one does not know the meaning of each individual shape, there is a general feeling that it must mean something special. Stripes and bands of the middle Chou period often end in animals heads; on them and between them appear horns and eyes that call to mind the *t'ao-t'ieh* masks,

50

but only for those who know the old examples; an uninitiated eye would hardly regard them as more than not particularly fantastic ornament. The art of the middle Chou period, bereft too of all the excitement of colour, may now appear poorer and more jejune than it in fact was. There are no compact groups of finds and, apart from the great number of bronzes, only a few jade objects have been attributed to this period on account of the same jejune ornament.

One looks for a reason for this striking phenomenon, and it comes to mind that king Kung-wang, in whose reign the Chou reached the zenith of their might, felt himself strong enough to employ his power in altering the religious foundations of the old order, no doubt with enduring success. He doubtless wished to establish conceptions peculiar to the Chou, which would prove a better foundation for the high ambitions of a politically conscious state than anything the old order could provide. An agricultural community could complacently concern itself only with the prosperity of its own fields and narrow family circle, but such an attitude undermined the strength of the state. However that may be too subtle an interpretation, wise after the event, which sees things contemporaries were unaware of. For the next hundred years the power of the Chou was steadily on the decline. King Hsüan-wang (827—782) was indeed famous for a punitive expedition against the barbarian Hsien-yün in the north. His successor Yu-wang, "the sad", was killed by these same barbarians in 772, and the Chou had to retreat to a new capital, Loyang, in the middle of the original Shang territory. There they continued to reside in a narrow royal domain which did not give them control of sufficient force to play an important part in a wider field of politics. In 704 the prince of Chu in central China adopted the title of king, and by so doing put in question the claim of the Son of Heaven to be the sole representative of the Chinese kingdom in the sight of heaven. In 680 it was necessary to appoint as dictator one of the feudal lords who had advanced from their original subsidiary condition *Northern peoples* to a state of greater, indeed almost complete, independence, in order to ward off the attacks of the nomads in the north. Again in 606 north China and the Chou king owed their survival to an expedition led by the King of Ch'u, who had been made dictator, and advanced past Loyang to the north where he attacked and defeated the invaders.

Chinese histories, of which the Tso-chuan is the most important, begin to give more reliable information about the period from about 900 to 600 B.C., and from 841 onwards their chronology, which can be checked by references to eclipses of the moon, is perfectly reliable. But the picture they paint is, in at least one substantial point, far from adequate. And

51

Sinologues who have a great work ahead of them in establishing sound texts, seldom take a chance to look out beyond their books and beyond China in order to understand the written word better in the light of realities. In the sources there are strikingly frequent allusions to "incursions" of nomadic peoples, and from 800 B.C. onwards there are frequent "punitive expeditions" against these unhappy rebellious barbarians. The battles are always played down as tiresome border affairs of merely local significance. But it is all too often mentioned as the result of these wars that the barbarians were granted land to live in inside China. The conquered were always settled as far away as possible in the south, especially in the Huai valley, and were allowed to become merged with the aboriginal population. In fact these incursions were bound up with a fundamental natural catastrophe of most far-reaching importance. A great force caused

Two-handled bronze cup cast together with its base. There is an inscription on this so-called Lü-kuei cup (s.O.A. 1956 p. 9ff). Middle Chou period, 9th—7th century B.C. *Musée Cernuschi, Paris (19 inches high)*

52

these invasions from the north, which disturbed the Near East and Europe no less than China. Indeed China is only one of the theatres in which a worldwide upheaval can be observed.

About the year 1,000 B.C. such a decided and enduring change took place in the climate that the steppe peoples from the Amur to the Don were compelled, simply to save their lives, to send at least the surplus of their population off to the south. This change of climate can now be most accurately observed in the land east of the Jordan, which was then turned back to desert. There is clear evidence of it too in Near Eastern historical sources. The climax came with the attacks of the northern peoples, regardless of their various racial origins, in the 7th century B.C. Jeremiah's lamentations about the Scythian invasions into Palestine in 625 B.C., from which the word "Jeremiad" is derived, might as easily have been composed in China. The great invasion of the Huns in Honan in 660 B.C. which for 90 years made it necessary to appoint dictators, shamefacedly described as "generals" (680—590 B.C.); the great diet of princes in 651 B.C. and several smaller diets; all of these are not so much matters of internal political intrigue and conflicting interests of comparatively unimportant cliques, as indications of the desperate necessities then facing north China. Conversely there is food for thought in the fact that the 7th century is one of the darkest periods in the history of Chinese art, for there is hardly a bronze that can be accurately dated, and not one of outstanding quality. Not only lovers of art are concerned with the fact that the technique of bronze casting grew visibly clumsier between 900 and 600 B.C., and that one finds stamps carelessly pressed one on top of another, and faults in casting left uncorrected, for it is more than a mere question of taste. There may be much truth in all the moral stories in the history books about rebellions of princes against their king, of peoples against their princes, about luxury and intrigues, and the gruesome details about the decay and decadence of the Chou kingdom. But we must put all that on one side if we want to understand the reason why, over three hundred years, Chinese antiquity broke down in the deadly sickness of artistic impotence, borne sometimes with pain, sometimes with euphoria. Discoveries in Persia, in the Altai, and in China, or at Ziwiye, Pazyryk and Ch'ang-sha-to mention only the best known excavations — give a much better picture of what was actually happening than all the commentaries on historical texts.

About 600 B.C. the pressure from the North seems to have slackened. From that time onwards the peoples who had been most unwillingly forced into contact with one another, begin to reap benefits from their misfortune. Necessity and war had driven them against each other but also

Disturbance of climate

53

together; they could begin to share their experiences and ideas and to exchange goods. Karlgren is right in placing the beginning of a new epoch in China at 590 B.C. when it was no longer necessary to submit to dictators, albeit called "generals", in the interests of defence. So the most brilliant epoch of Chinese art, the feudal period, begins in conditions that were far from peaceful, but a little more quiet.

ANCIENT TIMES

CHINA

III THE FEUDAL AGE

One can count it lucky for China and for the Chou dynasty that, from the 8th century onwards, their kings scarcely exercised any political power. From 770 B.C. they reigned in the city of Loyang and a small royal domain round it; with due ceremony they confirmed the appointments of princes over whose actions they had little control; they presided over the diets of princes; sometimes offered themselves as arbitrators; but there was nothing for them to rule. Just for that reason the thought of the king as the emblem of Chinese unity gained lasting power. Although in the 4th century others followed the example of the prince of Ch'u who proclaimed himself king in 704 B.C., and princes who had gained independence made wars and changed their alliances, and although they divided up north China by their earthworks, still "China" did not fall apart. For China did not yet exist except as a longing and an ideal embodied in the Chou kings.

It was the craft and power of the state of Ch'in in the Wei valley which united most of what is now the 18 provinces of China. King Chen-wang *Emperor* brought this process to completion in 221 B.C. He took the new title of "Huang-ti", or Emperor, while the old royal style of "Wang" came to mean a prince of the blood. He called himself, "the first Emperor of the house of Ch'in" (Ch'in Shih-huang-ti). He indeed ruled as an utter despot and ended in madness, but the world still calls the land "China" after his house. So we can give rather accurate dates for the feudal period; it began in 590 B.C. with the end of the rule of generals, when the defensive war in the north was substantially finished, and the great feudal lords had time to compete with each other in the arts of peace; it came to an end in 221 B.C. when unity was finally enforced, and feudal tenure and the hereditary nobility abolished. The Chou dynasty had been quietly liquidated in 250 B.C.

This is no place to dwell on the eventful histories of each separate feudal state, and the many men of parts among their princes and statesmen. But we must note that from the 6th century onwards central China comes within the orbit of written history; the Ch'u state in central China is especially important and, further south, that of Wu in Kiangsu, whose king, Ho-lü (514–496 B.C.) built a magnificent capital on the site of the modern Suchou which was later to become one of the leading art centres. These lands had a long and varied history behind them, but central China, being outside the Chou domain, was neglected in its archives, and ap-

Leg of low table in the shape of a bear, made of bronze with inlay of gold and silver. Probably from Chin-ts'un near Loyang. 3rd century B.C. *William Rockhill Nelson Gallery of Art, Atkins Museum, Kansas City (5 inches high)* parently had no system of writing of its own. So we must employ the methods of prehistory to study the interesting civilisation of Ch'u and the Yangtse valley.

Excavations Though the excavations have not been sufficiently scientific or adequately published, an astounding wealth of works of art from the feudal age has been brought to light. In the north finds have been made at Hsin-cheng, south of Ao, the most important dating from 575 B.C.: at Chin-ts'un near the old capital of Loyang (about 450–230 B.C.), and at Hui-hsien between Loyang and Anyang (5th – 4th century B.C.), all these being in northern Honan; also at Li-yü (3rd century B.C.) in northern Shensi. Then in the south there are these sites in the former state of Ch'u; Ch'ang-sha (5th – 2nd century B.C.) in Hunan; Hsin-yang and Ku-shih in southern Honan, south of the Huai river (4th – 3rd century B.C.); and Shou-chou, or Shouhsien, on the Huai river in Anhui (5th – 3rd century B.C.), and from 241–222 B.C. the last capital of the Ch'u state. But it is not advisable to draw general conclusions about the artistic development of these places until fuller publications are to hand.

Buildings We must not underestimate the brilliance of the capitals and palaces of the feudal age. Although the high falutin' literary descriptions of their pomp of sculpture and paintings may, in the total effect, be exaggerated, excavation confirms their details. As all their buildings were made of wood, none have remained nor are likely to be found. But ridge tiles have been unearthed and, in graves at Chin-ts'un, hollow tiles of grey pottery almost 5 feet long. Some of those coming from the tomb walls were decorated with impressed patterns and pictures which give some idea of contemporary painting. Excavations at Lin-tzu in 1941 laid bare the capital of the important state of Ch'i in Shantung; an earthwork about one mile by two enclosed some 1800 acres of land in an irregular quadrilateral. Again there may be some exaggeration in the story that the First Emperor transferred 120,000 of his richest subjects to his capital Hsien-yang somewhere in the neighbourhood of the modern Hsian-fu, and that when foes burnt it in 206 B.C., the city and the famous A-fang palace burnt for three months continously. But certainly this metropolis was, even by modern standards, a great city reaching perhaps the million mark; the total population of the empire in Shih-huang-ti's reign may be estimated at 50,000.000. It would be quite a mistake to assume that the feudal princes and their great lords could usually read and write, but one is struck by the evidence of learned or literary circles which seem, generally speaking, to have existed at individual courts; for instance that of king Hsüan-wang of Ch'i (332–314 B.C.), and that of the First Emperor at Hsien-yang. The existence of these let-

58

tered people and the use of writing, since about 500 B.C., for the business of this world, are important innovations deserving closer examination. The "archives" of the oracle inscriptions on bone or tortoiseshell, dating *Inscriptions* from between 1,300–1,000 B.C. at Anyang provide us with some 100,000 specimens using about 3,000 ideograms. There is evidence that both brush and Indian ink were already in use. From the first millenium B.C. there are hundreds of inscriptions cast on sacrificial bronze vessels, more enduring than parchment or paper; they were often specifically intended for the "archives" of the temples of ancestors. There is a remarkable tendency, especially in the 10th century, for the writer to be expressly mentioned. In those days his was a rare accomplishment. Boards and tablets of bamboo are often mentioned as writing materials in feudal times, and we now know just what these and the writing on them looked like in the 4th century B.C. from the excavations at Hsin-yang, where there was a grave with an inventory on bamboo tablets of everything in it. So we can well understand why a learned man then needed a wagon to move his library of wooden and bamboo books. But presumably rolls of silk must already have been in use for writing and painting, and paper is first mentioned in the 2nd century B.C. Presumably this was made from silk waste, and then, about the 1st century A.D. paper made from rags and vegetable fibre was invented. But even in the 3rd century A.D. it was still a costly rarity.

We should be rash to suppose that anything resembling books or libraries existed in China before the 5th century. Up to that time writing had been employed almost exclusively for religious purposes, that is to say dealings with spirits, ancestors and gods (if deified ancestors may be so called). The aim was sometimes to ask their advice by means of an oracle, sometimes to invest an appointment, a victory or a treaty with special dignity by means of a "letter to the gods", which would give it the stamp of their approval, and sometimes to record eclipses of the moon, floods and suchlike phenomena. In this way a partnership evolved between religion and science which, in China, has from the very beginning been astonish- *Science* ingly rationalistic and moreover has treated history as its basic theme. Chinese religion knows nothing of god the creator as a powerful and arbitrary being; it shows no interest in myths about the creation. Demons and gods are conceived as subordinate to the same *Tao*, the same law, as are spring and autumn, seed and harvest. Admittedly these laws cannot always or easily be discovered. So the reason for composing chronicles and compiling archives was, to put it in modern terms, to provide statistics of phenomena from which conclusions could be drawn about the laws governing them. So the first true book in China is the Ch'un-ch'iu, "the Spring and Autumn Annals" which is, for good reasons, attributed to K'ung-tse, our Confucius. It seems to us to contain nothing but dry accounts of unimportant events in and around western Shantung, but there is something astonishing in the method behind its composition, something not unworthy of 19th century positivism. The impeccable source used in these short annals has been the original inscriptions preserved in the temples of ancestors throughout the land. We do not know how it came about that K'ung-tse and others like him resolved to make collections of sources. His "sayings" (Lun-yü) were not written down by him but by his followers in the 5th century. Later commentaries of solid historical worth in addition to their moralising interpretations, were appended to the Chun-ch'iu. We cannot here go into the question whether Confucius himself, as tradition says, instigated the collection of the 300 folksongs and sacrificial chants transcribed in the Shih-king, or "Book of Songs". The decisive fact which

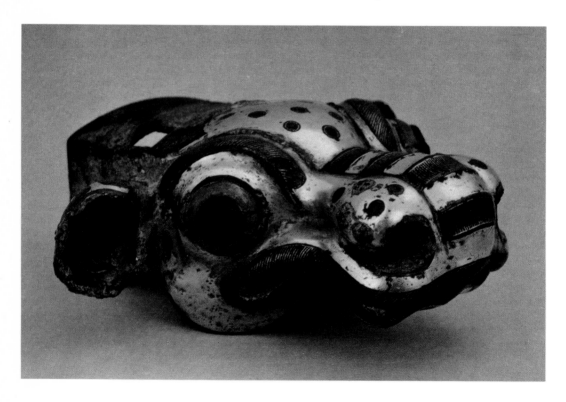

Ox head ornament presumably from a chariot. Made of bronze plated with gold and with silver inlay. From Chin-ts'un near Loyang the capital of the Chou dynasty. About 300 B.C. *British Museum, London (8½ inches high)*

60

needs to be emphasised is that in the 5th century writing had come to be used for mundane purposes, for the methodical and rational collection of historical material as well as for religious, moral and economic affairs. Art too in the feudal age is essentially rational and secular. As a result of this tendency, morals, the wordly aspect of religion, were raised to the conscious level and, by that very fact, largely severed from religion. K'ung-tse was one of the first Chinese moralists who tried to exercise political influence at court, without, in his own life time, any success worth mentioning. So he had to limit his activities to teaching a private circle of disciples, who in turn taught others, with the result that 400 years later his teaching won general recognition and was regarded as the basis of Chinese social morality.

Especially in the 4th century, there is a crop of political theorists, economists, moralists and publicists, some with practical turns of mind and others speculative, some hard headed and others paradoxical, some with *Lao-tse* successful and others with unsuccessful schools. There are now good grounds for placing Lao-tse too in the 4th century. His book, later to be called the "Tao-te-king", a title that emphasised its anti-Confucian tendencies, was rooted in mystical conceptions sometimes harking back to ancient myths, and used extreme paradox to attack those theories of the state which were then struggling for recognition. It is true that the text, as often happens, raises almost insoluble problems of date and authenticity. At the same time, that is to say the 4th century at latest, there began to be a marked demand for more exact instruction. So the Yü-kung, a long chapter in the classical book of "Ancient Records", gave for the first time a general account of the geography and economic life of all the then known world. Tsou Yen's "Doctrine of the Five Elements" dates from about 330 B.C. and, speculative though much of it still is, marks the beginning of the scientific study of nature. It is unfortunate that at that time there were also speculative theorists about religion, who were all too successful in burying the genuine old conceptions under a mythology invented in their libraries and a rationalising theology. So there is no reason to be surprised when we find that the religious art of the feudal age was deeply tainted with mundane rationalism.

Finally we have to note a far-reaching change in society, which began to be *Merchants* very important in the feudal age, namely the social advance of merchants and tradesmen. Nothing is more typical of China then and always than the history of her coinage. The "cash", round coins of copper or, more often, bronze with a rectangular hole in the middle, which had been cast since the 6th century, remained the same, the inscriptions apart, until the be-

61

ginning of the present century. So a Chinese man in 1900 A.D. could pay a debt with a coin Confucius might have used. It is not just that the Chinese are conservative, but also that they are fundamentally practical, and so they found a solution of the currency problem that lasted for two and a half millenia. The advance to importance of the merchant class was due to three reasons which have partial parallels in Europe in the age of absolutism. The conduct of war had become more expensive; apart from infantry and war-chariots, the wars with the nomads in the north had made a considerable force of cavalry essential. Wars did not stop after 600 B.C. and war chests were ever in need of cash and credit. Moreover the merchants had been quick to realise the advantages of reading and writing; consequently the revenues were pledged to them and they became both tax farmers and, by the same token, the first semi-public officials with a knowledge of writing and of accounts. Thirdly, at that time land could be freely sold, and Chinese merchants would have belied their calling had they not taken the opportunity to put their surplus capital into land as the safest investment. So they became great landowners; however, and this is typical of China, they had no huge continuous domains, but widely scattered properties which the former owners continued to cultivate as tenants. That is at the root of the system which for two thousand years has been the hallmark of Chinese society, and goes by the rather unfortunate name of the "Gentry system". The wealth of the gentry consisted primarily in leasehold land. They might own a country house somewhere and either live in it or retreat to it when their town house was in danger. But even the most successful of them did not want to be sole owners. Land and wealth belonged to the family or kinship group which was often very large. Its disposal was under the control of the head of the family whose position did not always come to him simply by hereditary precedence. As a rule the temple of the ancestors, often quite an unpretentious building, was the centre of family life. There the senior members of the family would assemble from time to time, discuss the yield from the property and the possibilities of new enterprises, and appoint a head of the family, who would have a casting vote in case of dispute. But the eldest son did not automatically inherit rights and responsibilities; if he appeared unsuitable, a more reliable person, who might be quite a distant relation, was adopted in his place. The family was also concerned with the training and marriage of the children, the care of the sick, the weak and the old, and it also often paid for tutors and the upkeep of schools. This system, which has both good and bad points, became more widespread as the merchant class lost the privileges it had enjoyed in feudal times. In time it became

62

the basis for the learned and independent bureaucracy of China. That is the reason why — and this again is a typical Chinese correlative — everyone is glad to have a numerous progeny, and takes pleasure in old age and the evening of life, and sees in it above all the fulfilment of existence. Recently there has been much harsh criticism by the Chinese of the inhuman and immoral institutions of Europe, our impersonal hospitals and asylums, and our old age pensions which can be swept away by an equally inhuman and impersonal inflation. No doubt the Chinese gentry system has its weak sides and, as everywhere, its members may be righteous or unjust. However that may be, for two thousand years it has never refused to bear the weight of the highest civilisation known to man.

Tiger's head which probably formed part of the decoration of a chariot. Dark bronze inlaid with silver. There is an inscription, inlaid in silver, underneath, which gives the owner's rank. About 300 B.C. *Museum of Far Eastern Art, Cologne (length 2 inches)*

63

Surrounding world   At this time, relations with the outside world begin to take on importance. The peoples of the steppe, from the Amur to the Don, were in all probability forced by an enduring deterioration of the climate to keep on the move, and tried, in considerable numbers, to find new lands to settle in the south. This upheaval included peoples of all races, Tungus, Mongolian, Turco-Mongolian and Indo-Iranian, and it seems pointless to try and sort out these races and groups by measuring skulls and observing linguistic survivals, or to try and follow their trails, for every name we meet has to be put into inverted commas. But there are some ways in which the story of these movements, as far as we now know it, is relevant to the history of art.

The artistic remains of the Scythians have long excited the greatest interest, since magnificent gold work was found in their tumuli (Kurgans) in southern Russia together with Greek export pieces and other treasures.

Scythians   The recent finds at Ziwiye near Sakiz, presumably an ancient Scythian capital in Persia south of lake Urmia, give us a better understanding of the origin and derivation of Scythian art. We know from literary sources that the Assyrian king Asarhaddon (680–669 B.C.) made an alliance with the Scythians who were then invading Western Persia, against the Medes who were of the same stock as themselves, and against the Cimmerians, whose armies harried Asia Minor in the 8th Century B.C. He went so far as to give a daughter in marriage to the Scythian King Partatua, whom Herodotus mentions as Protothyas. About half a century later, in 616 B.C. the Medes defeated the Scythians decisively, and drove them out of Persia. They rode back into South Russia. Presumably it was then that the Ziwiye hoard was buried. It contained, apart from pottery and other things of purely Assyrian type, magnificent gold work which in all probability was made by Assyrian artists for their Scythian allies. So deer and other animals suited to Scythian taste were added to the usual Assyrian repertory. Hence it is almost certain that many of the magnificent golden scabbards found in the kurgans of southern Russia are also of Assyrian workmanship, and that the Scythians learnt the goldsmiths' art and adopted many motifs from the Assyrians. However we cannot trace similar influences in the other scarce remains of the early period except, possibly, in the pottery. But K. Jettmar and others concerned with this special study have recently pointed out that the whole Scythian people did not go on the move together. Some of them always remained at home, and indeed there were occasions when only the age groups called to military service went fighting in the east and brought the gold and other plunder home. How far this home of theirs stretched towards the east is far from clear, but they must at least have had connections with the Altai region. And about 4,000 feet up in the

64

mountains of the Altai, kurgans have been found which are the pre-historians' delight, and of which eight at Pazyryk have so far been excavated. These barrows were partially robbed soon after they were finished, but then they filled with water which turned to permanent ice. This ice preserved the contents of the tombs so perfectly that even the tattoo marks on the bodies were quite fresh in colour. The 2nd kurgan at Pazyryk contained a princely pair of whom the man was emphatically Mongolian and the woman Indo-iranian in type, which goes to show how easily racial questions were solved in those days. The kurgans so far excavated date from about 300 B.C. and their gay contents give a vivid impression of the great variety of things which war and plunder, and peaceful trade too, brought to the Altai. Some of the textiles were pure Persian, while others were local imitations of Near Eastern designs whose original significance was, often enough, misunderstood, and there were others too of no identifiable derivation or resemblance. There was also a fragment of a Chinese bronze mirror with exactly the same pattern as is found in the Huai valley in central China, the oldest piece of Chinese silk yet known with diamond pattern, and other things derived directly or indirectly from China.

It is true that we have only got two excavations, that at Ziwiye and that *Altai* in the Altai, to serve as a basis of comparison with the finds in South Russia, and they are separated widely in space and by three hundred years in time. But still they give so vivid an impression of interconnection and exchange of ideas between Assyria and the Altai and China that one can no longer consider Chinese art of the Feudal age without a glance over the border. No doubt further excavations, at Pazyryk especially, will fill in the gaps and complete the picture; at present we are, for instance, completely ignorant of what was happening at that time in East and West Turkestan. There is however literary evidence that the Chinese were already prepared, and had to be prepared, to learn something from their enemies, those "barbarians" who none the less enjoyed a truly international luxury. In 307 B.C. Duke Wu-ling of Chao in Northern Shensi, which borders on the Ordos tribal area, in the great bend of the Huangho, took over the tight breeches of the nomad horsemen and the tactics of light-armed mounted archers. It was a matter of life and death that compelled him to imitate the enemy's strongest weapon, but imitation was not confined to the military field. A number of motifs and patterns appear in Chinese art of the Feudal age which would be hard to explain without a knowledge of their contacts with the nomads of the steppe and, through them, with the Near East. Far the most important motif is the animal fight, and it is not a chance that it is often found on the clasps of belts and hooks for clothes

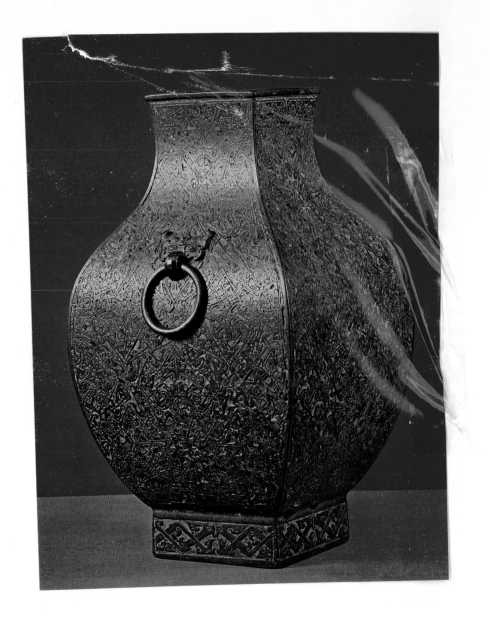

Bronze sacrificial vessel inlaid with malachite. The incised inscription shows that the vessel was made in 279 B.C., presumably somewhere near modern Peking, and came as plunder into the hands of its owner. Bronzes resembling it have been found in the graves at Chin-Ts'un, near Loyang, the Chou dynasty capital. *University Museum, Philadelphia (15 inches high)*

66

which were a new fashion in Chinese dress. The animal fight is one of the most ancient religious themes in the art of the Near East; for all its variations, the basic motif maintains its continual vitality from Early Sumerian down to Sassanian times. The Greeks and Etruscans borrowed this motif from there, and so did the Scythians and the men of Pazyryk and then, from the 6th century B.C. onwards, the nomads of the Ordos and the Chinese. Now it is very significant that this motif is never found on Shang bronzes, although there were representations of thousands of animals which could have had reason enough to bite and kill each other. So it would be interesting to discover just why this motif came to the fore in China in the Feudal age. In the Near East, deep religious meanings may be symbolised in hunting scenes. But the Chinese seem to have had no sense of this significance, and to have taken over simply the external form. Moreover, in China it is not until the 4th century that battle scenes, of a type that had long been usual in the Near East, appear. That is to say, battles on land and water and also the storming of city walls. A simple representation in outline on a bronze might, with but little alteration, have been found in Assyria. The motif of the flying gallop, which is first found in Chin-Ts'un may have a deeper significance than Reinach saw in it. It may be that this partiality for the representation of actual happenings was in some way connected with the contemporary awakening of Chinese interest in historical research.

DRAWING ON P. 68

One can never draw a clear line between ornamental representation and pure ornament. But when for the first time a plant-motif makes its appearance at Pazyryk, and in China too, it is unmistakably a rosette. This is significant evidence of Western Asian influence. The most striking example is found on the lid, probably coming from one of the then fashionable bronze boxes, now belonging to the King of Sweden. A rosette fills the centre of the circle, and this rosette is very true to nature; it has, so to say, been revivified. Its round chalice and double row of petals are framed in a plaited ribbon pattern. This ribbon pattern too is among the commonest of Near Eastern designs. That might indeed be a chance, for such a simple pattern may be found anywhere and any time. But it cannot be chance that rosette, animal fight and hunting scene are all found together. One might have supposed that a plant motif was something so simple and so pleasing that it would be used everywhere and always; but that was just what did not happen in China. These new finds have put an end to the doubt about the heart-shaped four-petal pattern which constantly recurs on mirrors and textiles from the Feudal age to Han times; plants must be intended. But these plant patterns and diagrammatic petals long remained in China as isolated decoration. Simple trees apart, they were slow to attempt the representation of plants, until, in T'ang times, they were freely accepted and indeed from thenceforth became one of the favourite themes of Chinese art. All of which indicates that this motif, which one would have supposed to be universally understood, must originally have struck the Chinese as strange and unattractive, and that it took a long time for them to change their minds.

Ornament Besides these patterns there are some quite new ornaments such as drops, commas, points, circles, points in a circle, beans and triangles, for the most part framed by a heavy line, which are especially suited to indicate the fur and joints of animals. These motifs are very often found among the steppe peoples, the Scythians and Sarmatians, whereas in the Near East they are only occasionally seen. The glazed tiles from about 400 B.C. now in the Louvre, which decorated the walls of the palace at Susa, more especially the winged bull and the griffin, provide a regular pattern-card of these decorations. They were all very cleverly used to emphasise the joints and the flecks of colour in the skin, and the organic shape of the animals. In the Near East and in Persia, even in the palace of Susa itself, these patterns are something of an exception to the general rule but they are leit-motifs among the steppe peoples in the Ordos territory and in China in the Feu-

Storming of a city wall. 4th Century B.C. *Copy from the representation on a bronze in the National Museum of Peking (Drawing by Professor E. Consten)*

68

dal age. Admittedly, one can draw no sharp line between China and the Ordos territory, and we cannot say how long these patterns stayed in fashion.

There was a great taste for precious stones, especially turquoises which were imported ready cut, sometimes triangular, sometimes round and sometimes bean-shaped, and inlaid into the skins, ears and joints of bronze or golden animals. It is often impossible to tell, when one finds these patterns cut out of the bronze, whether they were originally intended to be filled with jewels, or whether they are cheap substitutes following a style originally made fashionable by the coloured inlays. So the thought suggests itself that the steppe peoples may have got the stones ready cut from the south and, not wanting to waste any of such costly materials, invented a style with plenty of uses for them. The Chinese then enjoyed adopting and developing this technique. In any event Chinese art of the Feudal age was open to influences from the furthest parts of Asia which reached them across the steppes. This could only happen, or at least is most likely to have happened, if the Chinese were already in a mood to appreciate the rational and geometrical shapes underlying this style, a style indeed of transparent intelligibility. So these timely influences throw light on the essential nature of Chinese art at that time, its susceptibility to external influences and its secular mood. That is not to say that these foreign contacts and stimuli were all important. Internal evolution had set things going along the same path. That is clearly proved by the evolution of purely Chinese ornament both in detail and in general structure, in its vocabulary as well as in its grammar. The leit-motif of the Feudal age is the "triangular volute", generally an acute angled open triangle one of whose sides curls inwards. Next in importance comes a system of interlocking T-shapes. There is no end to the variations and combinations of these basic motifs which evolve to form diamonds and diapers filled with volutes in a way which is difficult to describe, but might be made clear by a template. Animal shapes are often altered beyond recognition to take their part in this fantastic linear decoration. Both triangular volutes and T-shapes can be traced by the careful observer in their descent back from Shang times. They are surely there both in the bronzes and in the white pottery excavated at Anyang. There is for instance a clear anticipation of a triangular volute on the wings of the bird on the lid in the Musée Guimet (plate on p. 35), in which case it may be meant for a snake, and there is a more recognisable, though headless, snake on Mr Kawai's bronze (plate on p. 32). From the 6th century onwards this linear spiral-loving decoration is once more firm and taut; bands and braids are

69

Tripod with cover, made of bronze with silver inlay in an exceptionally spirited style. Three small animals executed in the round form the handles of the lid, and their skins are enlivened by drop-shaped inlays. Excavated at Chin-ts'un near Loyang. About 300 B.C. *The Minneapolis Institute of Art (6 inches high)*

70

again in fashion, but they are very different from the smooth and feeble Middle Chou versions.

The earliest examples of sculpture in wood, bronze and pottery date from *Meaning* this time and are usually small objects. They represent animals and men in many forms. So man is accepted as one, though not the most important, of the possible subjects of art. Moreover the finds at Hsin-yang and Ch'ang-sha give us direct evidence about the painting of the period, though not perhaps about its greatest manifestations. Linear transcriptions of paintings on to bronze or brick, such as we find at Chin-ts'un, and similar copies on stone in the Han sanctuaries must supplement what we know from literary sources.

But it is the bronzes with their many-coloured inlays of turquoise, malachite, jade, silver and gold that give us the most vivid sense of the brilliance of the Feudal age. Less costly objects imitate this effect of polychromy by means of flecked and broken surfaces. Pottery is more closely than ever linked to bronze shapes, but thin hard felspar glazes, first used at the ancient Yueh (modern Chekiang), long antedate anything similar in the West. The opaque coloured glazes are harmonious in their polychromy.

The great number of lacquer objects recently found are a glory of the age, and constitute a new and original branch of art. Jade too has never been carved into more spirited or elegant shapes. The swinging curves of their fantastic lines are like nothing that has gone before and have never been equalled since; there is in them a freedom and spirit that even the calligraphers of later ages scarcely attained. The mood of the age was in harmony with the actual world; spiritual feeling found direct expression; there was playful delight in the invention of aesthetic formulas; and an universal rivalry in excellence forbade the trivial and stimulated bold creation. In such circumstances religion fell into the background and its voice was drowned. In Shang times every utensil had a sacred purpose: but now sacred things were turned secular, being needed for the shrine of understanding and pressed into the service of a spiritual debate which, as was almost bound to happen, shifted the accent on to morality. But this morality then was one of high pretensions, not of quiet modesty.

Though so much is preserved from this age, it is difficult to sort out the *The State of Ch'u* objects intended for religious use, and it is no chance that this is less difficult in southern and central China than in the north. The great agricultural state of Ch'u kept the conceptions of the Shang age more vividly alive than did the warlike Chou with its feudal lords. Thus in a tomb-

71

chamber at Hsin-yang we find a squatting lacquered wooden figure of a guardian spirit with tiger's body, great round eyes and long tongue hanging out; on its head are real deer's antlers. This must be derived from the earlier *T'ao-t'ieh* earth demons such as we find on the Cernuschi bronze. And it is tempting to suppose that the tongue stands for the spirit in the sense of speech; for it is in the writings of the 4th century that we first hear the authentic voice of Chinese self-expression. This demon is much more naturalistic than anything from Shang times, and indeed the real antlers, other specimens of which have been excavated at Ch'ang-sha, substitute actuality for art. Moreover the earth demon has the very face of a man. In the British Museum there is the wooden bust of a man, found at Ch'ang-sha, with long tongue hanging out and antlers on the head, which is no great work of art, but is a significant example of the changed ideas of the period. Also at Ch'ang-sha was found a huge wooden sculpture representing the old motif of bird and snake, painted in red and white lacquer on a black lacker ground; it is now in the Cleveland Museum.

Return to nature There again one is struck by its extraordinary closeness to reality, indeed by the return to nature of an ancient motif never so naturalistically represented in China before. One cannot doubt that the birds are cranes, and only the peacock feathers planted on the wings bring to mind the erstwhile taste for crowds of symbols. Different patterns emphasise a contrast between the bodies of one snake and another, one crane and another, and must symbolise the *yin* and the *yang*, the female and male of each pair. Apart from the return to nature and the actual world, there has been at work a movement for the rational purification and indeed for the theorising of ancient mythical themes. We find again cicadas and owls which, at first sight, are not distinguishable from those of Shang times; but there are no more snakes on their wings, and only someone familiar with antiquity would recognise the ancient meaning of the decoration that takes their place. Now it is above all the animals themselves which are represented, and it is not quite certain whether they are in fact there in the service of religion. At any rate the *t'ao-t'ieh* masks lose all their demonic character and have turned into useful decorative motifs; they often hold rings or

PLATE ON PAGE 57 handles in their jaws. There are even almost human demons serving as legs for tables, which at that time were still low on the ground. Magnificent examples have been found at Chin-ts'un. The well constructed body of the almost human bear (plate on p. 57), firmly articulated and vividly outlined, is enriched with inlays of gold and silver which, while they are in harmony with its forms, yet have a decorative life of their own with

72

Jade ornament or amulet found at Chin-ts'un near Loyang. About 250 B.C. *William Rockhill Nelson Gallery of Art, Atkins Museum, Kansas City (6½ inches in diameter)*

waving curves, sharp triangles and volutes, and with a thickening and thinning of line that enlivens the swing of the design.

Chariot fittings too, such as shafts and axles, are enriched with more costly ornament of higher aesthetic pretensions. The ox head (plate on p. 60), also found at Chin-ts'un, is vividly enriched in plastic form and in colour by its inlays of gold and silver. There are triangular volutes of pure Chinese style in its ears, while the dotted circles between forehead and nostrils are a near Eastern pattern, and the nostrils themselves, though organic and naturalistic, also form a truly classical comma pattern. The little tiger's head in the museum at Cologne with its flat silver inlays harmonises volutes, triangular volutes and the comma patterns for the hairs with the swinging curves of the interlocking planes. Round bronze mirrors first appear in the Feudal age. One surface was polished, while the back was often richly decorated in relief, and sometimes had inlays of gold and silver. There is a knob in the middle through which a cord

PLATE ON PAGE 60

PLATE ON PAGE 63

Vase with lid of reddish pottery and glass drops on the slip. Probably found at Shou-hsien in the Huai valley. One of the earliest known examples of the use of glass in Chinese art. 3rd century B.C. *Museum of Fine Arts, Boston (5 inches high)*

74

could be passed. The great number of these mirrors leads one to suppose that bronze was no longer so rare and costly that it could not be used for all manner of luxury goods. But it is certain that all the mirrors of this and the following age were not just articles of luxury. Some of them *Luxury* are very large, almost three feet in diameter, and many of them have spiral ornaments with some connection with the calendar, whose meaning astronomers are trying to discover. Many of them must have served religious purposes. That was certainly the case later in Japan where mirrors are placed in the most holy part of Shinto shrines, but as yet we know nothing of their function in ancient Chinese religion.

The same doubt arises about many other utensils. The tall bronze in the Philadelphia museum is much the same shape as many sacrificial vessels PLATE ON PAGE 66 of Shang times, though they have round bases. The square base is a change, but not a fundamental innovation. The outline has regained the tautness lost in Middle Chou times, and the curves have the characteristic elegance of the Feudal age. The costly malachite inlay shows all the magnificence and the spirited variation of the regular ground pattern of which no previous age was capable. The *t'ao-t'ieh* masks supporting the handles are again brought back close to nature. One wonders whether such a magnificent bronze was simply intended for religious use, for the reverence of an earth born demon or of the ancestors. Is it not more likely that it was placed in the high rooms of a palace or the hall of ancestors attached thereto? We learn from the inscription that it was made in 279 B.C. and probably carried off as booty from the state of Yen, the most northern of the states in the neighbourhood of modern Peking and southern Manchuria. That argues in favour of a secular use for the vessel but does not prove it, and we must leave the matter open. One is left wondering whether this costly and elegant though restrained magnificence, which suits the secular spirit of the age, can be brought into harmony with our former conception of the simple taste of Chinese religious feeling.

One can ask the same question about the lovely three-footed bronze in the *Linear fantasies* Minneapolis Museum. It comes from the burial area at Chin-ts'un, near PLATE ON PAGE 70 the old capital of Loyang which continued to be an important artistic centre. It dates from the 3rd century B.C. Time has turned the bronze to a decidedly reddish hue from which the silver inlay stands out boldly. Was there ever a more spirited linear fantasy, although nothing more than the ordinary current motifs are used. The pattern is easier to see, or copy by a drawing, than to describe. Is it diamonds whose sides have twirled into heart-shaped volutes; are the half-diamonds underneath intended as eyebrows, and the little volutes that spring from them intended

75

Round covered box for toilet requisites or the like. Lacquer on wood. Probably from Ch'ang-sha in central China. 3rd century B.C. *William Rockhill Nelson Gallery of Art, Atkins Museum, Kansas City (height 3½ inches: diameter 8 inches)*

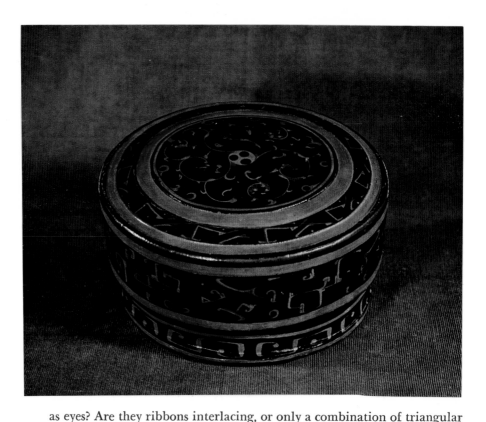

as eyes? Are they ribbons interlacing, or only a combination of triangular volutes of varying sizes? Can one discover in this decoration an abstract version of the old *t'ao-t'ieh* masks? What could be more spirited than the scaly snake dragons on the lid? Could anything be more sensitive than the comma inlay on the hide of the animal handles moulded in the round?

Jade

PLATE ON PAGE 73

The jade disk in the Kansas City Museum may have been either for religious use or a refined ornament. In any case it is the most beautiful surviving example of Chinese carving. Broad jade disks were found as early as the prehistoric settlements in Kansu, and there is a not entirely reliable tradition that these sumptuous objects were intended as symbols of heaven. We know representations from Han times in which they are clearly used as amulets hanging from beds, and they are found in graves on the breasts of the dead.

76

The living too may have worn them as talismans but it would be difficult to imagine anyone wearing this unbelievably finely carved disk. We must remember that jade is more brittle than glass, to appreciate the skill required to cut the tiny roundels ornamenting the surface. The outer ring is of the usual size; within it is a smaller ring, and the two are joined by a splendid dragon and a cloud pattern; the curling outlines are sharply defined, and the drawing of this fretwork is brilliant. Advantage has been taken of the chance shape of the jade to add two similar dragons on the outer rim, both delightfully fantastic, and both executed with a sure mastery of subtle curves. Perhaps the maker had not forgotten the meaning of its original religious significance, but one can hardly see it now as anything but a jewel of refined elegance.

Very simple geometrical designs were also in fashion at this time. Some- *PLATE ON PAGE 74* times the ground was divided up into quadrilaterals each of which contained a circle, and each of these circles was in turn filled by three or seven smaller circles. It is a simple but attractive design, and well suited to decorate, but not to spoil, the simple, comely shape of the covered pot illustrated on page 74. This pot is made of reddish clay covered by a slip on to which drops of opaque glass have been applied, a technique which was probably an expensive innovation at the time.

Lacquer begins a new and glorious chapter of its history in the Feudal age. *Lacquer* Lacquer and silk are the two happiest of Chinese discoveries; things which add two noble media to the raw materials of art. The resin of the true lacquer tree which is native to China, has qualities which recommend it for preservation as well as for beauty. It is consistently firm and almost completely resistant to acids. Two thousand year old lacquer skins, whose wooden backing has long perished, have been excavated and cleaned with hydrochloric acid so that they are as fresh as on the day they were made. Almost any material can be given a lacquer skin; wood is the most usual, but textiles, paper, bronze and pottery are among the other possibilities. Lacquer is viscous and slow in drying to complete hardness. It is a fine foundation for colours more brilliant, but a little more tacky, than those available in European oil paint. Its finest effects are obtained by careful repeated polishing. There are fragments to prove that lacquer was known in Shang times, but no complete piece is preserved. The supply increases in the Feudal age, both in the north and in central China. A wonderful lot of lacquer has been found in the recent excavations at Ch'ang-sha and Hsin-yang, and we may hope that in the near future further excavations will be more carefully recorded. Then we may see as a piece of luck that all the things dug up in the war years at Ch'ang-sha were so recklessly scattered

77

over the world. Thus every country will be able to get an idea of Chinese achievement in this branch of art whose appeal is not to the eye only, but also to the sense of touch; there is hardly any other art which gives so great and so varied a delight to this sense. That is why so many articles of everyday use were decorated with lacquer; caskets and all manner of boxes, especially those for rouge and powder and the dressing table generally, the holders for ornamental combs and all the other things that bring beauty into daily life. The 3rd century B.C. toilet box from Ch'ang-sha, now in the Kansas City Museum, is one delightful example out of a great number of such things made by an army of craftsmen. In outline it is simple but very spirited; the crooks and circles and curves of its ornament are sure and never tedious; this free and playful disciplined linear fantasy is characteristic of the Feudal age.

PLATE ON PAGE 76

Lacquer Painting Lacquer was also in fashion at that time for painting. A magnificent example comes from a 4th century grave at Hsin-yang. It is the fragment of

78

a broken lute, made of wood covered by a black lacquer ground on which hunting scenes have been painted in a few vividly contrasting colours. The fragment here illustrated shows two scenes; in one two men are carrying their game slung on a pole, accompanied by two dogs rather like bulldogs.

The other scene is placed in an angle to the right of the first and shows a large bearlike animal and a dog with an ornamental collar; one can just see the tip of a spear presumably belonging to a huntsman who was giving the beast its deathblow. Only three colours are used, a purply blue, flesh-red and yellow; on the bear's head there are places where these colours have been laid one top of the other and rubbed away to make a good transition. The almost grotesque figures of men and beasts, with the taut curves of their silhouettes, bring the jade dragon from Chin-ts'un at once to mind, and give one a very good idea of the fashion and style of the age. For, as has been said already, this highly spirited and fantastic style is capable of the boldest and most grotesque paradoxes.

There must have been many more things of use and beauty than the few *Literary evidence* chance has saved for us. A poem attributed to Ch'u Yüan, an ill-fated poet and statesman who lived in central China about 300 B.C., gives us some real insight into this question. It seems that he has been given the credit for all the verse that could be collected from central China, and in this way has won fame as an immortal poet. The long poem entitled "Heaven Questions" *(T'ien-wen)* describes among other things fallen palaces in which there were pictures of the great kings of antiquity and of their deeds, and also of tyrants and their misdeeds; besides this there are representations of the great historical figures in the land, such as King Ho-lü of Wu, the founder of Suchou. Now no direct evidence of such high art has come to light, but the themes maintained their vitality in the following Han period, and we have copies, transcriptions and drawings from that period among the decorations of the stone walls of Han grave chapels. They are only dry copies, but their historical value is inestimable, even though they have little charm as works of art, and do not give an inkling of the life and movement and spirit of the originals. For every work of art from the Feudal age was bubbling over almost to excess with high-spirited creative power.

◄ Two hunting scenes painted in lacquer on the fragments of a broken lute. Excavated at Hsin-yang in southern Honan. 4th cent. B.C. *Published in Wen-wu, September 1957*

79

CHINA AND THE WEST

IV THE UNIFIED STATE

In the year 221 B.C. all the states of China were conquered and unified *Shih-huang-ti* by the King of Ch'in who took the title of "First Emperor", Shih-huang-ti. Four years after the death of this forceful and unscrupulous founder of Chinese unity, his dynasty was pushed aside and his capital went up in flames. A struggle followed which ended in the foundation of the Han Dynasty by Liu Pang in 202 B.C. He had no intention of restoring the old system, but appointed officials responsible to the central government instead of the Feudal lords. The Han dynasty maintained the unity of China for 400 years and the whole of the present 18 provinces was brought within its domain. At this time the foundations of the state and of society were laid on a basis that has endured for 2,000 years, a basis to which China has always returned, in spite of many sad deviations and troubles. There were enough internal struggles for power and attempted revolutions both in Han times and the 2,000 years thereafter. A naval battle at Red Rocks on the Yangtse in 208 A.D. marks the final end of the Han dynasty. But during its rule the unity of the state in all essential matters had been so firmly established that it remained ever after as an ideal in Chinese minds. The magnitude of this achievement can be grasped if we remember that the Han Empire was as large and as populous as that of Rome.

The First Emperor in 221 B.C. had taken decisive steps to secure the unity of the state. Of these steps four are important in our context. First the axle width of carts was standardised and a network of roads laid out. That this should have been necessary gives an idea of how China was before. One of the most important highways was the military ring road along the northern frontier. It performed the same task as the Roman "limes" which was originally just a military ring road round the frontier. Strongpoints were placed along it, and the Emperor joined up the already existing stretches of wall so that they formed one continuous line along the frontier. So he built the "great wall" which was to be rebuilt in stone in the 16th century. The whole of the Huangho was not included inside the frontier, for in its great northern bend what is called the Ordos territory was left out, and this was done not only because it was held by tribes from Mongolia, but also so as to have a surplus area of meadow land to use in case of necessity. The Ordos territory was both before and long after this time important in art history as a place of contact between China and Mongolia and the world beyond.

81

Nobility of office All privileges of the nobility and feudal functions were abolished, and duties entrusted as far as possible to people with the requisite specialist education, or else to members of the Imperial Family. Naturally this bureaucracy was hardly like that of 20th century Europe, but similar principles had already been enunciated. In practice there was not an adequate educational basis or enough competitors to satisfy the needs. It was often necessary to call on experienced merchants, and the highly educated chancellor and adviser of the Emperor, Lü Pu-wei, was also the greatest merchant prince of China. Like many a duke in earlier times, he gathered a learned circle in his palace, and stimulated them to publish an encyclopedia, the Lü-shih ch'un-ch'iu, which has remained one of the most influential books in China, though its modern editions are not in all respects like the ancient one. Richard Wilhelm made it his great task to translate it. But it shows up the present state of Chinese studies, that there is a margin of 600 years in different estimates of the date of the manuscripts, though there is litte doubt that the thoughts expressed in it are substantially those that held the field about the year 200 B.C.

Writing Ch'in Shih-huang-ti also paid particular attention to the question of the script. In the interest of Chinese unity, he ordered the standardisation of the shape and meaning of ideograms. In the conditions of social chaos in which literacy had spread in the Feudal age, there was a great danger that strong local variations of script would become established. The Emperor banished this danger, and it is only the simplifications very recently introduced for supposedly practical reasons that have once more made it difficult to read the books of the last 2,000 years without a special dictionary. But after that Shih-huang-ti tried to do something which has an all too familiar ring in modern ears. He condemned and destroyed all books that did not suit his political line. He had the archives of the individual states brought together in his capital, Hsien-yang, with the understandable object of getting the title deeds of other claimants to hereditary power into his hands, and then ordered the writings of any political theorist of whom he disapproved to be kept in one example under lock and key in the archives, and all copies to be burnt. The only books permitted were ones dealing with technical questions, economics, medicine or the like. At the same time 460 men of learning, intellectuals as we should say, were executed because they would not approve his new policy.

Politics So he and his chancellor Li Sse who supplanted Lü Pu-wei and drove him to suicide, are branded as enemies of the spirit and, later, especially of the Confucianists. These two did not realise that they were paying a great tribute to intellect, in that they took writings so seriously that they

82

Model of a tower house with courtyard and gateway, placed as one of the offerings in a rich tomb. It is made of pottery, in several pieces, and painted with unfired colours. Han period, about 200 B.C.—200 A.D. *William Rockhill Nelson Gallery of Art, Atkins Museum, Kansas City (4 feet high)*

attempted the impossible task of destroying the spirit by force. But no one seems to have learnt anything from this story. The following tale illustrates the great importance already attached by Chinese statesmen to public opinion. The story is found in "Political Dialogues", and concerns an argument in the state of Ch'in, which took place about 100 years before Shih-huang-ti. Ch'in, a state in the Wei valley in the north west, was then following a policy of unifying China by attacking one of the secession states after another. The question was whether to attack the rich and highly civilised state of Ch'u, perhaps the strongest opponent in central China, or the out-of-the-way and backward state of Shu hemmed in by mountains on the upper Yangtse in the modern province of Ssech'uan. The argument ran on these lines: to attack Ch'u which was more civilised even than Ch'in itself, would unite everyone in opposition: but to conquer Shu and bring it into the system of the secession states, would be approved by all including Ch'u; in that way Ch'in territory and power could be increased so that Ch'u could more surely be conquered. This calculation won the day.

The Emperor issued many ordinances against pretentious luxury, but that did not prevent his spending huge sums on his A-fang palace and on his sepulchre. The immense barrow was plundered soon after his death, but has not yet been excavated, and it is likely that the huge stone sarcophagus lies there intact. When the Emperor disarmed all the former Feudal states, he melted down the weapons and probably other bronze objects, and cast twelve colossal figures out of the bronze, which he set up outside his palace as symbols of the unity of the state. That is typical fate for Chinese bronze work. The sheer material value of the bronze "cash" coins made it a temptation to turn bronze works of art into money, and vice versa. When China was prosperous more and more works of art were made of bronze: when money was short, the temples — and later the Buddhist monasteries — were stripped of their ornaments which were treated as a currency reserve. This was all done in due form with proper bureaucratic punctilio. Shih-huang-ti also established an imperial factory with a regular staff under official supervision. This system continued under the Han dynasty and indeed in hardly altered form down to K'ang-hsi and Ch'ienlung in the 18th century.

His weak successor survived this brilliant father by only four years. Then the storm broke on all sides against his despotism. In 206 B.C. Hsien-yang lay in ashes. In 202 B.C. the founder of the Han dynasty had defeated all his rivals and ascended the imperial throne at Ch'ang-an which he rebuilt to take the place of Hsien-yang. The Han were prudently determined not to allow the feudal system back again, and suppressed a number of rebellions with slaughter, when nobles, some of them princes of the imperial family, got control of districts and tried to set themselves up as feudal lords. At the same time the ban on books was lifted, and so a beginning was made of a collection of the writings that had been secretly preserved. On the other hand merchants were forbidden in 199 B.C. to carry arms, or ride, or wear costly brocades or richly patterned and embroidered silk. The training of the bureaucracy was not put in hand so quickly or with so little friction as is sometimes supposed. When the school in Ch'ang-an, one of the oldest universities in the world, was founded to set an example for education, it was at that time intended as a school for knights in which the military training of the body was as important as the writer's brush.

Pair of portraitlike pottery tomb figures with coloured glaze. 1st or 2nd century A.D. *Museum of Ethnography, Munich (25 inches high)*

Neither the principles of Confucian morality nor the text of its "classical" books were as yet established, though there were collections and some commentaries in Han times. The Confucian claim for advancement for every worthy man without reference to his origin, remained an ideal, or rather an exception. Meanwhile as time passed it became usual for the gentry, the owners of rented land, to employ tutors and support private schools, so that in practice they were the strongest upholders of literary education; they entered their most gifted sons for the examinations and so opened the highest positions for them.

The disadvantage of this system is easily recognised: the solidarity of a class bound together by ties of wealth, education and political feeling, which reacts most sensitively against any attempt to share its privileges. But there were these advantages; the foundation of wealth made possible an independent bureaucracy with an educational ideal of firm moral standing *Morality* and self-reliant decision. So examples of corruption in China are balanced by as many instances of true courage in facing the sovereign, and petty, dependent menials are hardly found among Chinese officials. The Chinese state beat all records for the minimum number of laws and regulations, and the smallest possible band of officials. The Chinese have often achieved in practice things which are only wishes for other peoples, and it seems that Tacitus's comment "corruptissima respublica, plurimae leges" (the more corrupt the state, the more numerous the laws), which Europe has treated as rhetoric, was taken literally and applied in China. They put morality and knowledge of life in the place of law; this knowledge they gained from history which they also quite literally took to mean the judgement of the world on themselves.

Remarkable work was done in Han times in the field of philology in order to establish the basis of the Confucian canon. But even greater was the achievement of Sse-ma Ch'ien (about 145—80 B.C.) the father of Chinese history. He edited a work of history in 130 volumes from antiquity down to the year 85 B.C. with such a careful attention to sources as is only equalled sometimes in our own day. The most astonishing thing is the methodical way in which he analyses the process and value of historical writing. His methods can be applied unaltered today. He analyses his historical material under three headings:

1. The analytical narration of historical events, including the almost verbatim quotation of documents without further interpretation;

2. The biographies of all important people who played a part in history with all their gifts and idiosyncracies;

3. Monographs about any special subject from astronomy to finance.

86

In an appendix to his work this usage is recommended: no history of its achievements should be written while a dynasty still rules, but archivists and entirely independent Censors should keep the relevant documents locked up.

When each dynasty ended, a commission of historians should be appointed to write about it, as far as possible without either favour or malice, and using the tested methods of Sse-ma Ch'ien. Their work would then provide text books on statesmanship unrivalled in the whole world for their objectivity. The oracle archives of the Shang dynasty, the bronze inscriptions of the Chou, and the debates of Feudal times were all striving to detect laws of events in human society; the same effort was renewed under the Han in a form that was methodical, bureaucratic and unexceptionable. We are doubtful whether there are laws of history, and whether it is possible for man to formulate them in their completeness; the Chinese limited themselves to noting as accurately as possible what they believed mattered. It was sufficient achievement to sustain and expand a high civilisation for 2,000 years with a minimum number of laws and officials. In China the essentials of history and morality were not just subjects for discussion; they were things that counted, things for which there were always men ready to die as the 460 had done under Shih-huang-ti.

The concentration of power and the comparative freedom from internal fights and tensions, made it possible to think of turning the tables on the Huns and going over to the offensive. By the 2nd century B.C. the Chinese had gained some knowledge of the more important lands to the west, in east and west Turkestan, Persia and western Asia: about Rome and the lands between Rome and themselves they may not have known much, but certainly more than Romans knew of them. Direct contact was prevented by the Parthians, who held the Romans back along the Euphrates, and who enjoyed a substantial increase of strength from their trade with China and their position as middlemen. Here we need only mention the main points in the exciting story of the wars with the Huns and the establishment of the silk road from Loyang and Ch'ang-an by Lou-lan, the Pamirs, Hama- *Huns* dan, Palmyra and Antioch. In 110 B.C. the Huns were decisively beaten and most of them driven back to the west. From 102 B.C. the Chinese were riding the powerful "horses of heaven", which substantially strengthened their cavalry. They had brought the horses from Ferghana, and from there too they introduced lupines which were the normal food to give them extra strength. Many other new plants and flowers reached China from Persia along the silk road. The road was kept open for the 200 years of Parthian rule, and even after that more trade passed that way than one

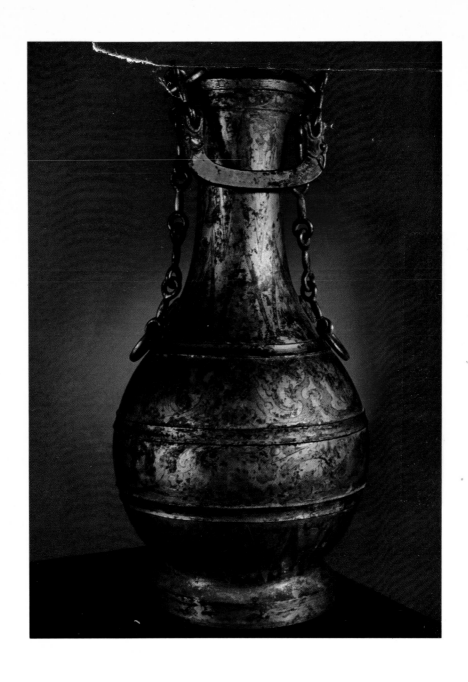

Covered bronze vase with gold and silver inlay and an inscription in Han ideograms. 200 B.C.—200 A.D.
Musée Guimet, Paris (14 inches high)

would have expected, judging from the stories of wars and revolutions. Northern Korea too was conquered in 108 B.C. and remained as a Chinese colony for 400 years. It was clearly a very rich colony; astonishingly magnificent finds come from the tombs near the old capital of Lo-lang which is often called the Chinese Pompeii.

Lo-lang provides the earliest direct evidence about ancient architecture. The tombs were partly built of wood, but they often had rooms built of brick on which rich patterns were impressed. The contents of the rooms were astonishingly well preserved; there were small wooden objects and a great deal of silk. But the lacquer articles and their inscriptions were the greatest suprise. Most of them had been brought from Ssech'uan well over a thousand miles away, and so we may expect to find similar things all the way along that route. Many things have been found in the excavations which Lo-lang, in its former days of isolation, lacked, but we still know nothing about the centres of craftsmanship in China herself in Han times. In Han times Chinese civilisation begins to radiate out as it had never done before. Probably as a result of the conquests of Alexander the Great, the West had learnt about silk which became a coveted luxury in Mediterranean lands. For its sake the Romans fought the Parthians, though they, like the Germans, were never completely conquered. For its sake Roman merchants established trading posts on the east coast of India in about 100 A.D. For its sake the Byzantines, or rather the Syrians, sent a trading expedition to find the seaway to China in 166 A.D. Roman coins and gems have been found at Oc-eo at the mouth of the Mekong. Roman satirists lampooned the luxury of Chinese silk which made the body look naked, and Pliny is concerned at the drain of four million pieces of gold going to the East. Such a figure represents a very appreciable passive burden on the finances of Rome at that time. Chinese silk, probably mostly unspun raw silk, went to Syria. But the Parthians too loved it. The Romans were impressed by the silken banners of their armies. Chinese silk reached Afghanistan, where some has recently been found, Mongolia and Siberia, where the Hun tribes threatening the silk road demanded it as customs duty or plunder or, often enough, tribute. Though we do not know in detail exactly where the millions of Roman gold sent to the East went to, it is a striking fact that, payment in gold apart, the Romans had hardly anything to offer to the East.

Radiation of civilisation

Great numbers of Chinese bronzes, especially mirrors, have been found everywhere from Siberia to southern Russia. There they help in dating Sarmatian excavations. And the Huns as well as the Sarmatians, following in the footsteps of the Scythians, soon tried to make their own copies of

Chinese originals. A recent excavation revealed a purely Chinese house with tiled roof and central heating built by a prosperous Hun at Abakan near Minussinsk. The popularity of lacquer is attested not only by many finds in China and especially Korea, but also by finds at Noin-Ula in northern Mongolia and Begram in Afghanistan. The lacquer is often accurately dated by inscriptions scratched on the bottom. By this means we can, with bureaucratic exactitude, trace the names of founders and overseers of the imperial factories from 85 B.C. to 102 A.D. It gives one a good idea of the impact of the new bureaucratic state on the arts.

Buildings When we come to Han times we can get a good idea of the architecture. Admittedly there are no great buildings standing above ground, but in the tombs, especially at Lo-lang, there are brickbuilt chambers as well as wooden ones. Almost as soon as brick appears in China, men learnt to construct vaults and true and sham domes out of overlapping bricks. But the aesthetic possibilities of the material were neglected for the sake of fashions dictated by wood. Even in much later times brick buildings were at pains to imitate forms appropriate to wood, with balconies and elaborately carved capitals. Architecture in stone goes even further in this direction. For instance, the tomb chambers at Nan-yang in southern Honan are built of stone, but one might say beams of stone, so easy would it be to copy them in wood. The same can be said about the tomb chapels of which a particularly large number have been found in Shantung. They consist of simple single rooms with saddle-shaped roof and one open side, in the middle of which is a pillar supporting the roof. These chapels stood in front of the graves, and in them visitors made their offerings to the dead. As architecture they are of little interest, but their large stones are engraved with copies in outline of well known paintings. As there are many copies of the same picture, one can get at least a hint of the themes of the outstanding paintings of the day. Presumably there were copy books from which they were derived. The representations of buildings on them tell us a great deal about Han architecture, and it is striking how much has remained unaltered down to the present day. We are further helped to see the old buildings in three dimensions by the numerous pottery models of houses and towers placed in the graves. Some of them are in undecorated pottery, but others are glazed or painted, and details of construction and even the painting on the walls are often truly rendered. All manner of things are represented in these gifts to the tomb; houses, stables and pleasure domes, and everything a home needs from cattle to spoons, from wagons to dogs. The custom of putting such figures in the tombs seems to have become very general by Han times. They give a good idea of the daily

life of the time, and the varying costliness of the gifts tells us something about social distinctions.

The tower with courtyard and gateway in the Kansas City Museum is one of the grandest and best of the model buildings. It has four floors and a mezzanine; there are fine "cloud roofs" overhanging all the upper stories; and the proportions and all the details are so faithfully shown that one would have no difficulty in having a real tower built from this model. There is much literary evidence showing the Chinese delight in such towers from Han times onwards. In the height of summer one could enjoy the freshness of a cool wind in the top stories. One could go there too for peace and quiet; there is a 5th century anecdote about the painter Kp Chün-chih who used to retreat to one of these towers and pull up the ladder, so that he could work undisturbed by wife and child. Books mention wall-paintings too, and our model gives a good idea of what they looked like. Near the gateway there are some trees indicated in bold outline, with birds in them; the gates themselves are decorated with a remarkable pattern of curving lines, and the walls right up to the highest roof are decorated with a great variety of diamond patterns. It is clear that colour and painting played a great part in architecture in Han times and, probably, long before. Maybe, a Chinese city, or a rich man's house, looked almost as gay then as it does today.

Because almost without exception the great quantity of tomb furniture, which provides such inexhaustible data for the history of civilisation, came from the uncontrolled plunder of graves, we have very little chance of grouping finds together and establishing more precise dates. As so often happens in China, we can generally tell with reasonable accuracy when an innovation started, but not for how long it lasted or in what form it took on new life. It seems reasonably clear that models of houses and pottery figures came into fashion in Han times, but it is difficult to give reliable answers to the many questions that greatly interest a Western reader — when were humans first represented, how did the style of representation develop, and how did the fashion in clothes change? There are hundreds of grave figures, of companions, servants, jugglers and dancing girls, which we can attribute with some confidence to Han times. It seems clear from literary sources that there was some marked change in fashions, and efforts have been made to find out what the change was. But it is only occasionally that we know for certain that a figure really does come from the Han period, or whether it is in fact more recent by anything from a hundred to three hundred years. There is a blank in our knowledge about Chinese tomb figures and other aspects of Chinese art between 200 and

Tomb figures
PLATE ON PAGE 83

91

Fragment of silk. The design shows wild geese in flight and tigers between patterns representing clouds and mountains; there are also ideograms of lucky import. Found at Lou-lan in eastern Turkestan, the point of departure for the silk road to the West, by Sir Aurel Stein. 100 B.C.—100 A.D. *Central Asian Antiquities Museum, New Delhi*

92

400 A.D. There is little help to be got from literary sources, so that it often happens that one cannot say with a good conscience whether a figure belongs, for instance, to the first or fourth century A.D., or whether a certain concept of figure and face is characteristic of a particular century. We may hope that scientific excavation will reveal tomb inscriptions. Until then, the best approach is to try to link fashions in clothes with other dateable representations, a task which has not yet been carried very far. As far as we can judge from the pictures on the stones of the tomb chapels, the usual dress in the 2nd century B.C. was like the present day Japanese kimono, with a long robe brought together under the breast and girdle, but with less wide sleeves. I cannot hope to satisfy readers interested in fashion, but can only suggest that to judge by their dress the stately pair in the Munich Museum of Ethnography probably date from late Han times (1st to 2nd century A.D.). These figures stand out from the army of those rightly or wrongly attributed to the Han period by their individuality. Their faces are so full of character that they confirm the maturity of the civilisation that produced them, and this impression is so strong that one cannot help wondering if they are portraits, although that cannot be proved. There are some indications that in Han times portrait sculptures were made for tombs, but it cannot be said to have been the general rule, and the only undoubted portrait sculpture that we yet know of dates from the year 918 A.D. and from the tomb of Wang Chien in Ssech'uan. Nor can we know whether the maker of the Munich pair was a sculptor in any specialised sense of the word. Certainly whoever made the figures was a born artist, but none of his contemporaries would have thought of him as one, or have singled him out from among the many craftsmen who produced so many varieties of excellent and aesthetically delightful works without anyone thinking it worth mentioning their names. When, for instance, lacquer work from the Imperial workshops was signed, the name that stands first is that of the official inspector who was responsible for every specimen produced. The other craftsmen concerned in the product were mentioned with reference to their particular duties, but not singled out as individual artists. The strict division of labour which the inscriptions clearly imply, rules out any idea of that sort.

The bronze workers were subject to an even more harassing control, for they had to mark the exact weight of the object made, lest a few grains of bronze that might have been turned into coin, should be missing. In Han times, bronzes were made almost exclusively for the bureaucracy. They were intelligent and demanding clients, but there were no outstand-

Representations of humans

PLATE ON PAGE 85

Workshops

93

PLATE ON PAGE 88

ing art patrons. The style of the bronze vessel, illustrated on page 88, descends from Feudal types. Its lid and handle are attached by a chain to two naturalistic *t'ao-t'ieh* masks on the body. The body is smooth and simple and the thin neck sharply defined and elegant. Simple and discreet rings run round the body. The demands of luxury are met by inlays of silver and gold. The linear cloud-pattern decoration of the two middle bands is as good as anything similar from the Feudal age, but adds nothing new. The generous use of pointed triangles is typical of a new Han fashion, for though the triangles are filled with twirling spirals, they are kept in neat rows. The technique is perfect. The vessel is a more elegant variation of the classical *hu,* and would grace a religious festival anywhere in the world. But it probably was not intended for religious use, as the inscription names the owner and gives its capacity of two measures and its weight of $10\frac{1}{4}$ pounds. There are a great many similar Han bronzes without the inlay and generally fatter. Such vessels are described in the inscriptions as measures for corn, and their capacity and dead weight is always given. These *chung,* many of which come from the imperial workshops, are nevertheless too costly objects for use in daily life. It may be that they were only used when rents were paid with festal ceremony: One could take that as indicating that the boundary between religion and business had been obliterated, and it is, in fact, difficult to find out anything about the religion, or even the religiosity, of the Han period. In the study of Shang art one has to make religion one's point of departure in order to understand the sense and the full meaning of its grandeur. But in the orderly, solid, worthy art of Han times and long afterwards there is

Drawing after the design on a gold-inlaid and engr

94

hardly a hint of religious content. In Feudal times the serious arguments about religious questions were certainly speculative, but also full of inspiration. But this spirit gave place under the Han to a scepticism, dull rather than pugnacious, which finds its chief exponent in Wang Ch'ung (27—97 A.D.).

As was natural in an age ruled by the small minded rationalism of a highly *Bureaucracy* competent bureaucracy, on the one hand every conceivable form of superstition flourished, and on the other people took refuge in a morality which was often strict. Anyone anxious to explore the tangles of superstition will find endless material in the secret practices of Han magicians. However there is a correlative to that tendency in the historicism which attempted to project everything that could not be understood back into antiquity, and to explain and interpret it in historical terms. From the pictures in the tomb chapels we learn much about the legendary interpretations and elaborations grafted on to the old religious forms. And we have to be careful not to put too much faith in these interpretations, though they may incorporate some true ideas. Figures of gods are found in these pictures, but they are usually the lower gods, or rather demons, who are now often portrayed with human faces. Moralising historical pictures are also very frequent. It is not only the kings and "emperors", great princes and statesmen of antiquity and their deeds which are portrayed; there are also examples of tyrants and criminals to stand as warnings.

The Han age saw itself in historical terms to an extent which is not only striking, but sometimes quite out of proportion. In 163 B.C. a new system was introduced by which epochs were measured by "dispensations" or

pipe. Found at Lo-lang. *Academy of Art, Tokyo*

95

reign names. From that time onwards each emperor, when he ascended the throne, gave his reign a lucky motto which he could alter in exceptional circumstances, or change to a new motto to usher in a new situation. However from Ming times onwards the emperors never changed the "dispensation" once given, and so one can be sure, for instance, that the 40th year of K'ang-hsi corresponds to our year 1701 A.D. In the year 116 A.D. an event of such importance occurred that the reign name was changed. A bronze tripod, then supposed to be the insignium of rule of the kings of antiquity, was found, and the years following were known as Yüan-ting or "new tripod".

We may think that that was an event of no more than archaeological interest. But it raises the interesting question for us whether ancient tripods really were so rare then, and whether perhaps Shih-huan-ti may purposefully and systematically have melted them all down, and whether their simple ancient use as sacrificial vessels was so completely forgotten that an exaggerated importance came to be attached to them. The usurper Wang Mang (6–23 A.D.) certainly did carry historicism to unreasonable

Historicism lengths. He was a nephew of the empress, who set himself on the throne, and he thought that he could renew the vitality of the state by reviving the ancient forms of ceremonial and sacrifice in a way that was more superstitious than romantic, getting his ideas from books of wild speculation. His decision to build a *Ming-t'ang,* or "hall of light", in accordance with classical prototypes, is important in the history of art, for his advisers could not agree what it ought to look like. From this we learn that in Han times no one either knew or could find out what this type of building, which probably originated in Chou times, had been like. The same was presumably true of much else that had been familiar in antiquity.

Their sense of history included the present too in its purview. The emperors often had portraits made of statesmen, generals and virtuous women; they were particularly eager so to honour those who gave examples of filial piety. Contemporaries too were represented as patterns of this particularly Chinese virtue, not only to do them honour, but also to incite others to follow their lead. One of the best known specimens of Han painting, the lacquer basket with a very well preserved frieze of figures excavated at Lo-lang, shows Li Shan who lived in the first century B.C., among examples of filial piety. This famous painted basket may have been made in that century, or shortly afterwards. A usage, which has lasted almost to our own day, began at this time, by which the emperor would designate saints, and gods too, and give them titles with different ranks. Every place or district that felt it had good reason to be grateful

96

to a living citizen, could ask the emperor to designate him as a saint. If he assented, a temple was built to the man as a guardian or local god. Many of them won more than local fame, and were reverenced for decades or even centuries throughout the kingdom. Such bureaucratic regimentation presiding over this and many other things under the Han, often drove the spirit out to seek its home elsewhere. This tendency is very clearly reflected in art.

There are a great many meritorious works from Han times, but they are one like another and turned out to a formula. Very few that are outstand- *Uniformity* ing or astonishing in their individuality. This may be partly due to the chances of survival, for there are occasional exceptions, and one can hope for more. But there must be something more than chance at work, and if art history is the history of the spirit, that is only what one would expect as a result of the general conceptions current in the Han age. There is a key to understanding in the fact that this period hardly invented a single new decorative motif, for that is the surest and most decisive test of creative power. Almost everything that was, until recently, assumed to be typical Han ornament, the simple geometrical patterns such as repetitions of plain diamonds, and the swelling and swaying curves and bands, were anticipated in Feudal times and then often employed with more spirit. Han artists did indeed make good and effective use of these prototypes, and the mere fact of sticking to long established conventions must never in itself be mistaken for poverty of spirit or lack of inventive power. But in the age in which the unity of the state was being forged, the drive towards regimentation in the arts did not only affect small things. China put her house in order so that her influence could radiate out over her borders, and the surrounding world could turn to Chinese craftsmen for solid, good, uniform work. If the China of the Feudal age had acquired many patterns and, presumably, many techniques from abroad, she now set herself to make use of what she had learnt, and give all this back in a cultivated and refined form. If the Feudal age breathed in, the Han breathed out. What she had turned to her own use, was now given back to the new countries and peoples then moving on to the historical scene. The golden belt clasps found at Lo-lang in north Korea, have often been illustrated and are among the masterpieces of goldsmiths work: the dragons which ornament them are perfect in form and technique, using granulation and filigree, an invention not found in earlier works; there are also inlays of turquoise in the shapes of dots, commas and drops, which fully maintain the sureness of touch of Feudal polychromy.

Another of the rare masterpieces of individual character is the bronze

97

pipe inlayed with gold, which was also found at Lo-lang and is now in the Academy of Art in Tokyo. The pipe, for that it clearly is, is 10 inches long, and is ornamented with four encircling bands of engraving so fine that

PLATE ON PAGE 94 only a drawing can give an impression of the scale and fantasy of its pictorial invention. One of the two strips illustrated here shows a hunting scene. A mounted archer whose horse is shown in the "flying gallop" convention, that is to say with fore and hind legs outstretched, as never happens in nature, and flying over the earth without touching it, is aiming a Parthian shot at a tiger goaded to chase him. Stags, roes, hares and a wild boar rush in the same direction through the landscape which is indicated as mountainous by strange, uneven, wavy bands. Behind one of the mountains rises another tiger with a fine "comma" on his front shoulder joint; close to him is a bear caught in very lifelike movement. Birds fly through the air which is full of fantastic patterns derived from the old

PLATE ON PAGE 95 triangular volutes. The other strip also shows a mountain landscape, two bands representing crossing mountain chains; there are many animals, a two-humped camel on to whose back a monkey jumps, a stag, a wild bull, a tiger half hidden by the mountain, and underneath an elegantly twisting dragon; many birds and a tree to the left. Its trunk is at first hard to distinguish from the bands representing mountains, but the curving twigs and flowers and the birds sitting on them make it clear that it is a tree transformed into a swirling decoration. We know of no tree so conceived in Feudal times; then trees were depicted upright and stiff, in a formula that seems foreign to us. The basic form here derives from the Feudal age, but it has been twisted and transformed into a fantastic linear fugue; and it would seem that the men of Feudal times had not discovered how to adapt a shape such as that of this pipe to sustain a fugue of weaving lines. When an epoch in art finds itself and treads its own spiritual way, one can recognise its manifestation in every painted twig.

Han silk and lacquer are an unmixed aesthetic delight. Lucky circumstances have brought to light many sumptuous and richly coloured fragments of silk. They have mostly been found at the eastern point of departure of the silk road, in or near Lou-Lan, where the road from China turns towards Eastern Turkestan, and at the Western terminus of Palmyra, not far from Damascus, where the road through the Parthian kingdom leads into the Roman East, and in the Parthian Dura-Europos on the Euphrates. The graves of Hun princes at Noin-Ula in Northern Mongolia and in Siberia have often yielded magnificent silk stuffs which have been adapted to make clothes and even slippers and sometimes been decorated with native embroidery. Balls of silk had long counted as currency in China;

98

the Chinese paid their tribute to the Huns with them when they were defeated. The finds at Lo-Lang in Korea also enrich our knowledge. The decoration of these stuffs is not fundamentally different from that of other categories of art and we can only admire how freely and naturally complicated curves and waving lines were adapted to the technique of weaving. The diamonds loved by the Han present fewer difficulties even when they are used in the most varied permutations. The playful spirit of the Feudal age rings true in the decoration of a piece of stuff found at Lou-Lan. That people argue seriously whether the rolling, swelling bands PLATE ON PAGE 92

Round covered box with lacquer painting and silver inlay on a base of lacquer soaked canvas. Excavated at Hai-chou in northern Kiangsu. 1st-2nd century A.D. *British Museum, London (5 inches high)*

99

represent mountains or clouds just shows how strong the playful element is; they could perfectly well be either or both together. Wild ducks are flying under the lower bow-shaped curves, and tigers walk through the more gently curved bands above. These cloud-mountain bands are found on other objects, even on bronzes. They are very common on the pottery which was put as a modest substitute for bronze vessels in the tombs. What is most astonishing in the silks is the pictorial freedom with which the ducks, for instance, are represented; the way neck and head twist downwards catches a vivid snapshot of a characteristic movement most unexpectedly in such a technique, and yet it is in sensitive harmony with the decorative pattern. No wonder that the world was enchanted with these stuffs.

Luxury goods The decoration of the lacquer too is never monotonous. Probably this provided the finer utensils of household luxury, and was, as nowadays in Japan, preferred to pottery. The very technique of their making forbade close copying of a pattern. Lacquer work is a form of painting, and uses it with great freedom. The vessels are mostly made on a thin wooden core, covered with linen; but many are simply based on lacquer soaked linen, and these are just as firm, but even lighter, than the others. A first coating of lacquer, usually black, forms the background on which one can paint rather more slowly, but just as freely, as on paper or silk. Of course most lacquer articles are things of utility and applied art, whether they come from China herself, or were exported to the military capital at Lo-lang in Korea, or for the tombs of Hun princes, or to Begram or to Than-hoa. There are often inscriptions, especially on those from Lo-lang, which show that they were made in the imperial workshops, mostly in Ssech'uan. They must have travelled over more than 1,000 miles to reach the graves of the distinguished and fastidious officials who could not be without such a luxury.

PLATE ON PAGE 99 A fine Han specimen of a round lacquer toiletbox, now in the British Museum, was found in China herself, in northern Kiangsu. Its core is simply lacquer-soaked linen but an inlay of silver, including a large quatrefoil pattern on the lid, has been let into the superimposed layers of lacquer. The whole surface is woven over, but never overloaded, with patterns and figures. The main zone round the body is decorated with wavy cloud-mountain patterns between which mounted archers in flying gallop are shooting backwards. Some of the animals they are hunting are shown on the outer rim of the lid. The simple, comely shape of the box is emphasised by framing bands. The painter has treated these with restraint, confining himself to variations of diamonds in circles and triangles filled with volutes. These are motifs long familiar from the inlays of Feudal

100

times, and they lose none of their playfulness when brush strokes take the place of precisely cut metal, and there is no need to bother about mathematical accuracy and balance.

The themes of Han lacquer painting are various and spirited; bears and dragons are full of spring and often gaiety too; the figures of people, for all their simplicity, give a strong impression of character. In pure decoration there is no falling back from the heights of the Feudal age, and indeed artists learnt to take advantage of qualities peculiar to lacquer to increase their decorative repertory with mock granulation and other tricks. There are some lacquer masterpieces that tell us a good deal that we should not have known just from the tomb engravings about contemporary painting and, because they really are painted, they give us a better idea of what could then be done with the brush. But none of the outstanding works are signed, or even carry the mark of the imperial workshops. Can one draw the conclusion that amateurs followed their personal tastes in ordering pieces from gifted lacquer painters, of whom some may have worked as free lances? However that may be there is certainly a difference between the army of competent craftsmen and the small band of individual artists, even though we know neither their names nor anything else about them. *Themes of painting*

The very large number of somewhat uniform Han products surviving, tends to make us feel that the bubbling creative activity inherited from Feudal times has been put to admirably solid use, and to impress us with the grandeur of the concept of the unified state. But we must not be deceived into the misconception that conformity inhibited growth. The Han not only won world recognition for Chinese art, but also led the way to the high tableland from which yet higher peaks could be scaled. *Significance*

V THE TIME OF TROUBLES

There was no inner law that made it inevitable for the Han empire to decay, degenerate and fall. Before 200 A.D. there had been weak rulers who survived intrigues, internal struggles for power and peasant rebellions. Such rebellions occur with almost rhythmic regularity throughout Chinese history, and some historians see them as the effective motive force in its development. But the more precise information now available almost seems to prove that there is no solution for the universal problem of how to make peasants contented. About the year 200 A.D. three generals who had come to control substantial armies raised to quell risings, felt themselves called upon to save the state by mounting the imperial throne. These contestants for power were all men of more than average ability and they had more success than previous rebels, but not enough to reach their ultimate goal. They suffered great losses fighting bravely with each other to make the people happy, but the naval battle at "Red Rocks" in 208 A.D. clarified the situation enough to show that neither the reigning dynasty nor any of the country's saviours was strong enough to hold the helm alone. Finally in 220 A.D. the Han abdicated de jure, and the three saviours divided China between them; one ruled the Wei kingdom in the north with its capital at Loyang; another Shu in the west with its capital at Ch'eng-tu; the third Wu in the south with Nanking as capital.

Peasant rebellions

Three kingdoms

For centuries afterwards yarns were spun about their heroic deeds, and men laughed about their diplomatic tricks, and finally, in the 14th century, an anonymous editor gathered all the tales into one great book. This romance of "The three Kingdoms" became the favourite reading of the common people. By far the most popular of the three saviours is the sly peasant Liu Pei with his friends; but the former barrowboy Kuan Yü who was strong as a bear, has actually become the Chinese war-god. The clever and cruel Ts'ao Ts'ao is less sympathetic; but that same man was an outstanding poet and man of letters, and his son inherited these gifts. So the old Han capital, Loyang, where the new dynasty reigned for 45 years, was distinguished by the most cultivated court and literary centre in China then. The third of the rivals, Sun Ch'üan (181–252) the king of Wu and founder of Nanking, is the least talked of, but in the history both of art and of literature he and the city he founded count for most of all. But the city was sacked many times and what remained was so thoroughly destroyed in the T'ai-p'ing rebellion of 1860, that now there is little of its ancient brilliance to be seen. There are only the huge stone animals of the royal tombs nearby. Nanking was then the brilliant, lively and entertaining centre of spiritual and aesthetic innovations. The very air was so penetrated with this spirit that again and again, and especially twelve hundred years later, the arts that flourished there had their own particular atmosphere.

Seen from that point of view the fall of the Han Empire and the subsequent decentralisation had some positive advantages. Provincial centres developed their own very real and lively aesthetic life. It may be that we shall soon come to think of the five hundred years of troubles and changes between 200 and 700 A.D. as one of the most fruitful and independent epochs of Chinese art and civilisation. In politics and government everything was falling to pieces, and the unfortunate historians who must concentrate their attention on the leading personalities find a tale of nothing but murder and violence. Otto Franke took the trouble to work out that of twenty-six "Emperors" of this time thirteen were murdered, four dethroned, and only nine died a natural death. It hardly seems to matter whether one calls this period after the six "legitimate" dynasties (Liu-ch'ao) reigning in Nanking, or counts the sixteen smaller "illegitimate" dynasties, or calls it the time of division between North and South. What passed for a dynasty at that time generally meant an usurper who was seldom followed by more than two or three successors. But it is all a wonderful illustration of the truth of Confucius' maxim (Lun-yü XVI. 2) "when over-powerful servants seize the rule in a state, they lose their power within three generations". But no doubt many of them intended the best for their country, and many did do good. The fate of Hou-chu, the last Nanking Emperor, who reigned as a fourth ruler of the Ch'en dynasty from 583—589 A.D. is striking and ironical. He counts as one of the greatest wastrels and Don Juans of China, but with fastidious taste he appreciated music and musicians and had the best of all good things. He drew a circle of great painters too around his court, and their flowery verses won fame as a special style. Fate was kind to him; he survived his fall from power and lived happily surrounded by luxury and beauty until he died a natural death. Chinese painters who care more for him and his like than for heroes, continued for hundreds of years to paint him, surrounded by his musicians (plate on p. 183).

In 589 A.D. China was again united under the Sui dynasty which, for all its striving, was unable to last for more than thirty years. In 618 A.D. the T'ang supplanted the Sui and again established a stable government. They had to fight for nearly a hudred years to establish the basis of power

Decentralisation

103

inherited by the Emperor Ming-huang when he came to the throne in 713 A.D. His reign was the apex of Chinese art, its classical age. So the time of troubles may be taken as beginning with " Red Rocks" in 208 A.D. and ending with enthronment of Ming-huang in 713 A.D.

Northern peoples It is hard to see through the fog of events and figures what really happened. In spite of all setbacks life clearly not only continued but, so far as trade and intercourse with foreign nations, especially India and Persia, was concerned, made progress. Spiritual life too, like trade, found its own way despite all the upheavals among the ruling classes and the mad way in which they fought and killed each other. Just one phenomenon of the time must be briefly mentioned. Turco-mongolian peoples from the steppes again burst into northern China and played their part in the foundation of dynasties. The T'o-pa had some substantial success and maintained the rule of their dynasty, disguised with the good Chinese name of Wei, for 200 years, for 80 of which they reigned from the venerated ancient capital, Loyang (452–534 A.D.). However by now there was nothing the "barbarians" wanted more than to become Chinese as soon as possible, to marry into the old Chinese families and to speak Chinese. W. Eberhard has made a detailed study of the T'o-pa kingdom, and he has shown how the

Detail from the frescoes in the 'Tomb of the Dancers' at T'ung-kou north of the middle Yalu. Until 427 A.D. it was the capital of the Korean kingdom of Kokuryo. The date is still uncertain, but is probably nearer 400 than the date of 500 A.D. often suggested.

Chinese gentry managed not only to keep their positions but even to bring their new rulers over to their side. These were not only quick to make their own officials learn Chinese, but were themselves eager students of Chinese classical literature, and were anxious to continue its traditions. For all the similarities between these inroads and those of 1,000 years earlier, their significance was quite different. For one thing the climatic conditions were reversed. Throughout the whole of the first millenium and up to about 1,100 A.D. the climate, in Asia at any rate, must have been more propitious than now. Parts of eastern Turkestan were then very fruitful, if we may judge by the few surviving oases, and Russian western Turkestan too was much more fruitful then, as we have learnt from the recent excavations undertaken in connection with the plan to water those parts again. A little time ago no one imagined that there were such large and richly decorated castles and cities in those deserts. Perhaps the investigations of the next few years will give us a new and fuller picture of Kharezmian, Persian and also Chinese art of that period. Chinese civilisation, as well as natural conditions, had greatly changed between 700 B.C. and 300 A.D. It was both more firmly established and more differentiated, more urban and more cosmopolitan. The situation of the T'o-pa and other Turkish peoples throw indirect light on the great Han achievement of the unified state. It was no longer the sheer necessity to keep alive that forced the steppe peoples to fight for room to settle in China. Instead they were attracted by an undoubtedly higher civilisation and a better way of life in which they wished to take part. While for the Chinese there was no longer any need to define and defend boundaries; their millions could absorb a few tens of thousands of Turco-mongolians without any substantial disturbance of society. Indeed they sometimes discovered that their new citizens were more Chinese than the Chinese, and found that they worked as a ferment for the many changes which were anyhow in train.

Change of climate

To understand an epoch one must start from its greatest and most unmistakeable achievements. The excellence of the poetry of this time is not disputed, and the only question is whether or not the prose was better still. A good many Chinese consider the poetry of the six dynasties as the fairest flower of all in their literature; Li T'ai-po was among this number, and reverenced these poets as models he could never equal. Even those whose main interest is the plastic arts, ought to know something about the general character of the literature of the period. This for two reasons; first, the same attitudes of mind are dominant in both; second, very few important original works of art have so far been found, but literary sources begin at this time to give us substantial information about the intentions and achievements of artists. These four seem the most important characteristics:

1. Poets lose their anonymity and reveal their subjective feelings. We do, of course, know the names of some poets even in Han times, but the folk songs are as often as not anonymous, and the works of the known poets are very like the folk songs and conform to an accepted moral code. T'ao Yüan-ming is the first great lyric poet; he is very subjective and lived his life just as we all expect an unworldly poet to do.

2. The *fu* which we translate as "essay" for want of a better word, was a Han literary form, but it specially suited the mood of this age and came fully into its own. The *fu* stands half way between prose and poetry, using high-flown language and often rhythmic tone. It generally starts off from a description of a place, or person or happening, often expressed with astonishing sharpness of vision. It is very literary with frequent allusions to poetry and the classics, so that it is often hard to tell what are quotations or variations on a theme; often some personal point of view is then voiced, and it may end with a more general observation and turn of thought. There is a surprising charm in the way these essays play around with proverbial quotations and, most successfully, subjects and analogies of enduring interest; they are never tedious, and always add vivid and revealing touches.

3. As one would expect from what has just been said, nature poetry and lyrical descriptions of landscape come into their own. After T'ao Yüan-ming (365–427 A.D.) his contemporary Hsieh Ling-yün (385–433 A.D.) counts as the earliest great poet of nature. It is no chance that there is included in the collected works of T'ao Yüan-ming a poem by the painter Ku K'ai-chih (about 346–406 A.D.) pregnant with a new conception of landscape painting.

4. Criticism comes into play as a correlative of the individual to complete his new-found independence. Aesthetics and questions of form come under discussion, at least as far as they concern poetry, painting and calligraphy. Anyone accustomed to European categories of thought tends to see a contradiction in this emphasis on the independence of the individual, and the interest in set-themes, fixed forms, symbols and quotations even in nature poetry. We are now all too much inclined to value an artist's achievement by the extent to which he has broken free from the forms and themes embedded in tradition. Hence there are many amateurs of Chinese poetry who argue as to whether it is not just a conscious, not to say pedantic, variation on classical themes, without claim to true insight

106

or feeling. It is often difficult for us to be clear about such distinctions, and in translating Chinese poetry great learning is needed to reveal its simplicity. But the contradiction vanishes if we appreciate that the Chinese of the Time of Troubles were forging forms to express a previously unknown spiritual independence, and that thereafter these forms became themselves classical. T'ao Yüan-ming's life and work is the best demonstration of this. He only fulfilled the duties of his humble official position for a short time, and used the plot of land enjoyed as a perquisite of his post to build himself a retreat where he made the very best wine. Feeling himself useless in the great world, he soon retired to his tiny property. There what time was left over from writing poetry and drinking, he de-

The Emperor Ch'en Hsüan-ti who held court in Nanking from 569-582 A.D. being carried by his servants, accompanied by two courtiers. Probably the copy of a contemporary portrait. Detail from a roll of 'Portraits of thirteen emperors'. *Museum of Fine Arts, Boston (Colour on silk, 20 inches by 17 feet 5 inches)*

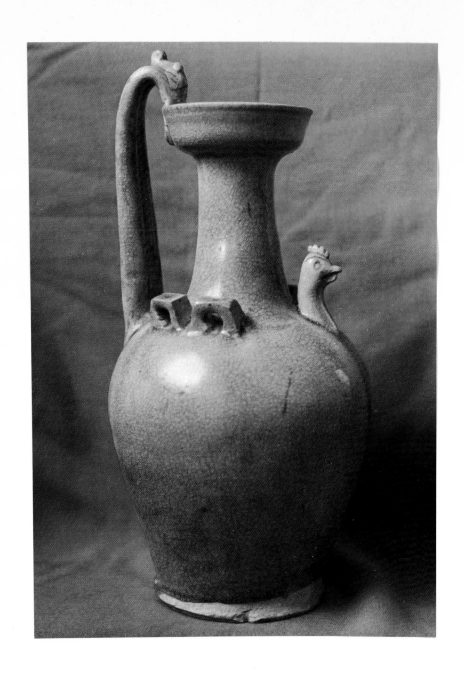

Jug with a cock's head added as ornament. Light coloured pottery with a thin transparent felspar glaze. 5th-6th century A.D. *Museum of Far Eastern Art, Cologne. (Height 23 inches)*

108

voted to his hobby of growing chrysanthemums. His little garden with its three paths, five willows and a bamboo fence on the eastern side, that and the poems he wrote there were his whole world. Among his "Twenty Drinking Songs" is one called "The Song of the Eastern Fence":

I built my house in the midst of the haunts of men,
But there is no portico here for their carriages.
And if you ask why that is so, I say,
"My heart lives far away, and keeps itself for company".
Lazily I pick chrysanthemums by the eastern fence,
In peace I look towards the mountains to the south;
The mountain breeze is delicious in the fading light;
Wandering birds fly out in pairs.
Somewhere there lies a deeper meaning.
I would like to say it, but have forgotten the word.

What is the essense of this poem which has become one of the most famous in China and provided painters with a classical theme down to our own day? Does it express delight in the simple contemplative life, renunciation, flight from the world, insight into the uselessness of all anxious striving, escape from tears and troubles, the independence of self-sufficient natures, the return to nature, or just the melancholy of autumn? There are all these notes in it, and perhaps Schubert's song "Who chooses loneliness . . ." ("Wer sich der Einsamkeit ergibt") comes nearest to its mood. All who live quietly in the country, the disenchanted, the lonely, the lovers of independence, shade and peace in all the world claim kinship with T'ao Yüan-ming and see themselves in his mirror. In any Chinese picture a man sitting or walking under five willows, or reciting a poem about "three paths", must be T'ao Yüan-ming and every one shares his feelings. A chrysanthemum by a bamboo hedge, or on a rock, or even alone (plate on p. 226) always carries this overtone of autumn melancholy and also of a way of escape from troubles and tears; it speaks in praise of quietness, of delight in the simple life and in growing flowers, with a suggestion, as we should put it, of the reserves of nature's power; in a word, it speaks of T'ao Yüan-ming. But it also orders retreat and withdrawal from where a man cannot obey his own conscience; not to stay on to no good, where only madness and evil reign; to renounce, if inaction impedes the better part. T'ao Yüan-ming may have been a lyrical character to whom renunciation came easy. However in Liu-ch'ao times there were a striking number of poets whom one finds to have been statesmen, politicians or

Flight from the world

109

Detail from a letter written by the
famous calligrapher Wang Hsi-chih
(321-379 A.D.). T'ang copy. *In the
possession of Marquis Maeda, Tokyo*

九月十七日羲之報且因

孔侍中信書皆至必至不

弓領軍疾後问

ministers, who went into retirement, brooking no compromises and refusing to toe the line, even if it cost them their heads.

In spite of all set-backs Confucius had repeatedly required that the man of noble character, if he was gifted with wisdom, property or power, should live and work for society; but he admired the wisdom of hermits and never depreciated it. This attitude was now turned into the opposite. There lived *Opposition* in the 3rd century the renowned "Seven sages of the bamboo grove", men of learning, statesmen and officials, who demonstratively devoted themselves to drinking and poetry in order to escape the cares of office. The group is often painted in cheerful mood, but that can hardly have been the way the most important of them, Hsi King, felt about his own execution. From thenceforth there are continual examples of cultivated men, not necessarily poets or painters, refusing to live at court. The scholarly emperor Liang Wu-ti (502—549 A.D.), afterwards famed for his humanity, once asked a painter to come to his court at Nanking, and received as answer a picture of two oxen, one of them running free, and the other tied by a golden chain and guarded by a herdsman. Some narrow-minded sociologists can see nothing but political motives and opposition to the ruling class in the aesthetic and religious manifestations of this age.

The system of state examinations in the fundamentals of the Confucian classics, which had been introduced in Han times, had many ups and downs in the next five centuries; high schools were founded, and then again dispersed; classical texts were made a mock of and then, be it noted under the half-Turkish T'o-pa and their successors in north China, edited with commentaries. At the same time Taoist thought comes into prominence. Chuang-tse and Lao-tse were quoted more often than K'ung-tse and Meng-tse, and indeed it has been suggested that it was just in these centuries that the greater part of the Taoist writings were first brought to birth. From the 2nd century A.D. Buddhist scriptures too were not only translated, but made the subject of earnest and fruitful discussion. Buddhist missionaries had arrived by sea in central China in the 1st century. In 325 A.D. permission was for the first time given for Chinese to enter a monastery. Intercourse with foreign lands seems to have been very lively in Liu-ch'ao times, which was one of the rare periods of sea travel in Chinese history. An East Roman embassy actually visited Sun Ch'üan in Nanking in 226 A.D. We do not know what the substance of the negotiations was, but it is recorded that ten pairs of dwarfs were considered a suitable present for the Roman Emperor. It is perhaps significant for China's position in the world that about the year 451 A.D. when Attila, King of *Abroad* the Huns, was defeated at Châlons, not far from Paris, Chinese ships were anchored off Ceylon and on the Euphrates, and Sassanian embassy from Persia came overland to Northern China just at the time when the first great persecution of the Buddhists and the destruction of their monasteries was taking place. Recent excavations have revealed substantial hoards of Sassanian coins in north-west China. So it is understandable that under the assault of so many new influences and the breakdown of the political ruling class, wise and gifted men held aloof from public life, bought their independence at the price of renunciation, and fought for a freedom whose sole object was the reunion of the Chinese people on the solid ground of their common civilisation. It is astonishing that both the Confucianists and the gentry not only resisted the assaults on them during these centuries, but actually emerged strengthened with new freedoms and traditions. The time of troubles, when the ruling class, with few exceptions failed to perform its duty, drove individuality out of society. This tendency was enhanced by the practical difficulty of circumscribing personal freedom, for by that time there were already considerable numbers of people of independent means, who did not find it necessary for their self-respect to take any part in the activities of the ruling class. So the Time of Troubles was also the time when China's freeest and finest spirits were put to the test.

Landscape It was in landscape that artists most clearly felt the power of nature transcending the authority of rulers and all mankind, as they watched the predestined and unalterable change of the seasons. The freedom that they loved and fought for, had as its correlative the freedom of nature which is no untrammelled freedom, for it is bound by *Tao*. In this context the painter Ku K'ai-chih's simple verses take on the quality of a declaration of principle:

> *In the spring the lakes are full of water,*
> *In summer clouds gather round the mountain tops,*
> *In autumn the moon shines in all her splendour,*
> *In winter the snow displays its beauty on the mountains.*

Besides being a painter, Ku K'ai-chih had the reputation of the greatest wit and madcap of his age. These lines set the tone for Chinese landscape painting and its subjects from his day to ours. So, if the moon is in a picture, it must be autumn; there probably is not a single picture with a spring or summer moon in it. Nonetheless Ku K'ai-chih himself hardly ventured into landscape painting. People were the usual subjects of his pictures, and landscape was no more than incidental background. The same was true generally of his contemporaries. Besides portraits and illustrations of historical or other stories, sacred Buddhist pictures were beginning to come into fashion. But these were not the only subjects. In Nanking the young Emperor Chin Ming-ti (323—335) enjoyed painting sparrows and crickets, and the brothers Liu Yin-tsu and Liu Shao-ku imitated the Emperor's taste for sparrows and crickets, and added mice to the repertory. The theme had lasting popularity. The great painter Lu T'an-wei (about 440—500 A.D.) tried his hand at it, and so did the Emperor Liang Yüan-ti (552—555) who painted it on round silk fans. We have not the slightest idea what these pictures looked like, but the popularity of the theme attested by literary sources shows that men were concerned to study the little things of nature as well as the great, so as to understand reality for its own sake and not, as in Han times, with some moral end in view. We must bear this significant interest in tiny things in mind if we are to understand the most important of all Chinese works of aesthetic criticism. The first critic of Chinese painting was Hsieh Ho (about 500 A.D.) and it is no chance that he particularly mentions the sparrow and cricket pictures of two painters, although he does not count them the greatest masters.

Hsieh Ho's little book, the Ku-hua p'in-lu is the Magna Carta of Chinese *Aesthetics* aesthetic criticism of the plastic arts, which in practice means painting. It has accumulated extensive commentaries, but its setting in art history has not been made clear. It was written in Nanking and the author, himself a well known portrait painter, only mentions painters and pictures which he could see in and around Nanking. He deals with twenty-seven painters, starting with Ts'ao Pu-hsing, who painted dragons in the palace of Sun Ch'üan, the founder of Nanking, and continuing down to his own day. Hsieh Ho's essential achievement was the division of painters into six categories, and he noted that only a few of them were successful in all alike, and many attained pre-eminence only in one.

He tabulates the following values;

1. Spirit and Life. 2. Outlines ("bones") and control of the brush. 3. Form and Shape. 4. Harmony and colour. 5. Division and arrangement. 6. Prototypes and copying.

To take these categories in reverse order; a painter's execution must be up to the standard of the classical models; he must be able to arrange his subject matter, that is, to compose; the colours and shapes of his subject matter must be harmonious; he must make proper use of the possibilities of brushwork; and, with portraits and figure subjects especially in mind, he must achieve a living image which expresses the spirit. No doubt Hseih Ho borrowed the word he used for "spirit", *ch'i-yün,* from the lively contemporary aesthetic criticism of poetry in which the word was used to signify

113

the highest value in a poem. The Chinese word can be broken down into the meanings "atmosphere, mood, content" and "rhyme, sound, rhythm", but one can also take it — and this is in the best old Chinese tradition — as "echo, correlative" of the spirit, of the "atmosphere". Moreover, this double word, whose first half can stand by itself and carry the same meaning, signifies that highest quality in any work of art that no teaching can impart. The meaning of this conception is very clear so long as one is only concerned with portraits and figure subjects and the painting of sparrows and crickets. One can easily see that a representation may be perfectly correct in execution, colour and shape, and yet lack the essential "life" of the spirit. But it is more difficult to follow the argument when, later on, the conception "ch'i-yün" had been taken over without modification in the criticism of landscape painting; for it is not such a simple matter to say in what the spirit of a place consists, and whether or not it has been ex-

Hsieh Ho pressed. Hsieh Ho did not set out to establish new principles of art, and he would not have enjoyed such enduring success in China, if he had not been discreet in his approach, with a practical understanding of the matter in hand. The same task was undertaken twelve hundred years later, and it is surprising how similar the results were. Henri Testelin, secretary of the French Academy, found it necessary, in order to have some standard by which to judge the pictures offered, to work out "tables de préceptes". His table was made in 1680, and its six categories are, with one significant exception, almost the same as those of Hsieh Ho:
"1. le trait. 2. l'expression. 3. la proportion. 4. le clair et l'obscur. 5. l'ordonnance. 6. la couleur."
The great point of difference between Europe and China is chiaroscuro or shading; China knew nothing of this quality and, in the 18th century, consciously turned it down. On the other hand in China not simply drawing, but control of the brush was demanded; the "brush" or, to use an expression fashionable later, the "power of the brush" was something that showed in the "bones", that is to say the main outer and inner lines, of a picture. Now the word "bones" used to mean powerful structural lines, had its origin in the aesthetic criticism of calligraphy, a field of art peculiar to the Far East. The first treatise about the nature of calligraphy

Calligraphy was written by Lady Wei Shao in about 320 A.D. She made it clear that an ideogram must neither have too much bone (structure) nor flesh (consistency) nor sinews (composition), but that all these elements should be in the right relationship with one another. Such observations may sound well enough, but they only come to life when an artist of genius transforms them into actual shapes. Such an artist was Lady Wei's nephew,

114

The Bodhisattva Matreya with Mandorla. Gilt bronze with a dedicatory inscription of 536 A.D. for a temple near Ting-chou in Hopei. *University Museum, Philadelphia (height 24 inches)*

115

General Wang Hsi-chih (321—379 A.D.). He once saw geese strutting on a riverbank, and looking at their footmarks in the wet sand, he intuitively grasped the way in which the ideal of personal writing could be made reality. Wang Hsi-chih, the poet of the "Orchid Pavilion", won the reputation of prince of calligraphers by his cursive, or so-called "grass" writing. It turned the straight beams of the ancient writing into spirited curves, freed it from the constraints of rectangularity, but at the same time subjected it to the discipline of a fastidious ideal. There has never been a fashion for subjective and unreadable writing in China, but neither has a limited external beauty been approved; only that spirit is praised which sets itself fastidious standards and rejects cheap success. The Chinese brush, whether for writing or painting, is soft with a wedge-shaped tip. The hand is usually held perpendicular and unsupported over the paper, so it is easy to get effects by raising or lowering the hand, by drawing it towards one or flicking it away. One can make fascinatingly amusing shapes with a Chinese brush, which almost does the work on its own. But the reader may well smile and say to himself that this is too cheap and that is too undisciplined. The true calligrapher is recognised by what he turns down and where he is silent. Unlike us, the Chinese adept first practises by copying the style of, say, Huang Shan-ku, Su Tung-p'o, or Chao Meng-fu. He long continues to copy these models, some of which have even

IDEOGRAMS ON PAGE 110   been engraved on stone, before he ventures to choose a style and develop a personal handwriting. His ideal is the innovator Wang Hsi-chih, the "Master of the three arts" calligraphy, poetry and painting. Wang Hsi-chih specialised in figure painting and, we are told, self portraits. Crowds of friends would come to him asking him to compose a few verses for a fan and write a line on it. The Japanese nation counts as one of its most precious treasures, which may not leave the country, a few lines of Wang Hsi-chi, although they are only an eighth century copy. The same standard holds good for painting as for calligraphy in Liu-ch'ao times and long afterwards; the living and personal brushstroke has been the result of a fastidious discipline, often working inconspicuously and secretly; as with an ideogram, its formal qualities come first, and its power of expression last. Colour does no more than add beauty and emphasis; European painting without outlines is called "boneless" by the Chinese. Only a few outstanding masters have occasionally, from the 10th century onwards, attempted this style of painting too.

Unfortunately almost all the great paintings of Liu-ch'ao times have perished, and we have to fall back on a few copies and the frescoes in Korean tombs and Buddhist cave temples, the work of craftsmen rather

116

than artists, when we try to picture what the painters in Nanking were *Painters*
striving for and what they achieved. To recapitulate what we know from literary sources. Painting was then in the hands of a small and cultivated literary elite who practiced it as a hobby, as a free aesthetic experience, and not to earn their living. The same class wrote poetry and essays, got excited about the style of an ideogram, and cared about music; if they had a useful profession, they were generals, ministers or statesmen. Emperors themselves took part in this rivalry, and sought, not always successfully, to draw inspired painters to their courts. Painting and writing were close allied, but the latter held all the rights of a mother or elder sister over the former, and paintings, unless they reached the highest degree of inspiration, were judged by whether or not they were well "written". Their arguments about style in poetry, prose, calligraphy and painting, may seem unrewarding to us. But they were not just the refuge of politically disappointed or contrary spirits. They exercised and multiplied China's greatest advantage, the high intelligence of her people.

Moreover the Chinese talent for patient collection and historical comprehension showed to special advantage at Nanking in those days. Consider the achievements in art and science of the first years only of the reign of Liang Wu-ti (502—549 A.D.) in Nanking. The Emperor's adviser *Theory* and minister Shen Yo (441—513 A.D.) discussed the eight defects of poetry, and was the first to point out the importance of tone in speech; Chung Hung composed a table of values for poetry, and Hsieh Ho for painting; the Emperor's son, Prince Hsiao T'ung, set in train the collection of the Wen-hsüan, a comprehensive anthology of the best Chinese poetry and prose, with examples of every category. Erwin von Zach has made a wonderful German translation with commentary of 1,100 pages of this work. At the same time there were discussions about Buddhist theology and philosophy in Nanking. Fan Chen stood out as the most determined and able critic of the Buddhists, but his effect on the Emperor was the exact opposite of what he intended. Wu-ti, in his youth, had fought hard and cruelly against the Buddhists, but he suffered a Pauline conversion, and turned to a passionate support of monasteries and the copying of sutras. He abolished the death penalty and animal sacrifice, and even forbade the eating of meat; he actually had to listen to criticism from Bodhidharma, a visiting prince from Ceylon, who told him that such concentration on works led him away from the essence of Buddhahood. 200 years later Bodhidharma's followers were to form the contemplative school known as Ch'an, or more often by its Japanese name of Zen, which is the least Indian and the most Chinese form of Buddhism. Then in Nanking in 519 A.D. the Kao-

117

Kasyapa, one of the great disciples of Buddha. Marble with traces of unfired paint. About 600 A.D.
Musée Guimet, Paris (height 4 feet)

seng-chuan was compiled; it was a collection of the biographies of 450 Chinese Buddhist teachers, and from its publication can be dated the self-sufficient independence of Chinese Buddhism. The monk Chih-k'ai too was born at this time in the land of Wu, though not in Nanking itself. This inspired man retired to the mountains of Chekiang where he founded the most interesting of all the Buddhist schools. In true Chinese fashion he disregarded the hair-splittings of Indian theology, saw Buddha's teaching as a historical fact and as a body of creative and developing thought. Some general remarks about Buddhism would not seem out of place.

Buddhism

A new edition of E Zürcher's excellent book is shortly expected; D. Seckel has recently written a fine book about Buddhist art in the Far East and is going to contribute to this series. So it may be helpful here to call attention, no doubt onesidedly, to some of its negative aspects, not in order to obscure its good deeds, but to clarify, by contrast, the peculiar Chinese spirit of the epoch. There are some who see Buddhism as a foreign body in Chinese civilisation. This is especially true of the Chinese conception of society, which imposes the begetting of children and the maintenance of ancestor worship as a primary duty. For that reason monastic life and celibacy were bound to strike the Chinese as antisocial and basically immoral. A considerable time passed and very unreligious means were used before the Chinese were allowed, on payment of a tax to the State, to build and enter monasteries; between 450 and 850 A.D. the official persecutions of the Buddhists were ever and again specially directed against the monasteries, until their power was broken. This is not without its irony. For Buddhism had grown up in the India of pedantic Brahminical learning which had no idea of pity or of social feeling, and there it signified a bitter but necessary revolt of the social conscience which, however, soon petered out again. In China, on the other hand, Buddhism acted just like a Brahminical virus which erupted in a plethora of books. But Chinese good sense was quick to see through the waste of letters and grasp the spirit of Buddha perhaps more clearly than others had done. Not to mention minor sects, there were three main schools of Buddhism, which had no precursors in India, and count as peculiarly Chinese achievements. The friendly and popular school of Amida Buddha with its doctrine of paradise was founded by Hui-yüan (333—460 A.D.) and probably combines Persian with Indian ideas and is open to the laiety and understandable by them. The more philosophical T'ien-t'ai school or Chih-k'ai (—597 A.D.) and later the related school of Hui-kuo had something of the high reputation for learning of the Benedictines. The most Chinese of all the new schools is the Ch'an, the contemplative school, which renounced temples, cloisters and books, and opened the gates of Nirvana to flesh-eating and married lay people, for it taught an emotional and intuitive insight. It would be interesting to find out how far Ch'an Buddhism and its Japanese adaptation, Zen, have influenced thought and popular philosophy in Europe; and it would also be interesting to discuss how far this teaching can properly be called Buddhist at all; for basically it is a very old Chinese idea, and repeatedly found a ready welcome in the hearts and heads of the most gifted Chinese spirits, including the painters who found in it ever new inspiration. The 7th to 9th centuries were the great period of Buddhist intellectual influence in China. And the Liu-ch'ao period with the 7th century was a time of ferment in Chinese life when many new ideas were born and took shape. So one can hardly exaggerate the importance of this period in the history of art, but the study of it is cramped by the very small number of actual works of art of a high order known to us.

We may hope that excavations will soon substantially remedy this deficiency, but for the moment we have to turn to the tomb frescoes of north Korea, which are quite unpretentious works, to get any idea of the painting of the time. The Kokuryo dynasty, which was in close dependence on China, had its capital in the 3rd and 4th century at Wan-tu, the modern *Frescoes* Chian or T'ung-kou, to the north of the middle Yalu. In this district, now part of Chinese Manchuria, the kings and their great subjects built their

460-490   490-550

Stylistic development of s

120

tombs, many of which were decorated with frescoes whose painters were probably sometimes Chinese. In 313 A.D. internal disturbances forced the Chinese to give up their military colony at Lo-lang, the modern Pyöng-yang; a Buddhist mission reached Korea in 373 A.D. and in 427 A.D. the Kokuryo dynasty moved the capital to Pyöngyang. There too they built tombs, and though these have been robbed the frescoes have survived almost unharmed. So from the 4th century down to 668 A.D. T'ung-kou and Pyöngyang give us plenty of material to study, which must have been very like the fresco painting in China herself, but the rarity of inscriptions makes certain and accurate dating difficult. The "Tomb of the Dancer", from which a detail of a group of five dancing figures is given in our illus- PLATE ON PAGE 104 tration, must be nearer in date to 400 than to 500 A.D. It is a simple painting, only using two colours, and gives one very little impression of the personal brushwork that might have been expected from a contempor-ary of Ku K'ai-chih. But there is strikingly assured execution both in the out-lines, which catch the sense of movement well, and in the varied expres-sions of the faces. Compare this with one of the 2nd century stone tomb chapels in Shantung, and one is immediately struck with the much greater freedom and individuality both in subject and in conception, though the execution is craftsman's work. Imagination tells us what joy the great artists of the time must have found in inventing these innovations, and what life and inspiration they would have breathed into every brushstroke.

580-620   620-750

ist figures, *after S. Mizuno*

121

The roll now in the Boston Museum with the portraits of 13 emperors tells us something of how the figure and portrait painters of the time saw their task. It is certainly an old copy of high aesthetic quality and gives us a better idea of the painter's intention than do the frescoes, but one cannot say anything definite about the ascription to Yen Li-pen (—673 A.D.) who was a high court official in early T'ang times and is said to have painted similar subjects. The roll seems to have been made up out of a collection of copies, differing in size as well as execution, after ancient portraits; they must somehow have survived the storms of the 7th century, and were probably joined together at Ch'ang-an. The pictures do not form a consistent series of portraits of imperial ancestors; there are two Han emperors, six of those who reigned in Nanking including the first, Sun Ch'üan, and the last, Hou-chu, then three northern emperors followed by both those of the Siu dynasty which came immediately before the T'ang. There is every reason to suppose that the pictures are derived from contem-

PLATE ON PAGE 107 porary portraits. In the case of our illustration that of the Emperor Hsüan-ti who reigned at Nanking from 569—582 A.D., it is a real portrait which tells us something about the Emperor's spirit and character. The accompanying figures too, including the bearers of his chair, are so sharply characterised, and the nuances of their movements are so well caught, that one feels the painter was enjoying himself working all this out. The very brushstrokes, and still more the delicately added touches of colour, make us understand, even if we only have the copy of a copy to go on, what interested the painters of the 6th century, what they were capable of, and how much the world lost by the destruction of the originals. For all the objective attention to detail which makes every hair distinct in the Emperor's beard, there is none of the niggling quality of a miniature here, but freedom and assured restraint in the firm handling of the outlines; these firm brushstrokes give this picture of manners decorative value without the help of foreground or background and, copy though it is, we feel we know something of the spirit and life both of the people represented, and of the painter.

Ceramics We have to be content with a faint reflection of its former glory to let us know how painting at this time won the leading place among the plastic arts, which it never afterwards lost. But when it comes to pottery there is a rich supply of originals. Nevertheless much research will be needed before we can date specimens accurately and so trace developments better. We can at least be sure that there was no falling off after the Han dynasty; on the contrary, new shapes were invented and lead glaze gave place to felspar glaze, which is both harder and offers greater variety of colour;

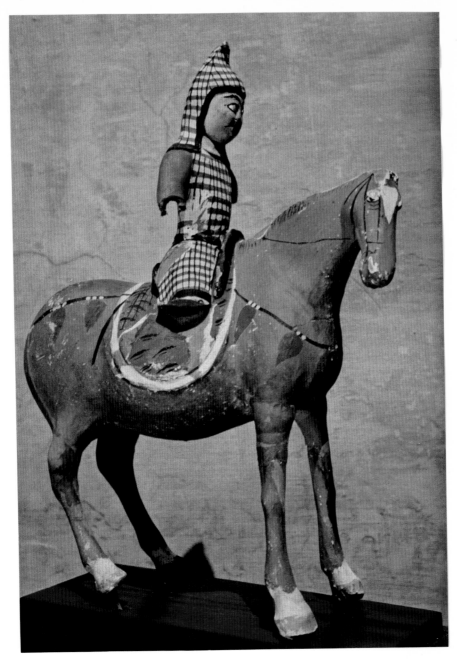

The Blue Rider of Astana. Painted figure. Found in a grave in the oasis of Turfan, East Turkestan. 7th century A.D. *Central Asian Antiquities Museum, New Delhi.*

PLATE ON PAGE 108 it may well be that porcelain was first made in Liu-ch'ao times. Recent excavations allow us to date the jug here illustrated to the 5th or 6th century. The cock's head on it is there for decoration, not as a spout. The finely crackled sea-green glaze, reminiscent of jade, is unevenly spread over the body of the jug which is of unusually hard pottery, and whose shape brings to mind Western, perhaps Hellenistic, prototypes. China traded with the Parthians and with the Sassanians who in 226 A.D. supplanted them in Persia, on a considerable scale, and the silverware, textiles and glass which reached them by this channel, could inspire copies. Unfortunately we do not know enough about Sassanian art yet to be able to analyse its influence on China precisely. Certainly many translations of Buddhist scriptures reached China from Persia, and China, as well as the West, derived many useful and beautiful plants from thence. The grape

Foreign influences vine had arrived under the Han; jasmin, narcissus, pomegranate, almond, fig, olive and watermelon now followed. In return China discovered tea which was first drunk in Ssech'uan in the 3rd century, and spread its aroma thence over China and the world. In Han times too the lotus motif had spread from Persia to the East. It is the generally accepted symbol of Buddhism; as its blossom rises from the mud of slimy lakes and marshes in perfect purity, so the essence of our being may ascend from the "dust of the world" to the purity of Nirvana. Together with the flowers themselves came the great new pleasure of using them in decoration. In the 6th century the old favourites of the West, tendrils, palmettes and half-palmettes, and flower-medallions were introduced; with them many Persian decorative motifs such as bands of pearls, framed medallions, peacocks and winged horses made their triumphant entry into China. China had to thank Buddhism for a new type of building, the pagoda. Admittedly Chinese pagodas do not look like Indian ones; in a sense they were transformations of the towers *(lou* or *t'ai)* which had long been popular; as they were generally built of brick and — this is the most significant of the awakened or, at least, greatly stimulated feeling for nature in Liu-ch'ao times — near the solitary monasteries in the countryside, they stood a better chance of survival than buildings in towns. For that reason pagodas are the earliest examples of full-scale architecture remaining above ground in China.

DRAWING ON PAGES Sculpture, especially Buddhist stone carving so much of which has been
112 & 113 preserved, provides the fullest, but not the best, witness to the art of this age. From about 450 A.D. onwards for some 300 years the wealth of material and of inscriptions makes it possible to date such works by the style of their draperies alone. But one looks in vain for an outstanding

124

sculpture among these simple mass-produced works, though any one of *Stone and bronze sculpture* them, taken by itself, has something moving about it. Compared to the Buddhist sculptures, the animals that guard the imperial tombs at Nanking seem imposing, free and genuinely Chinese. The earliest of them date from about 450 A.D. and they continued to be made for hundreds of years, but about the end of the 8th century there is a fall off from the original high standard. There can be no doubt that bronze sculpture was much more costly and much finer than that made from stone. But most of the great bronze figures that once stood in the temples have been mercilessly melted down into money, and but few survive, though these are certainly outstanding. As we do not know very much about Indian bronze sculpture of the first millenium, it is not easy to follow the stylistic development, or to know how much, within a strict iconographic tradition, is peculiarly Chinese. Certainly comparatively small works, and probably also books of iconographic patterns, must have reached China by sea from Ceylon and India, or come overland from Buddhist Gandara, the modern Punjab and Afghanistan. So it is often doubtful how closely Chinese works were tied to sacred models which, being in the nature of idols, forbade rather than encouraged artistic license. Nevertheless the Chinese with their talent for formulation were to adapt even these prototypes, making them more tense and inspired.

The tall Maitreya, the Buddha of future ages, made of gilt bronze and PLATE ON PAGE 115 dated to 536 A.D. which was found in Hopei, is now in the Museum of Philadelphia. It is one of the most outstanding works. It is a completely sacred and incorporeal symbol, the drapery being rich decoration without useful purpose; the gesture has its prescribed meaning, "fear not and be blessed". But the very folds of the drapery in their pointed ornamental arrangement show something of the Chinese sense of reality and their gift too for finding a convincing formula to express, in this case, pure rest, or, in the dancers from T'ung-kou, movement. The head could not be more dignified, and yet it is more personal than the theme warrants; for the Chinese, while they fully understood the feeling of this foreign world, nonetheless could not miss the chance of testing out their new sense of personal freedom in this context too. By the same token, the flame-surrounded mandorla has at its centre a Sassanian pearl-pattern enclosing a lively design of flowers.

In theory, Buddha and Bodhisattva had neither sex nor personality, neither material existence nor property. They lived from the alms of the faithful, but as Fan Chen protested in vain, they were masters in the art of exploiting a sense of guilt. In token of their poverty Buddhists wore

PLATE ON PAGE 118 only clothes of rags, but that did not prevent their priests from having costly brocades cut into rags and getting a skilful tailor to make a "rag-garment". We see such a garment on the figure of Kasyapa, Buddha's favourite disciple and the first patriarch of his followers. This stone figure, now in the Musée Guimet, is blocked out in the simple shapes which had returned to fashion under the Sui dynasty (about 600 A.D.), and which are well suited to express the gentle piety of this remarkable young man. For once considerable traces of the original paint remain to remind us how this finish must have softened and mellowed the downright roughness of much surviving stone carving. We should never forget that figures now lifeless and grey were once brightly coloured, and thereby more individual. The simple blocked-out Sui style, which is always easy to recognise, may be connected with a movement of taste grown tired of disintegrating experiments and four hundred years of turmoil. The 30 years of Sui rule again united the whole of China; after 628 A.D. the T'ang dynasty again took the offensive beyond the boundary and established China as a world power, greater, stronger and more brilliant than the Han. The 7th century was taken up with hard fighting, and does not seem to have had much time over for thinking about art, but among a fair number of painters of this time the reputations of Yen Li-pen and the landscape painter Li Ssu-hsün were outstanding.

Turfan A modest pottery figure, which would not have claimed to be a work of art, will serve to show that direct observation and invention were not hamstrung in the 7th century. It is one of a pair of figures on horseback excavated by Sir Aurel Stein at Astana in the oasis of Turfan to the north of Eastern Turkestan, and is known as "the blue rider of Astana". A coin of the K'ai-yuan period was found by the entrance to the tomb, and so our one foot high soldier, who is made of pottery on a core of wood, must have been put there a little before that, and represents one of those who conquered Turfan at the end of the 7th century. The same uniform is often seen in the frescoes in the cave of the thousand Buddhas at Tun-huang on the way from Kansu to Turfan. The colours are not fired, but they have kept their freshness. The humble craftsman who made it, without pretending to be an artist, had spirit enough to go beyond mere representation, and the very fact that he painted the horse blue strikes an individual note. For that reason this modest work may stand as a symbol of this freedom loving and inventive epoch.

Freedom In the epoch between 208 and 713 A.D. men had fought for spiritual freedom and attained an independence hitherto unknown. They took their delight in painting people, sparrows or crickets, and in all probability

126

laid the foundations of landscape painting which was to become the favourite theme and the great glory of Chinese art. No accident threw his independence into their laps. The world has produced very few works of art, and even less criticism, which attain this standard of self sufficiency and inspired objectivity. Certainly a rift formed between the free artist, who unlike his European counterpart really was free and did not work for his living, and the ruling class, though many of the latter were wise enough to bridge the gap. Ming-huang who ascended the throne in 713 A.D. established a true harmony between emperor and artist, and it is this harmony which ushered in the classical age of Chinese art.

We should underrate the Liu-ch'ao age, if we saw nothing but the freedom won from former bonds. It also prepared the ground for a far-reaching change of style and perhaps began to reap the harvest. Plants, especially flowers and fruit, came into their own not as mere decorative adjuncts, but as the essence of the created form. This was especially true of ceramics, and from this time onwards Chinese craftsmanship stands on a different level from anything that had gone before, though naturally many established techniques were used in the service of the new creative urge. One cannot fix a precise date for this change; it was not later than the 6th century and may have been earlier. More knowledge of Indian and Persian art, as well as Chinese, from the 3rd to the 5th century is needed before we can be more definite than that. Anyhow, it is clear that innovations were *Persia* absorbed in Liu-ch'ao times, and that many of them had come to maturity in Mediterranean lands long before. After the 6th century the craftsmanship of the Far East is more closely allied to that of Western Asia, and even of Europe, than it had never been before. But we do not yet know in detail the pedigree of this relationship, and cannot say exactly how mutual influences produced this result. However it is quite certain that the purest and most Chinese flowering of these new ideas came in the classical age of Ming-huang.

RECENT TIMES

CHINA

VI THE CLASSICAL AGE

The epoch of the Emperor Ming-huang, "His Radiant Majesty", has always counted as the apex of Chinese civilisation and power. Wu Tao-tse, the greatest painter, Li T'ai-po the most famous poet, and Yang Kuei-fei the most beautiful lady of China were among the many ornaments of his court. The capital Ch'ang-an, (the modern Hsian-fu) with close on two million inhabitants was by far the largest city in the world then; ambassadors, merchants, missionaries, painters, refugees and adventurers from the whole of Asia crowded its streets. The foundations of this greatness had been laid by the two emperors of the Sui dynasty, and the two first T'ang emperors, T'ai-tsung and Kao-tsung, in the first half of the seventh century, Mutatis mutandis, they had faced and solved much the *Retrospect* same problems as the Han. The Turco-Mongolian peoples of the steppe from lake Baikal to Byzantium, had become appreciably stronger but they had split into Eastern and Western Turks with the Altai mountains as a rough boundary between them. In some ways, they felt friendly towards China, where they were free to come and go, and where many of them had won thrones, but they also felt themselves to be the stronger party, indeed the rulers of China, and invaded her with their armies when everything did not go as they wanted. The same situation had developed in Eastern Turkestan, in Tibet and in Northern Korea, and there was a serious danger that the fate of China would be decided by Turks.

The two Emperors of the Sui dynasty exemplify opposite types of Chinese rulers. The first, Wen-ti (581—604 A.D.), transferred the capital to Chang-an in order to have a base of operations nearer the threat from the Turks and from Tibet. He was thrifty, just and financially wise; it was he who built the imperial canal which joined the rice-growing area of the Yangtse with the Huangho, to the great benefit of the economy. His son, Yang-ti (605—617 A.D.) showed an interest in the arts, and was extravagant, though his magnificence was not without its political value. He made a collection of pictures and a library of ninety thousand books, and he instructed Ho Chou as director of the Imperial factories to weave silk copies of Sassanian stuffs and gold brocades, and also to manufacture glass in the same taste, with such success that the Chinese soon came to prefer their native work to the original.

It would seem that Yang-ti's extravagance went too far; he was murdered in 617 A.D. and the provincial governor of T'ai-yüan in Shansi ascended the throne in Ch'ang-an as founder of the T'ang dynasty; he soon abdicated in favour of his son T'ai-tsung who is one of the greatest of emperors.

T'ang dynasty This was near to the date (622 A.D.) when Mohammed went to Mecca to found a new religion which was intended to make the peoples happy, by fire and sword, and forthwith set out to do so. The Arabs soon attacked Persia and the Turks, and swore that they would conquer China. It would seem as if the Turco-Mongolians had sensed the beginning of this earthquake, and were at the same time afraid that the new dynasty in China might put their influence in question, although the T'ang imperial family had enough Turkish blood in its veins. Twice Turco-Mongolian armies appeared before Ch'ang-an, but from 629 A.D. onwards T'ai-Tsung

Silver gilt box with an engraved design of lotus and flowers in medallions. Beginning of the 8th century. *On loan from H.E. Dr. R. Flaes, in the Museum of Asiatic Art, Amsterdam (4½ inches across)*

and his successors began to make the boundaries secure, partly by war and partly by diplomacy. The Turco-Mongolians were many times defeated, in 630 A.D. and in subsequent years. The conquest of East Turkestan began in 640 A.D. and the varying fortunes of war even brought the Chinese over the Pamyrs; in 641 A.D. Tibet recognised Chinese suzerainty; in 668 A.D. Korea and even Annam again belonged to the Chinese Empire. The Japanese had lived as children of nature, happily undisturbed by history, but in 645 A.D. they formed a state on the Chinese model and soon entered into relations with Ch'ang-an. In 638 A.D. Yezdegerd III, *Embassies* the last of the Sassanian kings, sent an embassy to China asking for help against the Arabs. In 640 A.D. an embassy came from the Byzantine Emperor Theodosius, but we do not know with what object. In the same year an Indian embassy arrived from Kanauj on the middle Ganges, not far from the modern Lucknow, where Harsha (606—47 A.D.), the greatest of the Gupta emperors, reigned. There are not yet any systematic excavations at Kanauj, but the magnificent statues that have been found there prove that this Emperor's reign saw the climax of the classical age of Indian sculpture. When we know more about it, we will be able to understand the development of Buddhist sculpture in China better. We owe a very vivid description of Kanauj to the well born and learned Chinese pilgrim Hsüan-tsang who lived in India from 630—645 A.D. and was often received by the Emperor Harsha, who put questions to him about China. He also lived and studied for five years in the Buddhist university at Malanda, where excavations have revealed the best of Gupta sculpture and architecture. On his return to Ch'ang-an, Hsüan-tsang wrote a full account of his journey, and later on, in the 16th century, Wu Ch'eng-in used it as the theme of a highly coloured romance. This book, called "Journey to the West" (Hsi-yu-chi) is one of the most spirited Chinese novels and has been excellently translated by Mr. Arthur Waley. Even the Islamic Calif Othman sent an embassy to Ch'ang-an in 651 A.D. and entered into diplomatic relations with China, which had, however, no immediate result.

It is a hallmark of Chinese political wisdom that they knew how to resist the attraction of war and annexation and were moderate in the extension of their power. They always saw war as a two-edged instrument. It might win plunder, export markets, taxpayers and recruits, but it was always very expensive, without reckoning the price in blood, and this especially when the Chinese had to go on the offensive beyond their own boundaries. Transport and communication lines were troublesome and costly when they had to cross the wastes of Mongolia or Turkestan, or the high mountains of Tibet. Such calculations always played a great part in Chinese financial policy, and even the most ambitious generals did not find it answered their aims to become seriously engaged, for instance, in the West beyond the Pamyrs, no matter what calls for help came from their subjects.

Empress Wu-hou Soon after the stabilisation of the frontier, a strange reaction set in in east China, and in this movement the Empress Wu-hou (625—705 A.D.) wife of the Emperor T'ai-tsung, played a leading part. In 658 A.D. she procured the transfer of the capital eastwards to Loyang, and there she supported the Buddhists on a scale that made everything colossal. In conjunction with the Emperor Kao-tsung, whom also she had married, she had made the gigantic statue of Buddha Vairochana in the cave of Lung-men near the capital, which the T'o-pa rulers had begun to turn into a temple. When the Emperor died in 638 A.D., she openly set about founding a new dynasty, and putting her own family on the throne. To this end she poisoned almost all her relations by marriage, and even her own son. At the same time she started on a building programme of disproportionate extent. In 688 A.D. she built a three-storied Ming-t'ang nearly 300 feet high, and next to it a still higher five-storied pagoda to house a colossal Buddha. From even the third story of the pagoda one could see over the roof of the Ming-t'ang or "hall of light". In 694 A.D. she had a huge pillar of bronze cast; it was 100 feet high with a diameter of 5 feet 3 inches, was called "The axis of heaven", and erected in front of her palace. There followed nine tripods, each 20 feet high, in 695 A.D. so that all the outward tokens traditionally supposed proper to a just ruler should be observed. In 697 A.D. she added 12 bronze animals over 10 feet high and, in the last year of her reign, a gigantic bronze Buddha. It was not until 704 A.D. that the ailing old lady of eighty was forced to abdicate, and she only lived a few months after that. Meanwhile the next Empress tried to play the same game, that is to say to put her own family on the throne. W. Eberhards has performed a useful service in pointing out that there was more to all this apparent madness and *folie de grandeur* than just the stubborness of a very old lady jealous of power to the very last. The real interests at stake were great and her motives intelligent, as is almost always the case in Chinese history. These vast expenses for the sake of world-denying Buddhism and these favours to the monasteries show that they had won not only power over the souls of men, but also over their wealth. It would seem that in the 7th century the great capitalists, especially in eastern China, used the Buddhist organisations as cover; monasteries and temples became the banks and places of safe keeping for their capital, and they also served as hotels and international exchange offices. They had

Back of a mirror. Dragons in clouds made from plates of silver cut out and engraved and let in to a lacquer background which is now almost entirely perished. First half of 8th century A.D. *City Art Gallery, Bristol.* *(Diameter 7½ inches)*

moreover been long free of taxes, and their landed property was as great as that of the great leasehold property owners. But, after Wu-hou's death, so great a danger threatened that, for better or worse, it was essential to re-impose taxes. In 642 A.D. the Moslem Arabs had conquered Persia; the last Sassanian Crown Prince served as a general in the Chinese army and died at Ch'ang-an. In 705 A.D. the Arabs and their allies crossed the Oxus, seized Buchara, Samarkand and Tashkent, which had accepted Chinese suzerainty, and left no doubt about their intention of going on to attack China. At that point even the greediest grandees had to think about the general welfare of the state.

Emperor Ming-huang In 713 A.D. a forceful, intelligent and able grandson of Wu-hou ascended the throne without a struggle on the abdication of his weak father. He took command of the situation and mastered it almost without trouble. He next confiscated the property of monasteries and drove out all those whose only reason for being there was tax evasion. At the same time he melted down all bronze statues of Buddha into money, and forbade the collection of money to make new ones. Wu-hou's "axis of heaven" was turned into coin too; that of itself provided money. He did not even spare the gold and silver ornaments of the palace, but put them in the melting pot. He was thus able to equip armies which defeated the Arabs in three campaigns in 714, 736 and 744 A.D. which consolidated his rule beyond the Pamirs and the Oxus, right up to the borders of India and Persia. As far as the sea of Aral the peoples acknowledged Chinese overlordship. However, Ming-huang was not over intent on military glory; hardly were the battles finish-ed than trade began. Between 713 and 750 A.D. ten embassies came from Islamic Persia bringing companies of dancers, who were certain to arouse the special interest of the Chinese court, and the Emperor who was an enthusiastic polo player, looked to the West for fine horses. Apart from reforms in agriculture, the army and the constitution, one can best see how Ming-huang conceived of his duties as a ruler by noticing where he economised and what he encouraged. He reduced the palace expenses, closed the imperial factories for silk and needlework, reduced the govern-ment corvee to about 120,000, and generally paid more attention than other rulers to the maxim of Confucius that he should make his people well-fed and contented (Lun-yü XII. 7). With the help of good harvests the number of the settled population, that is to say the registered tax-payers who alone were counted, rose steeply. Regarding Wu-hou's Ming-t'ang at Loyang as a symbol of crazy presumption, he had it taken down and another building substituted for it. On the other hand in 725 A.D. he anticipated Louis XIV by 900 years in his foundation of an academy of "immortals", which was developed from the idea of the famous Han-lin academy, the "grove of the brush"; his official bulletin (Ching-pao) was the first newspaper and it continued publication for nearly 1200 years; finally his "Pear Garden" was a sort of school for music, opera and ballet, in which he occasionally taught himself or at least tried out his ideas about music.

In 736 A.D. he definitely transferred the capital back to Ch'ang-an. The Emperor had a creditable reputation as a poet too, but then it was a matter of general education to be able to write a poem that was, at least, in good taste. Among the innumerable poets of China, there were more than 2,000 in T'ang times alone. Four of those who lived in Ming-huang's reign are among the greatest of "the golden age" of poetry: Meng Hao-jan (689—740 A.D.), Wang Wei (699—759 A.D.), Li T'ai-po (701—762 A.D.), and Tu Fu (712—770 A.D.). The Emperor's brothers, Prince Ning (—731 A.D.) and Prince Chi (702—761 A.D.) entertained painters and poets in their own houses more often than did the Emperor, and were thought of as their patrons. The Empress Mei-fei herself was famous for one poem. Ming-huang neglected her for the sake of his younger wives, but continued to be generous and once sent her a sack of pearls which had been brought as tribute to him. Mei-fei however sent it back with a few touching

The golden age of poetry

Hall of the Tōshōdaiji in Nara, built by Chinese workmen. 759 A.D.

135

lines of verse. A poem of Goethe's is based on an English translation of her verses:

You send treasures to adorn me.
It is long since I looked in the mirror.
Since I have been banished from your eyes,
I no longer know what suits me and what not.

Li T'ai-po's behaviour at court has become a legend embroidered with poetic licence. Friends introduced him there in 742 A.D.; he was given a sinecure and occasionally invited into the imperial presence, for the Emperor knew how to appreciate his brilliantly improvised verses, but they often had to fetch buckets of water from the market tap to souse him into decent sobriety first. After three years a festal party was given in his honour but he was told to leave the capital.

Sudden change In 742 A.D., the same year in which Charlemagne was born, Ming-huang himself proclaimed the break in his life; he announced a new reign-name *T'ien-pao,* "Heavenly Treasure"; the name referred to a Taoist relic which had been found under strange auspices and brought to the palace. From now onwards he took his dreams and his spiritualistic and pseudo-scientific investigations more seriously than the wise policy by which he had brought security and well-being to the land through thirty years. His new interests are generally described as Taoist, and people talk of the Emperor's conversion to Taoism, but that is only correct if we do not think of Taoism as a religion but as a miscellaneous collection of every imaginable irrational practice of magic, wizardry or conjuring. Apart from this, two definite events of the year 742 A.D. were to have serious consequences. The proclamation of Lady Yang as "Kuei-fei", a title roughly corresponding to that of *maîtresse en titre,* and the introduction of General An Lu-shan to the court. When the Emperor was fifty two years old, his beloved concubine died, and he met the twenty year old Yang Kuei-fei, who had originally been intended as a concubine for one of his numerous sons. He took her as supplementary wife and gave her the title of Kuei-fei. This Chinese

FRONTISPIECE *Madame de Pompadour* was musically very gifted and shared the Emperor's passion for polo and romantic rides by night. She looked well on horseback; her slim and elegant figure and her love of peonies, with which she decorated her hair, set the fashion. One knows that any lady in T'ang costume with these two characteristics is Yang Kuei-fei (see frontispiece). She took into favour General An Lu-shan, who had fought successfully in Mongolia; he insinuated himself into the Emperor's confidence which long remained unshaken, and he was given command of ever larger

Plate with three small feet. It is decorated with flying wild ducks in a lotus garland. The design is cut into the clay of the pot and heightened with coloured lead glazes. 8th to 9th century A.D. *Rücker-Embden loan in the Rietberg Museum, Zürich (11½ inches diameter)*

armies. It goes without saying that a cousin of Yang Kuei-fei was made Chancellor in 752 A.D. and her relations were provided for generously. Ming-huang, who for thirty years had been economical and farsighted, scarcely concerned himself any longer with affairs of state, to the great distress of his old officials. He was, indeed, still concerned to see that the common people were not excessively taxed, but he entirely neglected to notice that the Arabs were again on the offensive and in 751 A.D. they won a decisive victory at Samarkand. This victory brought Chinese crafts-men and the knowledge of the mystery of paper making and fine porcelain to Western Asia first, and thence to the West, but it marked a turning point for T'ang imperial power.

Rebellion In these circumstances, General An Lu-shan felt himself called on to save the country and himself from danger, and to make himself Emperor. He captured Loyang and Ch'ang-an, which he utterly devastated. The Em-peror fled in 756 A.D. to Ch'eng-tu in Ssech'uan, but on the way there the anger of his loyal soldiers wreaked itself against Yang Kuei-fei and her entourage who were held responsible for all that had gone wrong. Her cousin, the Chancellor, was killed, and the Emperor had to allow a minis-ter to strangle his beloved. Next year his son suppressed the rebellion, being greatly helped in this by a loyal and noble general, Kuo Tzu-i. This general was a Nestorian Christian, who in the troubled times that fol-lowed was to save the life of Li T'ai-po, and later provided a most popular and sympathetic subject for painters; he is always represented as a father surrounded by a vast company of sons. In 757 A.D., when the rebellion had been suppressed and An Lu-shan murdered by his own son, Ming-huang came back to Ch'ang-an, but immediately abdicated in favour of his successor. He sought, in spiritualistic seances, to see the ghost and form of Yang Kuei-fei again, and with his musicians composed elegies about his lost happiness. He died in his 78th year in 762 A.D. He had united in his person the two most outstanding characteristics of Chinese Emperors; In the K'ai-yüan period he was as frugal and farsighted as K'ang-hsi or Sui Wen-ti, but in the T'ien-pao period he was as wasteful and extravagant as Ch'ien-lung or Sui Yang-ti. However, he never lost the love of his people and of future generations. All his later weaknesses were forgiven; maybe people were glad to think that even the Son of Heaven could have such human frailties. People never forgot that Ming-huang reigned in an age of prosperity, justice and power, permeated with a high-spirited sense of self-confidence and worth.

That he should throw away all the glory of an empire for the sake of a girl could cast no shadow over his fame. The beauty and greatness of

138

Dignitary carrying a symbol of rank like a sceptre in his hand. Figure from the tomb of a man of importance. Splashes of lead-glaze over pottery. 8th century A.D. *Museum of Far Eastern Art, Cologne (height 22 inches)*

the age of this "Radiant Majesty" never faded from Chinese memory. *T'ang architecture* The palaces and temples of old Chang-an have perished, but we can get an idea of their appearance by turning to Japan. In 710 A.D. the Japanese Emperor had for the first time established a fixed capital at Nara, which he unhesitatingly planned on the model of Ch'ang-an. From 724–748 A.D. Shōmu-tenno reigned in Nara; he was a zealous Buddhist, and abdicated before his time in order to become a Buddhist priest. He summoned many Chinese priests and artists so that everything should be carried out correctly in accordance with the dominant Chinese taste. The great hall of DRAWING ON PAGE 135 the Tōshōdaiji in Nara built by Chinese craftsmen in 759 A.D., is not only an almost entirely pure example of the style of wooden architecture then prevailing in Ch'ang-an, but also one of the most magnificent and largest examples of wooden architecture existing in the world, being higher than the Pantheon in Rome. The Buddhist temples at Nara still contain great statues of bronze, dry lacquer and pottery, which are based on contemporary classical Chinese standards though nothing of the sort is preserved from China; they illustrate the full maturity of the classical style, sure and effortless in its plastic sense and at the same time with something of supernatural and intangible majesty and distinction. Perhaps one should regard the bronze Buddha of Healing in the Yakushiji, the pottery groups of the Tōdaiji and the lacquer Buddha of the Kōzanji as representing standards of absolute perfection in the classical sculpture of the Far East; their quality makes us wonder how much beauty was lost to the world in the destruction that has gone on in China. In 794 A.D. the Japanese capital was transferred to Kyoto, where it remained until 1868, but Ch'ang-an still remained the accepted ideal. Kyoto is a city of wide streets crossing at right angles; it is one of the most beautiful cities in the world, and perhaps the reason is that, in the best Chinese tradition, everything there inspires a sense of reverence for some great inner spiritual worth.

Shōsōin We have the greatest piece of exceptional luck in the preservation of the treasure house of the Shōsōin. It was erected by the widowed Empress of Shōmu-tenno in 756 A.D., the year of Ming-huang's flight. The treasury contains as a dedication to Buddha the entire household furniture of the Japanese imperial palace, and its more than 3,000 pieces, to which a few outstanding objects have been added later. They remain as fresh as on the day they were made; the lutes and games tables, the jugs and saddles, the boxes and chests, and the sword of state and the glasses could be used again at once. Nowhere else in the world has the household gear of an Emperor who died 1,200 years ago been preserved in such perfect and

140

complete condition. The great majority of the objects are Chinese, either brought from China or made by the numerous Chinese craftsmen summoned to Japan. So a good many of them could as easily have been used at Ming-huang's court, and would indeed have roused admiration anywhere in the world. Some of the articles of silver or silver gilt, and the glasses have, for the first time, a Western, that is to say Sassanian, look and indicate the inter-relation between East and West. Just a few pottery objects with splashes of three-coloured lead glaze are in the Shōsōin, and these help us to date the thousands of similar pots and figures dug up elsewhere to the T'ang dynasty. There were some pots of a class called "proto-porcelain", PLATE ON PAGE 137 which was not previously known, and which is older than the porcelain exported to Europe. The publication of the Shōsōin collection inspired the Chinese to look for things of like sort, at first only in uncontrolled plundering excavations.

Now, fifty years after the publication of the Shōsōin treasures, when we come to compare them with the objects excavated, two points strike us which seem at first surprising, but on further reflection throw some light, though not too clear a light, on the condition of the times. The first point is that pottery, China's great contribution to the world of art, is very sparsely represented; the Shōsōin has only a pair of Buddhist begging bowls, a jug and a small drum, all with the three-colour lead glaze which, while suitable enough, is certainly unpretentious. There are infinitely more and finer examples of this type found in Chinese tombs; moreover quantities of other and finer types of pottery have come to light, which are hard to date because there is no hint of anything like them in the Shōsōin. On the other hand the silverware in the Shosoin still holds its place among the very best examples known, though a surprising number of similar pieces, both earlier and later, have been found. Gyllensvärds has studied the *Silver and gold work* matter carefully and proved that from the 6th century at latest and throughout the T'ang dynasty silver was more in demand for use and ornament than had previously been supposed. There may be a simple reason for the striking contrast between the Emperor Shōmu's magnificent silver and his modest pottery. The Emperor was a pious and zealous Buddhist who would have followed Indian traditions. Now in India pottery made of burnt earth counts as something dirty and despicable; anyone who can afford it prefers to use metal, even if he cannot run to silver or gold plates, and over millenia there has never been any Indian pottery of aesthetic value.

So if Shōmu-tenno was thinking of himself as an ascetic, he had a contemptible beggar's bowl, but if he was Emperor and amusing himself playing *go*,

141

he enjoyed the finest materials Asia could supply, that is lacquer, and for his daily use silver and bronze were good enough if of the finest quality. Magnificent gold and silver work has been found dating back to the Han dynasty, but the quantity from the Sui and T'ang dynasties, from about 600 to 900 A.D., is so immensely greater than that from other centuries, that we cannot just attribute it to the chances of preservation. We know that the Persians were particularly fond of silver, and that costly silver plates are characteristic of Sassanian art. It would seem that Indian missionaries awakened a taste for gold and silver luxuries in the East, and that the Sassanian goldsmiths and merchants saw their chance to satisfy this demand; the Chinese gladly accepted the shapes and designs they were offered, adapted them and later under Ming-huang transfigured

Group of horsemen. A dignitary with his servant who holds a state umbrella. Painting on paper found in one of the sealed rooms at Tun-huang, the great Buddhist temple precinct in northwestern China, on the way to Turkestan. *Musée Guimet, Paris (6 by 9 inches)*

them into such lovely and such purely Chinese forms that no one could confuse them with Persian or Indian work. One may often be in doubt about the date of a particular object, but the general line of development is clear enough. The six-petalled partially gilt silver box, now in Amsterdam, illustrated here, may date from about 700 A.D., but its lovely shape PLATE ON PAGE 130 may have remained in fashion for another 50 years, and there is no reason why Ming-huang should not have used such a box. Its basic shape is plantlike, in outline like the diagram of a flower, and with the bulging body of a melon. In the middle there is a stylised lotus-rosette which echoes the basic shape. A medallion shape is formed on each of the six petals by the tendrils of a plant which twines round all of them; in alternate medallions there is either a lotus flower or fruit, or a bird; a peacock on a tendril that ends in a fruit, a phoenix on a lotus flower, and a goose on a pomegranate. Most of the silver background is enlivened with tiny punched circles, and the leaves, fruit and birds are gilt. All the individual elements are of Persian origin, or, like the lotus-rosette, perhaps Indian. But the sense of peace combined with the most lively and spirited taste, and the extraordinarily refined intertwining of the separate motifs, which can best be appreciated if one makes a drawing of the whole design, are not merely Chinese but the T'ang classical style at its best.

The ornament on the silver box in Amsterdam is clearly of Persian origin, *Ornament*
but no one would mistake it for a Persian work; it shows a pure Chinese taste for symmetry, naturalness and grace. On the other hand there are mirrors which in shape and technique could only be derived from the Chinese tradition. Round mirrors, and petal-shaped ones too, had been in fashion for more than 1,000 years. The backs are generally richly decorated, and none richer than the mirror in the Shōsōin with inlay of gold, silver, amber, mother-of-pearl and lacquer, can be imagined. At Ming-huang's court too, beautiful mirrors were so much appreciated that they were held worthy to be birthday gifts for the Emperor. In 736 A.D. all the great men competed with each other in the magnificence of their gifts including mirrors which are said to have been obtained at great expense from distant places. Unfortunately we do not know whence they came. We learn, for example that An Lu-shan was particularly fond of the *P'ing-t'o* technique, which was used for other things besides mirrors and which was so expensive that Ming-huang's successor Su-tsung immediately forbade it by his sumptuary laws. *P'ing-t'o* means "flat cut-out" and especially applies to gold and silver sheets cut out in the *à jour* technique and often engraved as well, and let into a lacquer background.

Bristol City Art Gallery possesses a mirror of this type that well may date

143

PLATE ON PAGE 133 to the time of Ming-huang. On the back, there are dragons playing round the central knob as if it were "a lucky pearl", which is a symbol of long life according to Chinese ideas, and which was later given a Buddhist interpretation. The lacquer in which the cut out sheets are laid has lost its colour and partly perished, but the drawing of the dragons remains sharp and clear. Their taut, clear-cut outlines would seem to have come first into fashion in the 6th century A.D. The harmonious balance between representation and decoration gives them a classical form, as the boundaries of the sharp lined drawing are held in check, and just for that reason a fine decoration of tense lines results. The frame as well as the dragons looks purely Chinese and at first sight more old fashioned than the then modish flowers and tendrils. The simple band of diamonds, the outer triangles of which are filled with parallel lines, could have been found as easily in Han times, but the tiny detail of the carefully drawn flowers in the diamonds could not. That just goes to show how completely plant patterns had come to be accepted as an element in Chinese decoration, for in other respects the mirror almost seems an expression of a reaction against foreign influence in the purity with which it keeps to Chinese tradition. Of course, no such thought would consciously have entered into the head of an artist of the time. If there was any sense of national pride in the reign of Ming-huang, it would have been based more on what was included rather than on what was excluded.

Pottery The Chinese never allowed themselves to be shaken in their affection for pottery, in which they have always excelled, by any Indian Buddhist ideas. They continued to make every vessel and utensil possible out of fine pottery, and this included pots and cups for tea, which had attained a wider popularity in the 8th century. If we can trust the classical "Book of tea" written by Lu Yü in the 8th century, the finest pottery must have been already in use in T'ang times and the imperial court must have had pure white true porcelain. But when we try to date the finest T'ang pottery we have to fall back on similarities of shape; and it is now usual and probably correct to date as T'ang all the bowls, cups, jugs and ewers whose profiles resemble contemporary silverware. These more exquisite works in turn aroused admiration in the Near East, which had a ceramic tradition as old as that of China and was very expert in such matters. There is literary evidence to show that Harun al Rashid (786—809 A.D.) already had a collection of Chinese ceramics, and the excavations of the palace of his successors who resided from 838—883 A.D. in Samarra, not far to the north of Baghdad, have brought to light potsherds which must have been made in Chekiang; to have a cabinet of Chinese porcelain has long been

144

a mark of good taste in the Near East and Moslem India, and was a necessary adjunct of any palace.

We know much more about the plainer sort of T'ang pottery with splashes of lead-glaze, of which much is preserved. The colours are the simplest possible; every beginner knows how to make green glaze with copper, yellow and brown with iron, and blue with cobalt. But see how the Chinese used these simple ingredients. They had no hesitation in throwing strong splashes of all three colours together, and letting the glaze flow and form drops. The world over potters face a problem which the Chinese solved; their shapes were so plain and dignified, simple and spirited, that they long endured. Probably this splashed lead-glaze ware found appreciative buyers for 500 years. Even fastidious households may well have used plates, bowls, jugs and vases of this sort. The patterns, often cut out in the clay, include besides flowers and garlands of lotus and leaves, cloud shapes and flying birds; sometimes too there are overlapping contours imitated from silverware. But it is in graves that we find the greatest number of vessels and even more figures, some small and some over three feet high, with this glaze. There are also plain unglazed tomb figures, often beautifully painted. So these pottery objects placed in the tombs have become generally known as "T'ang figures"; they may be attendants, horses or camels covered with gay splashes of brown, green, blue and white lead-glaze. People went to a great deal of expense to make these tomb offerings and there was a regular protocol for the number and height of the figures that might accompany a prince, a minister and so forth, to stand in counterfeit attendance in the next world. Most of the figures were mass produced from moulds. They therefore give a good impression of generally accepted manners and modes and of people's hopes and desires.

The figure of a dignitary, here reproduced, is one of many similar examples. He holds a symbol of rank, a sort of tablet or sceptre, in both hands in front of his breast. Compared to the hieratic and strongly stylised gilt bronze statues of Buddha of 200 years earlier, these figures are casual and natural. Their clothes are no longer unrealistic decorations but fall easily, and clearly show what they are made of. Especially the faces, which are never glazed, with their friendly and cheerful dignity, give an impression of the way T'ang people liked to conceive themselves.

The very ordinariness and popularity of these tomb figures is proof that this easy naturalness, these sensible, lively gestures and the friendly self-assurance of the faces were indeed characteristic of T'ang people in real life. The official waiting for an audience who looked so and stood so,

PLATE ON PAGE 137

Tomb figures

PLATE ON PAGE 139

145

with his easy and relaxed dignity, must have been the ideal of the society
to which a Li T'ai-po belonged.

Sculpture In the eighth century, in this unlike Han times, there were well-known
artists who had made a name for themselves by their statues and pottery
figures which were mostly portraits or Buddhist statues. However, Hardly

Hermit's hut. Drawing after the painted lacquer decoration on the inside of a bowl
in the Shōsōin at Nara. Before 736 A.D. *(Diameter 15½ inches)*

a single statue of this sort has been found and once again we must turn
to Japan, especially to the Tōdaiji, to get an idea of the grand and expressive pottery figures which were then made there, perhaps not by
Chinese craftsmen but certainly in completely Chinese taste. We do at least
know the name of one of the great painters of that time, Yang Hui-chih,

146

and a characteristically pointed Chinese anecdote about him throws a revealing light on the ideas then prevailing. Yang Hui-chih was at first a painter and tried to compete with Wu Tao-tse. When he realised the latter's transcendent superiority he gave up painting, and turned to making pottery figures, especially portraits.

There is no doubt that painting flourished much more than any other art in Ming-huang's reign, or that Wu Tao-tse has always counted as the greatest Chinese painter. And yet we hardly know more of him than of _Painting_ Apelles or Polygnotos. His great popular renown is due to the many wall paintings which he executed, more especially for the Buddhist temples in both capitals, Loyang and Ch'ang-an. But these were all destroyed in the great Buddhist persecution of 843 A.D. There are not even detailed descriptions of his pictures and the famous verses of Su Tung-p'o give no precise impression. If only a picture of his had been preserved, we should see the whole of Far Eastern painting differently. Though we have no precise information in detail, the vast influence of Wu Tao-tse and his school is something almost tangible. In the representations of Buddha's entry into Nirvana and in pictures of Hell, all of which are based on pictures of his which had become classical, one can see that about 730 A.D. a new conception broke through. This conception is clearly different not only from the hieratic style of the 6th century and the statuesque style of about 600 A.D., but also from everything we know of Indian or Persian painting. To put the point shortly, nearly half the figures in painting from this time forth are dressed in T'ang clothes, which gives an indication of the importance of this epoch. So we must try to get some idea of what Ming-huang and the painters of his time, especially Wu Tao-tse, mean for the art of China and the Far East, even though we have to rely on literary sources, what contemporary works there are and, albeit inadequate, copies and versions.

The Emperor Ming-huang was a man of an open and healthy disposition; _Ming-huang's_ he loved horses, hunting and polo, women, music and ballet. It would _court painter_ seem that his own strongest aesthetic interest was for music. He loved the world as he found it, and wanted to have himself and his surroundings recorded in pictures. He was liberal in praise and gifts to anyone who could paint what he wanted well, and what he wanted was pictures of himself, his ladies, his orchestra, his horses and hunting animals, and also his dreams. He did not care for antiquarian pursuits. It happened that the ship bearing the famous collection of pictures and the liberary of Sui Yang-ti from Loyang to Ch'ang-an sank in the Huangho, but, as far as is known, Ming-huang took no trouble to collect old pictures again and

147

build up a museum. In Chang-an there was the Ling-yen-ko which, like the Lin-kuang pavilion in Han times, resembled a National Portrait Gallery. Yen Li-pen in the 7th century, painted portraits for it and Ming-huang instructed a certain Ts'ao Pa to do the like. Besides this, Wu Tao-tse was commissioned to paint portraits of statesmen and generals which could be copied on stone blocks; from these printings rubbings could be taken and widely distributed.

If one were to judge by numbers, religious painting must have played the most important part at that time. But it is uncertain whether the Emperor was really interested in it, or whether reasons of state dictated his behaviour. The claims of Confucianists, Taoists and Buddhists were kept in balance without any one-sided favour to any of them. Wu Tao-tse chiefly painted Buddhist frescoes, but he also painted portraits of Confucius and his disciples, and Laotse too. Perhaps the Emperor's later interest in Laotse and the Taoists has been exaggerated. Some in good faith and others maliciously have made capital out of the fact that Laotse's family name of Li was the same as that of the T'ang imperial house, so that Ming-huang's feeling for Laotse could have been a matter of private but exaggerated reverence for ancestors. The Emperor had many reasons to be mistrustful and on the watch against the Buddhists; he had had thousands of their bronze statues melted down and forbade the collection of coin for new statues, but he did not prevent painters from painting Buddhist subjects in temples which were open to everyone. And the Emperor made no objection to the inclusion in these frescoes of his portrait and those of his ladies, or to painting distinguished Buddhist priests such as I-hsing, who advised him in his calendar reform. Ming-huang was the ideal emperor, who gave commissions, knew how to appreciate and reward successful work, did not harass painters with wishes and programmes that had nothing to do with art, and never interfered with those who went their own way.

We have some information about the circle of painters who gathered at Ming-huang's court. When he ascended the throne, he honoured the aged landscape painter Li Ssu-hsün by making him a general. Li Ssu-hsün had retired from the capital during Wu-hou's reign of terror, when the life of any member of the imperial family of Li was in danger. His son, "the little General Li", also won a reputation as a landscape painter. In the first part of his reign the Emperor esteemed most highly the painters Ts'ao Pa, Ch'en Hung, Chang Hsüan, Wei Wu-t'ien and Feng Shao-cheng. None of these was a specialist in any narrow sense of the word. The first three painted the Emperor and the ladies of the court, Ts'ao Pa and Ch'eng Hung also painted horses, more especially the Emperor's beloved white

Themes of the court painters

148

steed "Shining Night". Ch'en Hung and Wei Wu-t'ien were particularly celebrated for their pictures of the Emperor out hunting, or returning with the spoils of the chase. Feng Shao-cheng painted in the same genre, secialising in pheasants and other birds, hunting-falcons being favourites. Later Han Kan won the Emperor's special favour; he was a pupil of Ts'ao Pa and had the great poet Wang Wei as his patron. He is reputed one of the great horse-painters of China, and he painted "Shining Night", the Emperor inspecting his horses, or stag-hunting, or setting out on a night ride. However Han Kan was not a horse-painter only, but also made portraits of priests and frescoes in Buddhist temples. One of the most celebrated of his pictures showed the Lady Wang Chao-chün mounting a horse; the theme there was the story of a beautiful lady of the court, whose name means "Sunlight", who was sent in 33 B.C. as tribute to the Khan of the Huns. Many poems as well as pictures took as their theme the moment when she, escorted by a company of Huns and of Chinese, left civilisation for the barbarian land. Later versions and close echoes of this picture allow us to form a good impression of the original. One of these versions, now in Berlin, has substituted Yang Kuei-fei for Lady Chao-chün, and made the escort entirely Chinese. A fine picture, in the Freer Gallery, painted by Ch'ien Hsüan, may be based on an original by Han Kan or at least echoes his style and that in fashion at the court of Ming- FRONTISPIECE huang. Ch'en-hung too painted pictures of Yang Kuei-fei which must have delighted the Emperor.

We would like to know more about Wu Tao-tse's position in this circle, *Wu Tao-tse* but unfortunately there is no adequate biography either of him or of the Emperor. It may be that Wu was born at Yang-chai not far from Loyang in 690 A.D. as the son of poor parents who died young. The boy's gift for painting induced some high official to patronise him, as happened later to Li T'ai-po, and give him an education specialising in calligraphy. Wu has always been renowned for his wonderful "power of the brush" in that he filled his outlines with a life which, before him, had only been found in calligraphy. However enough copies exist to make it clear that Wu Tao-tse did not work himself out in the bravura of powerful, swelling lines, but also knew well how to use the gentler notes of delicate contours. The earliest information that we possess records that he painted a fresco in the Ching-ai temple in Loyang, and that an assistant, whose name is given, added the colour. It is several times recorded that his pictures were ruined by the colourists, and this would seem to imply that Wu often only painted the outlines, "the bones", and left the colour to assistants. We do not know the date when he was recommended to the Emperor, but it certainly proved a momentous event in art history. Ming-huang spent the winter solstice of 725 A.D. in Shantung, and while there performed a solemn official sacrifice on the T'ai-shan mountains. On his return next year he commissioned three painters to make a detailed record of his journey, and this became famous under the name of "the Golden Bridge". Ch'en Hung painted the Emperor and his white horse "Shining Night", Wei Wu-t'ien the animals, and Wu T'ao-tse the landscape. This may be taken as meaning that the master had not yet reached the height of his fame, and was only allowed a share in the common task which gave no scope for the figure painting for which he was later so famous. But one can also take it as showing that Wu Tao-tse already counted as the greatest landscape painter. It was just this side of his art that was celebrated in a delightful anecdote; in the Emperor's presence he painted a huge landscape in fresco, and then walked into it and disappeared for ever. We are nearer to reality with the information that the Emperor's brother and

Ladies making silk. Detail from a scroll. Old copy, perhaps by the Emperor Hui-tsung (1082-1135) after Chang Hsüan, about 740 A.D. *Museum of Fine Arts. Boston (Scroll 14½ inches wide)*

patron of the arts, Prince Ning, recommended him to the powerful Minister of War, Wei Tzu-li, and that the latter took him with him on a journey to Ch'eng-tu in Ssech'uan.

The Emperor often commissioned paintings from him and on one occasion he aroused his special admiration; the Emperor had seen the conqueror of demons, Chung K'uei, in a feverish dream which he described to the painter; the latter then painted an impressive picture of Chung K'uei which fully corresponded to the Emperor' dream. For a long time afterwards it was taken as a model for pictures of this hero who became extremely popular. The legend about him was as follows; once upon a time — perhaps a hundred years before Ming-huang — there was a very gifted, but very ugly, candidate called Chung K'uei, who wrote the best essay in the official examinations. According to custom the winner of this contest was summoned to an audience before the emperor to receive a belt as the symbol of his learning. But this candidate was so ugly that the emperor visibly shrank back, and hardly managed to hand the belt to him. Chung K'uei took this so much to heart that he committed suicide on the steps of the palace. This deeply distressed the emperor, and he ordered that the genius whom he had unintentionally insulted should be buried with the honours due to an imperial prince, and raised him posthumously to the highest rank of learning. Since then Chung K'uei was considered as the guardian against all evil spirits and demons, including that of the imperial fever. It was Wu Tao-tse's picture which caused his wide popularity.

The greatest gift of Wu Tao-tse would seem to have been his power to fill every figure, and every landscape too, with the sense of a direct intuition and genuine experience. All sources speak of the assured facility of his technical accomplishment; he is naively praised for drawing circles without a compass and lines without a ruler. It is more to the point to record the story that his Buddhist pictures of hell, a subject unknown in India but favoured by Chinese Buddhists in the 8th century, so worked on the feelings of the beholders that many sinners repented and turned to paths of righteousness. In Han times illustrations of moral stories had been considered edifying, but it was only the themes that mattered then; Wu Tao-tse was the first to make the expressive quality of the painting itself strike home. Of his pictures of hell there are but faint echoes in later versions. However we are luckier in the case of his equally famous picture of Buddha's death or entry into Nirvana. There are many illustrations of this theme, in sculpture as well as painting, in China and beyond her borders, and there is such a difference between those before and those after the 8th century, that we can be sure that a great Chinese painter

Chung K'uei

151

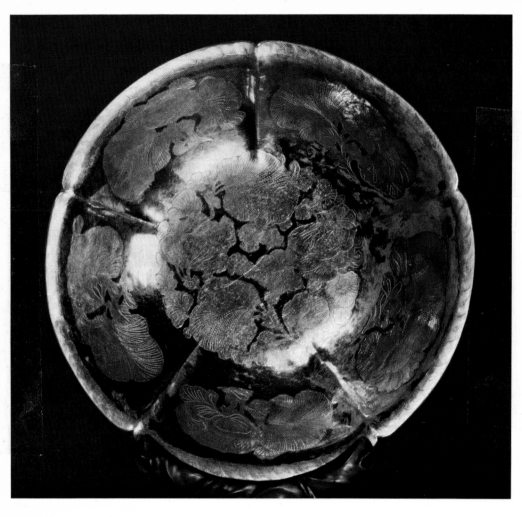

Cinquefoil silver bowl with gilding and a decoration of peony leaves and flowers. Inscription on the back, giving the weight. About 750-820 A.D. *City Art Gallery, Bristol (Diameter 9¾ inches)*

had lifted the theme on to a higher level, and that painter must have been Wu Tao-tse.

Literary sources and echoes down the ages are impressive testimony to the achievements of early 8th century painters, and to the effect of their new and free and fresh vision, but that is no substitute for actual pictures. Even modest originals give something, and something most important of the spirit and feeling of the age which cannot be derived from copies of masterpieces. A little paper picture found by P. Pelliot in a walled-up chamber in the caves of Tun-huang, is preserved in the Musée Guimet. It shows two figures on horseback, a dignitary and his attendant who holds an umbrella of state. A few trees on a bank and scattered plants indicate the surroundings. Naturally this simple little sketch of a picture gives us no idea of the famous T'ang calligraphy and the brilliance of expressive line, but the outlines are clear and crisp, without intersections, and the drawing of the tree trunks is spirited. There is something sure and vivid in the handling of the simple red and green which enliven the Indian ink. Even this unpretentious little sketch, being Chinese, makes use of formulas, but it also shows something of the free, natural assurance in the placing and proportion of the figures of which the best T'ang artists, and probably none before them, were capable.

PLATE ON PAGE 142

There are other significant originals in the Shōsōin. For instance 17 round, flat bowls decorated with landscapes, animals and figures. The technique of these objects of daily use is both highly refined and very unusual. Oxide of lead has been mixed with the white lacquer lining the bowl. The painting is in yellow lacquer sprinkled with gold dust, so a drawing is easier to follow than a photograph or even the original itself. Lacquer being a more tacky medium, one cannot expect to see free flowing brushwork, but still there is more than a hint of an Indian ink prototype. Our example shows a hermit's simple, open hut, with a dragon and a phoenix hastening towards it. The naturalness and simple effectiveness of the composition speak for themselves. It may not help us much when we try to imagine the huge landscapes which once decorated the walls of temples and palaces, but the fashionable round fans, usually of silk, must have been very like this in their freshness of feeling and unconstrained composition.

Lacquer painting

DRAWING ON PAGE 146

Neither these examples nor the numerous frescoes in cave temples in the provinces at Tun-huang and Turfan can give any idea of the aesthetic standing of T'ang painting. We must try to find a picture which, even if it does not come up to this standard, at least gives a hint of this quality. Perhaps the best example is the short scroll of "Ladies making Silk" in the museum of Fine Arts in Boston. This too is no more than an ancient

PLATE ON PAGE 150

153

copy, but one of high aesthetic value. We need not concern ourselves here with the doubtful ascription to the painter-emperor Hui-tsung (1101—1125). It clearly is a very faithful copy of a work of Chang Hsüan, the court painter of Ming-huang, who repeatedly painted the Emperor and Empress and probably stood highest in his patron's favour. The delicacy of the outlines is most striking and so is the sophisticated simplicity of the colour and the indescribable refinement of the composition. One does not know which to admire most, but perhaps one understands the quality of this masterpiece best if one compares it with the portraits of emperors also in the Boston Museum. The stylistic approach is much the same; these excellent portraits are incompassed by lines which never intersect and vary little in thickness. There the contour lines are thin, whereas those of Chang Hsüan are modulated with the greatest delicacy of feeling and most lively observation. There the colours are simple and subordinate, whereas Chang Hsüan has effortlessly contrived the most refined contrast. In neither case is there any indication of background or of foreground. However Chang Hsüan has not only achieved a more lively and more natural composition, but he holds each group together in such a way that one forgets to wonder about the background. More than this, gently and unobtrusively, he has put every figure and every group in such relationship with the next that, while they stand on their own, they also lead on to and harmonise with the next, so that the whole makes a melody which charms in every detail, and in its completeness makes one sad that no other such scroll exists. If it seems hair splitting to go into such details about every line and proportion, every contour and every twist, I can only say in painting it is just these tiny subtleties too small to measure and almost too small to express, which decide the quality of a masterpiece.

T'ang masterpieces have perished but we can see that these pictures were the peak of the achievement of a superbly creative age. Anyone who cares about art and inspiration, freedom and discipline, refinement, maturity and dignity, must turn to study the reign of Ming-huang.

VII TIME OF WITHDRAWAL

After the defeat at Samarkand in 751 A.D. and the abdication of the *Time of catastrophies*
Emperor Ming-huang in 756 A.D. one catastrophe followed on another
for 200 years, and there was no peace in the land, while army commanders
ruled almost as independent viceroys. The quondam concentration of
power and magnificence in the capitals, Loyang and Ch'ang-an, now
had sad results.

First An Lu-shan sacked them in 756 A.D. Then the foreign allies who
had helped to suppress his rebellion, themselves fell on the wealth of the
capitals. In 763 A.D. Tibetans, then a very warlike people, and Tanguts
burst into Ch'ang-an and plundered it thoroughly. In 784 A.D. it was again
the goal of plunderers; at that time the shortage was such that these
was no more silk to pay ransom money, and collectors were reduced to
cutting up silk pictures to make clothes. In that year too, first a tax on tea
and then a state monopoly of it was imposed. In 790 A.D. East Turkestan
was lost and the land route to the West was shut off or, at least, made hard
of access. The border peoples in Tibet, Turkestan and Mongolia as far
as the Yalu, themselves pressed from behind, more than ever turned their
thoughts towards China; greed was mingled with friendly admiration of
the civilisation on which they depended. Hence things so turned out that
the inner lands of China, all intensively cultivated and ploughed up, no
longer provided adequate grazing ground for horses; this put the Chinese
at a disadvantage in war with the nomads, and drove them to ever greater
financial sacrifices to make good the deficiency. Desperate attempts to
raise money for arms and armies led to the first issue of paper money in
806 A.D. and in A.D. 843 and 844 to a drastic measure, the great persecution of the Buddhists. The reason for this was purely financial. The *Persecution of*
property of all monasteries was expropriated, hundreds of temples were *Buddhists*
destroyed, and about a quarter of a million monks and nuns were forced
back into lay occupations, for manpower and tax payers were needed. It is
true that new temples were soon endowed and built again, but the "mort-
main" prohibition on the alienation of land remained, the monasteries
had to pay taxes, and a tax, this time a heavy one, was soon once more imposed on those entering monastries. In this way Buddhism lost its financial
and political power, but its spiritual side benefited from these trials.

There has not yet been an adequate study of the influence of Buddhist
thought on the best minds of this and subsequent ages, and the extent

155

to which it became a genuine spiritual strength for educated Chinese. All foreign religions were officially forbidden, but in the spiritual fields this *Withdrawal* prohibition was not seriously pressed. However all foreigners now had to wear Chinese dress and pay taxes, whereas formerly they had as a rule worn their own clothes, not paid taxes, and remained subject to their own laws. These changes show that the Chinese, who had been so expansive a hundred years before, were now withdrawing into themselves, and that stark necessity dictated the terms. The extensive secularisation of monastic property was not enough to improve the financial position fundamentally, and so 30 years later (874—884 A.D.) peasant revolts of unprecedented ferocity broke out. The great cities were plundered, and when Canton was taken in 879 A.D. it is thought that 120,000 foreigners were murdered, including many Arab merchants who had long had their depots there. We know from the excavations at Samarra what a quantity of fine ceramics were exported, probably by sea, from the Far East. The evidence is for the period after 838 A.D. but the trade must have started earlier. The news of the blood bath at Canton, the first terrible outbreak of xenophobia, was spread by the Arabs all over the world, and it is natural that for a long time after this China shut herself off from world trade and sea trade generally. In the next year wealthy Hangchou fell to the rebels, and in 880 A.D. Ch'ang-an. The emperor, like Ming-huang before him, fled to Ch'eng-tu in Ssech'uan, and this time 58 well-known painters went with him and remained there even after the emperor's return to Ch'ang-*Secession* an in 884 A.D. when the rebellion collapsed and its leaders were beheaded. In truth the T'ang dynasty was de facto at an end, and it is easy to understand why the Japanese chancellor Michizane, himself famous as a poet in the classical Chinese style, advised his master in 895 A.D. not to send another embassy to China. The generals did set yet another emperor on the throne and let him disappear again, but in 907 A.D. they forced his successor to abdicate.

The rule of the five Dynasties (Wu-tai) begins de jure from that date; they held power in the north, sometimes ruling from Loyang and sometimes from K'ai-feng, from 907—960 A.D., lasting from three to thirteen years each. Their writ did not run in central China; there ten other dynasties, known as "illegitimate", had set themselves up; among them were the Shu in Ssech'uan, the Nan-T'ang in Nanking, the Wu-Yüeh in Hangchou, and the Min in Fukien, which were all more important in art history than the "legitimate" dynasties. These powers of central China, especially the Wu-Yüeh at the mouth of the Yangtse, forged links with the outside world again. The north was left to deal with the nomads who,

156

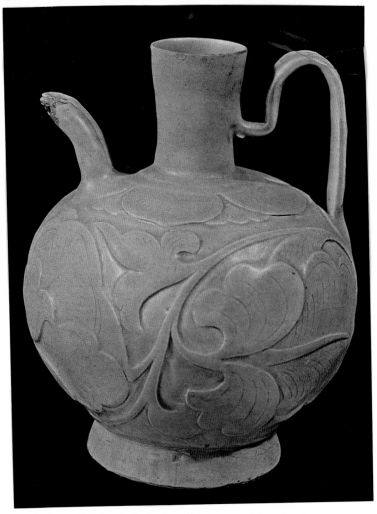

Jug. Peonies are cut in low relief out of the body which is covered by a hard, transparent, felspar glaze. Probably fired at Tung-yao, the 'eastern kiln', near the Sung capital, K'ai-feng. 11th century. *Museum of Fine Arts, Boston (height 7¾ inches)*

when the T'ang dynasty collapsed de facto, carved out more enduring states of their own on Chinese soil. The Tangus Ch'i-tan, forerunners of the Manchus, were the most important of these. From 936 A.D. onwards they called their kingdom Liao and ruled, for instance, over Yen-tu, the modern Peking, and that area. In 954 A.D. the emperor of the Hou-Chou dynasty, who had his capital and headquarters against the Ch'i-tan at K'ai-feng, began to make good progress towards unifying the whole of China and carrying on the war against Liao. He died suddenly, and the army elevated the sleeping General Chao K'uang-yin to the throne. In this way, almost against his will, he founded the Sung dynasty which was to bring some peace to the land for more than 300 years.

Sung dynasty The first Sung Emperor and the brother who succeeded him, T'ai-tsung (976–998 A.D.) fought hard but in vain to conquer Liao. They tried to provide for the war chest by state monopolies and, about 970 A.D., the issue of paper money. But their expeditions ended in repeated defeats. Finally in 1005 A.D. they made a treaty with Liao which stipulated a tribute of 50,000 ounces of silver and 200,000 bales of silk. Historians, concerned with the politics of power, consider this a shameful insult; sociologists point out that such a sum was small compared to the cost of arms and armies, and treat it as a move in the chess game of characteristically Chinese economy. At all events China had 100 years of peace in return for a small expense.

One cannot be sure whether this policy was adopted freely or from necessity, but certainly the first Sung Emperor, himself a general first, was wise in avoiding contests with any of the reigning kings and army commanders in his own land. He gave them generous sinecures and induced them to give up the profession of arms. Nonetheless the economic difficulties of the whole country continued on into the subsequent century, the 11th, and the famous attempt at state socialism introduced by the minister Wang An-shih, did not remove them. Apparently a deterioration of the climate in a land of intensive agriculture but still practically without machines, led to serious consequences. We are, for instance, informed that the last elephants crossed the Yangtse to the south about 1100 A.D.

The painter emperor Under the Sung the civil power had regained its control of the military.
Hui-tsung It is therefore an irony of history that it should have been a Sung emperor who, through a completely silly war, disintegrated the whole carefully balanced system. This man was the great painter-emperor Hui-tsung, whose artistic gifts were equalled by his military incompetence. The year of his ascent to the throne, 1101 A.D. marks the beginning of a new epoch in Chinese art. The three and a half centuries of darkness between Ming-

huang's abdication and the reign of Hui-tsung (756—1101 A.D.) may be treated, with some oversimplification, as a time when China, partly through her own fault and partly through the strength of her neighbours, was forced back and shrank into herself. The mood of that time was in marked contrast to the generous expansiveness of the classical age, but there was enough creative force at work within this half enforced, half self-chosen, withdrawal to keep aesthetic life alive in China, and even to inspire noble work abroad.

It speaks for the strength of Chinese art and civilisation that now more than ever the neighbouring peoples to the north were anxious to introduce Chinese education. This was specially important in the case of the Tungus Ch'i-tan, who in this respect were very like their Manchu successors. As the nature of their homeland dictated, they were nomad pastoralists and enthusiastic huntsmen; instead of one fixed metropolis they had five alternative capitals. They made their headquarters near the modern Barin (Chinese Pa-lin) on the upper reaches of the Liao river in eastern Mongolia, and it was in near-by Ch'ing-ling that they built their tombs and decorated them with frescoes. When they had conquered great parts of the provinces of Hopei and Shensi and become the masters of millions of Chinese subjects, they introduced the classical examinations for their Chinese officials, but did not allow any Chi-tan to compete in them. They also adapted Chinese writing to convey their language, but only meagre remains of their literature are preserved. They fostered the arts, and, far from destroying potters' kilns, they built fresh ones. Their sculpture, mostly Buddhist, which can be identified by inscriptions, stands out as a recognisable local style within the Chinese tradition, and painters too were encouraged as much as possible; there were even Liao emperors who tried to paint themselves. In the 11th century an enemy of the Liao in the west grew to strength; this was their Tangus neighbours known to the Chinese as the Hsi-Hsia who in 1032 A.D. established an independent kingdom, with its capital at the modern Ninghsia, which comprised the Ordos Territory, parts of Kansu etc. They too, extorted tribute from the Sung, devised their own script, translated Chinese and Buddhist books, and finally established an academy on the Chinese model.

This short explanation was needed to make some specific results understandable. The migration of painters from the ruins of Ch'ang-an and Loyang to Ssech'uan resulted in a decentralisation of art. In central China there was an old tradition, dating from Liu-ch'ao times, to encourage painters, and now a new interest was arising in the north, in Liao for instance. A specialisation of categories went together with decentral-

Decentralisation of art

159

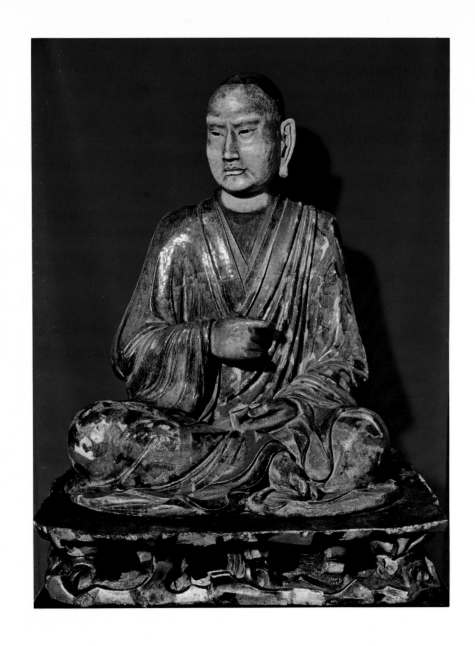

Lohan, a man who has come to an understanding of Nirvana. One of a group of pottery figures found at I-chou in Hopei. Perhaps 10th or 11th century. *University Museum, Philadelphia (3 foot 5 inches high)*

160

isation. Birds and flowers were worked up as a recognised theme, and so was landscape; almost all the centres competed with one another and supported local schools. Everywhere there were territorial princes, all of whom called themselves emperors, who warmly encouraged the arts, and never were there so many "emperors" and imperial princes who painted. There were for instance, Li Yü in Nanking (937—978 A.D.) who was also known as a poet, Jen-tsung of the Sung (1010—63 A.D.), and Hsing-tsung of the Liao (1016—55 A.D.). It seemed to be almost a matter of good manners for a man of standing to distinguish himself as a painter, and several of them became sons-in-law of emperors. There is a great deal of information about the academies, painting competitions, and collections of pictures, both imperial and private. One further result of the experience of these unhappy centuries was the formation of a belief that a climax of history had been passed, and that one should from henceforth take one's bearings from it. This thoroughly well-founded appreciation of the fact that in 800 or 900 or 1,000 A.D. one could never reach the heights attained in about 750 A.D., turned attention backwards to the "ancient masters". In this way the history of art began to take precedence over art criticism, antiquarian collecting interests were aroused, and there was a general wish to copy old masterpieces and make them widely known. At the same time there was a demand for encyclopedic summaries of knowledge.

It is striking that already in about 800 A.D. poets and painters were bewailing the Emperor Ming-huang and sympathising with him, and that all the abuse of Yang Kuei-fei was forgotten, and her harsh fate considered unjust. "The Everlasting Wrong" of Po Chü-i (772—846 A.D.), the great poet of the T'ang silver age, is the best known of many poems on this theme. We have already referred to the state of art criticism in the time of troubles about 500 A.D. Then, and for long afterwards, it was assumed, and sometimes explicitly stated, that the aim of criticism was an idealistic one, to foster and improve the practice of painting. Immediately after the great persecution of the Buddhist and the destruction of Wu Tao-tse's work, and that of his contemporaries, in the year 847 A.D. the first real history of painting, that of Chang Yen-yüan, which has been very well translated by W.R. Acker, made its appearance. It does include critical sections, but the greater part of the book describes the great masters of *History and criticism* the past and sings their praises for the benefit of future generations who only too often would be unable to see their actual works. The business of collecting names instead of essentially fine works begins in China at this time, and in the 11th century Mi Fu and Li Ch'ih made fun of the amateurs who would, in all seriousness, acquire at great cost and display

161

the very worst pictures of "ancient" masters. Chang Yen-yüan is the first of a long line of learned critics, and from his time onwards there was a continual argument about what was genuine and what not, and about the documentary value of copies. Next to pictures, bronzes were the chief passion of collectors, but furniture and other works of craftsmanship also attracted attention. As was to be expected, forgeries and casts from bronzes go hand in hand with the first important archaeological researches and publications. Every age finds what it is looking for and in this case, about 900 A.D., China discovered how to print books and reproduce pictures, using wood blocks in both cases.

Printing We must give a short account of printing and woodcuts which were two of the greatest contributions of China to civilisation. From as early as Han times it was a custom to engrave classical texts and pictures too on blocks of stone. Rubbings on paper could be taken from these then, just as our epigraphers do now, and they of course came out white on black. As far as we know it was in the ninth century that it became the custom to use the cheaper and more convenient wood blocks, and on these the representation was left standing out from the background, so that the impression taken from it stood out in black on white. The technique could be used equally easily for inscriptions, or for pictures drawn in outline; both operations required the same tools and skill, and the very large number of Chinese ideograms seems to have made this process more convenient and quicker than the assembly of moveable type. The Chinese did try out experiments in that direction, but gave them up. In the 9th century the Buddhists seem to have made most use of this invention for printed paper amulets, with or without illustrations, which were distributed widely. The oldest bit of printing preserved is a sutra scroll of the year

Woodcuts 868 A.D. with an elaborate "paste-down" illustration; it was found at Tun-uang by Sir Aurel Stein and is now in the British Museum. It was probably in Ssech'uan that printing from wood blocks was both first and most extensively used. Feng Tao (881—954 A.D.) is said to have suggested to the Emperor, after the conquest of Ssech'uan, that this technique should be used for the printing of classical literature. The relevant enactment was made in 932 A.D. and the Nine Confucian Classics were printed in 953 A.D. There followed an edition of the Tripitaka, the sacred Buddhist scriptures, in 5,000 volumes between 971 and 983 A.D., and one of the Taoist scriptures in 1019 A.D. in 4,565 volumes. No man's life would be long enough for him to read and understand all that has been printed in China up to the year 1019 A.D. alone. For there are not only the editions of the classics to consider, which would greatly exceed the total of Greek

A Guardian of the World, the Buddhist divine protector of the faithful. Cast in iron with remains of the basis for a coloured surface. Perhaps 9th or 10th century. *From the collection of Baron E. v. d. Heydt in the Rietberg Museum, Zürich (21 inches high)*

and Roman literature. Poets had their works printed, usually privately, and the voluminous collections of novels, diaries and so forth which began to pour forth in such quantities, owe their existence to the invention of this convenient method of reproduction. The year 1049 A.D. is an important date in the history of art, for then the Emperor Jan-tsung commissioned paintings of a hundred "edifying scenes from the history of the three (ancient) dynasties", and ordered woodcuts to be made from them. The Emperor distributed these hand-coloured woodcuts among his ministers and family.

There is no need to stress how the facility with which books could be acquired, spread a knowledge of the classics among ever wider circles; how each individual came to share a common background of knowledge and interest; or how books aided private study and genuine withdrawal from the world. Indeed they did not only foster this tendency, but actually made it possible. The Chinese would not have been true to themselves, if they had not used the new technique for a type of work very congenial to their way of thinking, that is the compilation of encyclopedias. It was not till 800 years later that the French took up the same idea and so re-shaped European thought. The distinction of editing the first encyclopedia in the modern sense of the word belongs to Li Fang (924–995 A.D.), the minister and adviser of the Sung Emperor T'ai-tsung, who published his T'ai-p'ing kuang-chi in 978 A.D. Many others followed, and among them were encyclopedias specialising in specific branches of knowledge. There is something of the quality of an encyclopedia about the Shih-ching, "the Book of Songs", which contains three hundred folk songs and sacrificial songs. In all these anthologies, for instance in the Wen-hsün of the Liu-ch'ao times, there is an eye on the future and a wish to provide standards for new work. But in the year 978 A.D. a great effort was felt to be long overdue to get together a thoroughly tested body of knowledge, in order first to regain the position that had been lost, and then to go forward from there. In these circumstances the new encyclopedic movement was not concerned to resurrect old and worn out spiritual

Concert of Ladies of the court in the presence of the Emperor. Old copy after Chou Wen-chü, court painter of the Emperor Li Yü in Nanking, in 970. Detail from a silk scroll. *Art Institute, Chicago (16½ inches high)*

165

values concealed in dusty books, but to prepare the ground for new researches and advances. It is no chance that a hundred years later the compass was discovered in China. In looking back to great prototypes and ancient masters, men had other ends than formerly in view. Confucius too had repeatedly stressed that he loved antiquity; but he thought of it as the golden age, an ideal paradise in which all knowledge came to perfection, and certainly not as actual history. Now his phrases took on a new meaning. K'ung-tse had said; "I myself have no widom from birth onwards; that is why I love antiquity and strive to understand it", or "He who has mastered the old and derived new wisdom from it, may be considered a learner" (Lun-yü VII,19 and II,11). But at this time men had a very clear conception of what an ancient master was, and, be he Confucius or another, strove to understand and go beyond him. In the history of Chinese literature and philosophy, we find that about the year 800 there was a return to the clarity of the classics, and that this coincided with a pronounced anti-Buddhist attitude. The protagonist of this movement was Han Yü, a contemporary of Po Chü-i. So the foundations were laid in the 11th century for what is called Neoconfucianism, which is in fact a very happy synthesis of Confucian and Buddhist thought. Its earliest representative is Chou Tun-i (1017—1073 A.D.) who was also known as a poet; he introduced the lotus as a theme for literature, whereas before him poets had neglected this flower. The "Time of Withdrawal", which covers in time the late T'ang, Five Dynasties and early Sung periods, with all its encyclopedic tendencies and its interest in the past, has nothing classicising or reactionary, still less retrogressive, about it. While popularising the idea that the ancients were worth attention, it made new discoveries in the immediate and actual present.

PLATE ON PAGE 152 A silver bowl, engraved and gilt, in the Bristol City Art Gallery, may be taken as a good example of the way in which these new ideas were worked out. Gyllensvärd has been able to produce convincing reasons for considering this specimen and others like it as dating from between 750 and 820 A.D. This is especially helpful as there are few works that can be dated to that period, and the details of stylistic development are hard to trace. The leaves and flowers of a peony radiate from the centre to the

Naturalism in art edge of the bowl which is itself shaped like five petals; they are so true to nature, so broadly spaced and so accurately drawn, that one scarcely likes to call them decorative ornament. It is instructive to compare this bowl with the box of a hundred years earlier in Amsterdam. There the flowers and leaves are kept in neat decorative compartments, but here such restraint has been abandoned for the sake of truth to nature. One

166

can speak of a return to nature, for, no longer statisfied with accepted decorative formulas, men have been looking again at the flowers themselves. It would be going too far to say that the strict symmetry of classical times had been altogether abandoned, but the division into evenly balanced sections, which had been the general rule, for bowls, mirrors and ceramics alike, is now often replaced by five- and seven-petalled shapes. But still it would be a mistake to regard these shapes as completely and fundamentally asymmetrical. All one can say is that asymmetry came to play a considerable and unprecedented part in Sung art.

The increasing importance attached to plants, especially the peonies *Plant and bird motifs* that Yang Kuei-fei brought into fashion, is illustrated by what we are told of the painter Pien Luan. About the year 800 he was court painter in Ch'ang-an and was one of the first to specialise in flowers and birds. In China flowers and birds went together and there were even almost fixed iconographical rules for the combinations, for instance, lotus and wagtails, willows and swallows, bamboos and sparrows. We cannot tell what the pictures of the famous Pien Luan looked like. There are flowers and birds from the second half of the eighth century in decorative pictures on screens in the Shōsōin, and we may hazard a guess that the painters around the year 800 A.D. shook themselves free from decorative conventions, and saw things for themselves in ways in which they had never been represented before. Pien Luan's fame rested particularly on pictures of peonies and peacocks.

There are many pots which show this new conception of plant life. However, we are still generally unable to give accurate dates for ceramics between 750 and 1100 A.D., though some progress has been made, especially by the excavation of kiln sites. Rich finds and full information are only available about the lively activity in Chekiang, the ancient Yüeh and the subsequent kingdom of Wu-Yüeh at the mouth of the Yangtse. It would seem that the first felspar glazes there date from early Han times; their colours, which run the whole range from jade green to olive green and blue, and the fine, often transparent glazes delight collectors. Probably most of the vases exported to Baghdad in the 9th century and found in fragments in Samarra came from there. One finds early so-called Celadon wares among them. Of course the better known later types do not have this transparent glaze. In the 10th century, at the time of the Five Dynasties, there must have been large-scale manufacture and export of ceramics, especially to south east Asia, and probably the Wu-yüeh emperors owed a great part of their wealth to this trade. We know that the last of them, who submitted to the Sung Emperor T'ai-tsung in 978 A.D., sent him fifty thousand pieces

167

of ceramics. Unfortunately we do not know of what types these were, but we do know that efforts were made in the north to imitate Yüeh glazes. A pottery was built at Ch'ien-Liu, not far to the east of K'ai-feng, and its products went under the name of Tung-yao, which means "Eastern Kiln".

PLATE ON PAGE 157

Some beautiful ceramics with transparent bluish glaze can now be attributed with some probability to this pottery and dated to the 11th

Glazes

century. The peonies, boldly cut out of the clay before it was covered with glaze, may claim descent from those on the silver cup in Bristol. They are as close to nature as one could possibly wish, but yet there is a change in the way the composition has been conceived. Representation has again been subordinated to the decorative intention, and details have been eliminated for the sake of the total effect of a jug which, without apparent effort, is delightful to handle and perfect to use.

In the north, in the kingdom of Liao, the splashy glazes of classical T'ang times remained in fashion rather longer, but the shapes are crisper and the glazes harder and more transparent. The almost life-size figure of

The Lohans

a Lohan which is believed to have been found near Jehol and made at I-chou not far from Peking is a masterpiece of Liao sculpture and pottery. Lohans are Buddhist priests or laymen who, usually by drastic ascetic practices, have won an insight into the nothingness of all earthly existence and so stand directly before Nirvana. It is worth recalling the story of the sculptor Yang Hui-chih who gave up painting and made pottery figures of Buddhist priests and saints instead. They may have looked like the

PLATE ON PAGE 160

Lohans from I-chou, but the wise and very individual expression of these portrait heads cannot be proved to belong to any particular century. Dates of any time between the 8th and 13th centuries have been suggested, and now a date about half way between these extremes seems likely. As the eye lingers on these heads, bodies and clothes, one realises the striving towards truth to nature which goes beyond the impersonal and detached dignity of the classical age, but which is never distracted by inessential detail, and achieves a complete work of art. These figures of Lohans fit naturally into the newly discovered conception of reality current at this time, but their quality surpasses everything else surviving from that age.

PLATE ON PAGE 163

The torso of a Guardian of the World in Baron E. v. d. Heydt's collection in the Rietberg Museum in Zürich, has also been attributed to dates varying from the 8th to 13th century, ever since it was discovered in 1926. The torso is of cast iron and shows traces of a chalky coating which originally covered the joins in the casting, and which was as usual painted. The athletic body is represented with almost too much truth to nature, and in this it is far removed from the powerful, but restrained, conception

168

Running deer in a landscape. Detail from a fresco in the tombs of the royal family of Liao at Ch'ing-ling in Mongolia. 1031 A.D.

of classical times. The Guardians of the World are supposed to protect the Buddhist faithful simply by the terror their appearance inspires in their enemies. In Buddhist thought this primitive power may have been thought of as the bodily form and expression of hidden and indescribable powers far surpassing anything visible. There is much more sculpture of the 9th century preserved in Japan, and the same ideas were at work there; almost intentionally coarse bodies and inscrutable faces seem to be the special expression of Buddhist mysticism.

Mysticism A doctrine intent on the secret workings of powers which only the inner eye can see, can well use an exaggeration of the coarseness of reality to hint at what lies behind superficial phenomena. We don't know enough to be dogmatic about such interpretations, but certainly at this time the Chinese spirit was perfectly capable of an objective grasp of reality, and was able to go beyond this and express a lot between the lines. Apart from lovely ceramics, some silver and a few pieces of sculpture, not numerous enough to draw general conclusions from them, there is hardly anything which can be safely or convincingly dated within these three and a half centuries. There is no lacquer work and no silk preserved, although we know from literary sources that these crafts flourished then. But the saddest contrast is between the few surviving paintings and the abundance of our information. We are told a great deal about the achievements of the painters, for instance that in the 9th century realistic tendencies in the figure painting of Ming-huang's reign were carried very much further, and that it was the monk Kuan-hsiu (832—912 A.D.) who broke new ground with his almost grotesque, ugly and contorted caricatures of fellow Buddhists. They were engraved on stone block, and rubbings from them have often been reproduced even in Europe. Kuan-hsiu was one of those who were

Shu school of painting forced into retreat in Shu, that is Ssech'uan, where a new school of painting soon flowered. One of the most highly esteemed representatives of this school was the flower painter Huang Ch'üan (active till 965 A.D.) who was also the first and most successful painter of "boneless" pictures, that is to say, he painted in colours only, as was to be done later in Europe, without any outline in Indian ink.

The school of Nanking rivalled that of Shu. The Emperor Li Yü (937—978 A.D.) was a learned amateur and collector. He was a poet too and A. Hoffmann has made excellent translations of his songs. Sometimes he painted himself, usually in collaboration with his court painters who seem to have specialised in figure subjects. But his circle included the flower- and bird-painter Hsü Hsi whose reputation stands next to that of Huang Ch'üan in this field. We are told that a new type of landscape

170

painting emerged in the north, at Ch'ang-an and Loyang, and that its *Landscape painting* founder was Ching Hao around the year 900, and that he was followed by Kuan T'ung and Li Ch'eng. But there was enthusiasm for landscape at Li Yü's court in Nanking too, where Tung Yüan and his pupil the monk Chü-jan had the highest reputation. There are dozens of copies of their works and even more pictures "in their manner", but we are still left guessing what was the real force of originality behind these great names. We know, for instance, that in many copies after Tung Yüan, bold blobs of ink indicate the leaves of trees. That fits in well with the information that the wilful Mi Fu, an 11th century landscape painter, studied Tung Yüan; but, if we had not been told that, we would hardly have seen a connection between the two masters, for the copies after Mi Fu are scarcely truer or more impressive than those after Tung Yüan.

When the second Sung Emperor re-united the whole realm by his victory over Li Yü (975 A.D.) and his other rivals, and took possession of the land of Wu-Yüeh, he did what he could to assemble at his capital, K'ai-feng, all the painters and all the art collections from the petty kingdoms. He bestowed on them the honourable title of members of the Academy, and chose as their President Huang Chü-ts'ai, a son of Huang Ch'üan of Shu. It would seem that the Sung imperial house, whose family name was *Sung emperors* Chao, inherited a pronounced talent for painting; the dozens of Sung painters of this name who fill the pages of the encyclopedia, most of whom belonged to the reigning house, are not there simply by reason of their high birth. The Emperor Jen-tsung (1010—1063 A.D.) who came to the throne at the age of thirteen, was outstanding both as painter and as patron. After him Shen-tsung (1049—1085, reigned from 1068 A.D.) was not himself a painter, but he was a strong supporter of the Academy and offered prizes, for flower pictures especially. His patronage supported the famous landscape painter Kuo Hsi; even more famous than Kuo Hsi's pictures, was a book about landscape painting edited by his son who played the part of a Boswell. A group of painters emerges at the end of the 11th century, who were critical towards the Academy and perhaps resented the pomp and vanity of patronage, although a son-in-law of the Emperor's, Wang Shen, belonged to the group which used to meet in his "Western Garden". There the famous painters Li Lung-mien and Mi Fu would meet the poet Su Tung-p'o, the "Li T'ai-po of the Sung dynasty", or Ch'ao Pu-chih who wrote the best essays of aesthetic criticism in all Chinese literature (cf. p. 6). These essays are indeed fine works deserving close attention, but how much more gladly would we possess a few un-doubted originals to show what these painters wanted to do and did. We

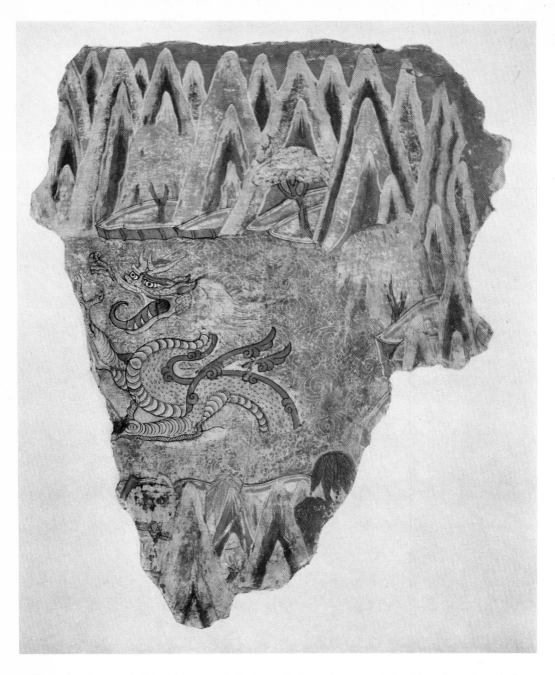

Dragon coming out of a lake. Tempera painting from the base of a stupa at Bäzäklik, in the oasis of Turfan in Eastern Turkestan. 9th—12th century. *Berlin Museum (26 by 21 inches)*

feel we are concerned with men of the highest inspiration, who had something important to express and accomplished splendid work. But the spirit quails before the more or less documentary copies which are all we have to go on; no amount of collectors' seals and genealogical pedantry can improve their aesthetic quality. Nor is it any use supposing that we can find out much about Kuo Hsi or Li Lung-mien from simple, mass-produced, provincial frescoes or from the sealed chambers of Tun-huang, contemporary though they be.

But the frescoes in the royal tombs of the Liao dynasty do reach a comparatively high aesthetic standard, and a good example is the vaulted tomb of Liao Shen-tsung at Ch'ing-ling. Here the deer and other animals PLATE ON PAGE 169 of the chase with their landscape background, are painted with the freshness of vision and accuracy of observation which one might have expected from such enthusiastic huntsmen as the Ch'i-tan rulers. It is even possible that an emperor himself did paint them; we know that Hsing-tsung (1016— *Frescoes* 1055 A.D.) who reigned from 1031, painted five scrolls of deer and, some time in the 1040's, sent them to K'ai-feng as a present for Shen-tsung, who was also both painter and emperor. At that time the Liao needed Sung help against their enemies the Hsi-Hsia. But it is also possible that the Ch'ing-ling frescoes were painted by Chinese subjects of the Liao, though there is no indisputable reason to suppose this. In any case they certainly derive from the Chinese T'ang tradition. Compare the little scrap of paper PLATE ON PAGE 142 found at Tun-huang and now in the Musée Guimet; it too is simple, fresh and gay in colour; there are no pretensions to calligraphy, but bright flicks of paint make each beast and plant stand out clearly, and there is a firm assurance in the spatial composition. These simple stylistic elements, used with disarming freedom, had meanwhile been made the vehicle of greater subtleties. For the style called "Yamato" in Japan is, basically, a refinement on this technique. It is true that the name means "Japanese painting", that the style was used for peculiarly Japanese subjects, their sacred egends and romances, and that it emerges at the beginning of the 12th century. However, in spite of all the emphasis on Japanese national subjec matter, the technique itself, this way of seeing landscape and its accessories, may have derived from a Chinese tradition. This must have been a stylistic method which the T'ang painters had thoroughly mastered, and which remained vital, and not much changed, at Ch'ing-ling in the 11th century. There is another surviving fragment of landscape painting which is harder and more intriguing to place in context Grünwedel and Le Coq brought back to Berlin a great many frescoes from Bäzäklik in the Turfan oasis to the north of Eastern Turkestan. Among them was the astonishing fragment of a tempera picture from the base of a stupa, which by good

PLATE ON PAGE 176 luck has survived both world wars. It shows a lake, from which a dragon emerges, in the middle of sharp cone-shaped mountains. The circumstances of excavation provided no closer date than between the 9th and 12th centuries, and it is still impossible to be more accurate than that about the chronology. We can see now that the dragon is clearly in the Chinese

PLATE ON PAGE 152 tradition, and might be a descendant of the one on the bowl in Bristol. The pattern that represents the waves on the lake is another indication that the artist knew Chinese works, even if only works of applied art. But the landscape is not only utterly un-Chinese, but also completely unreal. The mountain-cones look like separate clods of earth set up straight one beside another, and bring to mind the schematised versions of landscape that we can trace back to Akkad in Mesopotamia in the third millenium B.C. Only the lonely trees and the gazelle peeping out from behind a cone in the foreground show a remarkable degree of realism and remind one slightly of the Ch'ing-ling frescoes. But the reds, blues, greens and violets in the hills, and the red in the sky, are all completely unnaturalistic. We know neither the name of this painter nor when he lived, but peasant though he may have been, his work rises above the provincial level of watered down versions of metropolitan art. His naive yet bold colours bring to mind the Blue Horseman of Astana, and Astana is only a few miles from Bäzäklik. How such a work, sublime in its naivety, came to be made, remains an intriguing puzzle. We can only suppose that in the long centuries of Chinese rule over vast provinces, possibilities of artistic expression lay dormant and occasionally came to flower, which were in strong and colourful contrast to the dominant taste.

What picture can we find best to illustrate the peculiarly Chinese taste of this age, and help us to catch its unheard melodies? Among all the copies, many of them beautiful, which will show most of the essential quality of

PLATE ON PAGE 165 Sung art? Let us look at the "Concert" scroll in the Art Institute of Chicago. The scroll is certainly a copy, and so is the inscription purporting to be written by the Emperor Hui-tsung who had a taste for adding inscriptions to the pictures in his collection. Even without the inscription we could have identified the painter of the original as Chou Wen-chü, the friend and companion of Li Yü of Nanking. Various pictures of the same type are connected with his name, and it is known that Chou Wen-chü derived the theme from an older picture depicting the Emperor Ming-huang and Yang Kuei-fei listening to a concert of ladies of the court. Chang Hsüan himself had painted such musical entertainments at the imperial court. So perhaps by comparing the painting of Chang Hsüan with that of

174

Chou Wen-chü we may be able to understand the change that had taken place between 750 and 970 A.D. Details apart, there are some essential differences. The central figure in Chou Wen-chu's scroll is not Ming-huang but a contemporary of the painter, perhaps Li Yü himself who was equally fond of music. So much is clear from the clothes, especially the cylindrical cap, then in fashion, worn by the great man. The ladies' hair styles too, the furniture and the paintings on the screens, those pictures within pictures, are changed from Chang Hsüan's time; the screens are quite unlike those preserved in the Shōsōin. All this goes to show that Sung artists painted the contemporary scene. Chang Hsüan's ladies are just PLATE ON PAGE 150 as true to life, but they are all treated as individuals with a separate exist-ence each by herself, even when their gestures make a connection between them. But with Chou Wen-chü this isolation has been broken down, and they form such coherent groups that, if a single figure is taken on its own, it is often difficult to see what it is doing and why. The copy bears out what we have learnt from literary sources; that Chou Wen-chü's figures were more slender and their movements more lively; that there was more variety in the fall of drapery and the shape of outlines. Elegance, albeit refined and reserved elegance, has taken the place of calm dignity.

Perhaps what has been said above, taken in connection with the parallel achievements of ceramics and sculpture, can give some impression of the life-spring of art in the middle years of the Sung dynasty. China had been thrown back on herself and driven inwards; attention was directed to the past as well as to the contemporary world, and the history of paint-ing and poetry came to be studied. There was strength and inspiration enough to broadcast a better understanding of the values both of the present and of the proud heritage of the past; of this movement printing was the symbol. Art made progress. In its first wild flowering perhaps every plant and every figure tended to burst free of all restraint, but soon right measure and the golden mean reasserted themselves; a calm and disciplin-ed elegance, and a refined harmony of forms prevailed over all but the most contrary spirits. It evoked and still evokes the admiration of the world.

VIII THE AGE OF THE ACADEMY

Hui-tsung ascended the throne at the age of 19 in 1101 A.D. on the premature death of his elder brother. He was the most gifted and the most famous of all the Chinese rulers who have been painters as well. It is customary for us today to start a new chapter in Chinese art history at this point, though contemporaries may have noticed no abrupt change. For from this time onward we have real originals of everything, be it painting, ceramics or lacquer, to aid our studies, and make true art history possible. There are indeed plenty of gaps and open questions, but there are authentic works of fine quality to go on, and we need not be forever guessing or bewailing our losses.

The painter-emperor Hui-tsung

We have portraits of Hui-tsung and of the emperors who came after him and, more than that, we have numerous specimens of calligraphy some of which can be attributed with certainty to individual emperors, though other attributions are not certain. Moreover there exist pictures which Hui-tsung himself may possibly have painted. A signed and dated (1107 A.D.) picture of a dove may be safely accepted as Hui-tsung's work.

From that date onwards painting, which the Chinese themselves considered the highest form of art, can be followed from decade to decade down to the present day. Admittedly it is only after about 1500 that we have a rich harvest to illustrate the work of individual masters and schools, but from the 12th century onwards originals of sound quality can and should form the basis of art history.

It was not a lucky chance for the fate of the empire to have a downright aesthete as emperor. He tried his hand at one art that he did not understand, that of war. For he nurtured the dangerous illusion that the more millions are spent, the more certain is the outcome. That important question for all armies, the morale of the troops, was one that the Chinese were not fond of facing; even their moralists avoided or sidestepped it, and that is true of Confucius himself, a courageous man and a master of arms, but one who never used them. Whether it was Hui-tsung's own idea, or that of his entourage, is of no importance; in any event it was decided to conquer the Liao kingdom which lay not far to the north from the towers of the capital, K'ai-feng. The press gangs got to work, and an army of more than a million men was assembled. Political circumstances seemed favourable. To the north of Liao, in the district round the river Sungari, lived the Kin, a people who like the Ch'i-tan were of Tungus stock, but

Parrot and apricot. Painting and calligraphy by the Emperor Hui-tsung (1082-1135). There is a translation of the inscription on page 182. *Museum of Fine Arts, Boston (detail from a silk scroll 21 inches by 49)*

were hostile to the people of Liao, who by this time had become prosperous and unwarlike. A plot was spun in K'ai-feng for the Kin to attack Liao in the back simultaneously with the Chinese. All went according to plan except that the Chinese showed so little heart for the fight that they suffered a couple of reverses, and let the Kin see their bad morale and weakness. The result was what one would expect. They defeated Liao together, but the Kin continued their advance and in 1126 encircled K'ai-feng. Hui-tsung abdicated in favour of his son, so that the Kin, when the city fell, captured two Emperors and sent them off to Siberia, where Hui-tsung died as a prisoner in 1135. With difficulty his nephew succeeded in retreating over the Yangtse to the south; the Kin continued to pursue him even there, but in the end they concluded a treaty with the Chinese. Instead of the Liao kingdom in the north, they founded that of Kin with its capital in the beautiful city of K'ai-feng. This kingdom stretched as far

Southern Sung   as the Huai river in the south. The Sung dynasty carried on in the south with its capital at Hangchou, and paid tribute to Kin in place of Liao. Hence it is usual to speak of the Northern and the Southern Sung, for the same house reigned from 960—1126 in K'ai-feng, and from 1126—1278 in Hangchou. Now history repeated itself, in main outline, almost word for word. The Kin made themselves all too comfortable in K'ai-feng and in China generally. They no longer fought much; only in a narrow circle about the succession to the throne. One of their early emperors won a reputation for his remarkable capacity to hold his drink; thirty years later a crown prince is taking painting lessons from Liang K'ai. The Kin court painters, for the most part Chinese, were not inferior to those of the south, and the last of their emperors, Ch'ang-tsung (1190—1208) rivalled Hui-tsung as connoisseur and collector. When K'ai-feng was captured, the latter's famous collection was scattered but not destroyed, and it was brought together again and came into the hands of the Kin imperial house. Chang Hsüan's picture of "Ladies Working Silk", for example, bears the imperial seal of the Emperor Hui-tsung and next to it that of the Kin Emperor Chang-tsung.

This high standard of civilisation in Kin, which about the year 1200 was hardly below that of the Southern Sung, again attracted the greed of the

Jenghis Khan   untamed steppes. Jenghis Khan at the head of Mongolian and rebel Kin squadrons began his attack on China, overran Chin, captured Peking in 1216, and then turned back against the West. There, success came so easily that even after the death of the great Khan in 1227 the Mongol armies continued on the move, and by 1241 they had burnt Breslau and stood before the gates of Liegnitz. Neither the gallant little band of Silesian

178

Buffalo herdsman returning home with a pheasant on a stick through a winter landscape. An example of the suggestive and imaginative landscape painting in Indian ink of the Southern Sung dynasty. By Li Ti a painter at the imperial court in the 12th century. This picture was among the masterpieces in the collection of the Higashiyama princes from the 15th century, in Kyoto. On silk. *Yamato Bunka Museum, Osaka* *(9¼ by 9½ inches)*

179

knights who fell in this brave attempt, nor anything else could have prevented them riding on further into Europe, had it not been that a dispute about the succession to the throne lead them to turn back after they had levelled Budapest to the ground. Their leaders now knew the world from the Amur to the Oder, and they came to the understandable conclusion that China was the only country in all the world worth possessing. So Kublai declined to make any practical use of his title of Great Khan, with some difficulty succeeded in conquering China, dethroned the Sung dynasty in 1278 and established himself on the throne at Khan-Balik, the modern Peking, which he planned in magnificent style. The merchants and craftsmen of Europe without delay presented themselves before the "scourge of God" at Khan-Balik. The most intelligent of these was Marco Polo who lived from 1271—1294 at the court of Kublai. Kublai by then came up to Chinese standards of education and culture, and Polo, who was a wealthy man, was the first European to fall under the spell of China. When he came back and found himself a prisoner in Genoa, almost against his will he wrote an account of his experiences, anticipating that his story would not be believed and with some fear that he might be burned for his pains. His description of the city of Hangchou, whose brilliance as the Sung capital had not faded then, is the high point of his journey.

Mongol dynasty The Mongols in China, like the Liao and Chin before them, soon lost their taste for war. Kublai himself chose the Chinese name of Yüan for his dynasty. We have a complete series of portraits of the Yüan Emperors, in which it takes no expert knowledge of anthropology to see a perfect example of patent degeneration. The Mongol rulers had no insight into political economy, and China grew steadily poorer. It became only a question of time when the rightly incensed peasants would drive the emperors out, for from 1300 onwards they had clearly lost both will and power to defend themselves. Their rule continued de jure down to 1368, but in fact from about 1300 they controlled no more than Peking and a few garrison towns. The resistance of the cultivated classes is really more important than the political and economic revolts; they broke away from imperial patronage. The Chinese state had never evolved any proper constitution; it was based on the idea that Heaven, by giving the ruler power, thereby bestowed its "Mandate" upon him. It therefore did not matter whether the emperor came from a family of high standing or ancient lineage, or from one of foreign extraction. He was only concerned to see that his dignitaries and officials performed their duties with a view to the general good, and the cultivated classes, that is those with a classical education, had the right and the duty to work for the good of the people with the

180

emperor, so long as it was morally possible for them to do so. Repeated and celebrated examples of resistance to the emperor on moral grounds by high officials only prove the rule. But it was something new when Ni Tsan, a man of parts and of good family, celebrated as poet and painter, refused to come to court, and even refused to paint a picture commissioned by the ruler of his district. Many others of his circle did likewise. Moreover Ni Tsan and his friends evolved a new style of painting which marks an epoch in the history of art, beginning in 1341. In that year Ni Tsan gave his great fortune away to friends and relations; he abandoned everything for the sake of freedom of thought, art and spirit. Works of his are preserved from that date onwards. To understand what his decision meant to a man weak in body, though strong in spirit, it is helpful to think of other like-minded people; of Mozart who preferred to freeze rather than write music at the order of his Bishop and territorial lord, or of Lessing who fought with exemplary courage to fulfil the ideal of a man enlightened himself and bringing enlightenment to others. One should not press such analogies too far, but some such fundamental change took place in the spiritual world of the Chinese bourgeoisie about 1340, as occurred in Europe in 1789, and the contrast with the beginning of the epoch is very marked. The Emperor Hui-tsung is typical of this earlier period; he not only commissioned works from his painters, but painted himself, and was able himself to show what he meant by the high demands of art.

There are three works with serious claims to be considered as originals from the hand of Hui-tsung: the "Dove on a Peach Spray" of 1107, the "Wagtail among Narcissi" and a picture of "Parrots and Apricots" in the Museum of Fine Arts in Boston. All of them fall under the then well established and popular category of "Flowers and Birds"; the subjects are painted with the greatest accuracy so that they would serve as illustrations for a book of natural history, yet one sees at first glance that precision of detail has been subordinated to the discipline of an aesthetically demanding composition. There is never a hint of background. Every twig and every feather stands clearly outlined. Yet as we look more closely at the picture, it never occurs to us that we are simply looking at a careful miniature or text book illustration. The whole of spring comes with this flowering spray into the picture; the jewelled plumage of this brilliant bird brings all the gay magnificence of nature. The Emperor's own words are better than any analysis, when he describes the circumstance that moved him in the inscription which he has written on the scroll in his fine, rather precise handwriting; "The five-coloured parrot comes from Ling-piao (in the south of the kingdom). Brought up in the palace he was teachable

The painting of Hui-tsung

181

and friendly. He flew in and out of the garden singing as he went. Now the apricots are in full flower and he flies out over them. He shows his breeding in his natural dignity. As I look at him his appearance seems more subtle than any painting, so I wrote this poem:

Heaven made the parrot, this rare bird.
From far away he came as a present to the Imperial garden.
No commonplace form is this in the perfection of its five colours.
He can speak many words too in tuneful voice.
When he delights to fly, his feathers are a joy to see;
When he comes back, a few grains of corn suffice him for food.
The bright colours of his breast and the purple
of his claws are pure perfection;
So I write a new poem and sing it to the beat of my steps".

Epitome of all the arts   This is a complete example of what the Chinese would consider to be an "epitome of all the arts"; fine painting, calligraphy, prose and poetry sung in the freshness of a spring garden, are all combined here, and there is also the delight in a simple and beautiful natural object which is rare and choice too. The means of expression, especially the composition, imply more than is said, and rely on an esoteric symbolism which only like-minded spirits can understand. Here the kindly and over-romantic side of the great Emperor and his art are to the fore. Certainly there was a great deal of the romantic in him, but Hui-tsung was much too serious an aesthete to indulge in indiscriminate pleasure in everything pretty. He did not revolutionise painting, but he emphatically selected what appealed to him in nature, art and history. We know for instance, that he took no trouble to preserve landscapes by Kuo Hsi which his father had treasured, and just gave them away. He took no interest in the masters of the "Western Garden", but that may have been because they were political opponents. He did possess pictures by the famous Li Lung-mien, and those he was bound to value as the work of a great archaeologist able to appreciate his rich collection of bronzes. He naturally had pictures by his brother-in-law Wang Shen, but nothing of Mi Fu or Su Tung-p'o who, exiled for his opposition to Wang An-shih's reforms, remained on the political proscription list.

Hou-chu, the last Emperor of the Ch'en dynasty in Nanking and a famous Maecenas, (583-589 A.D.). Probably painted in the early 14th century and attributed to Sheng Mou. *British Museum, London (on silk, 6 foot 5 inches by 3 foot 5 inches)*

182

All this detailed information is available because the Emperor had a catalogue made of all the 6,192 pictures in his collection, and this catalogue came to be used as an excellent encyclopedia of Far Eastern art. The whole collection was divided into ten categories, and these categories came to be accepted as the proper divisions of classical art generally. They are:

Classical categories of painting

1. Taoist and Buddhist Themes.
2. Figures (that is to say, non-religious conversation pieces).
3. Palaces and Architecture.
4. Foreign peoples.
5. Dragons and fishes.
6. Landscapes.
7. Domestic and wild animals.
8. Flowers and Birds.
9. Bamboos in Indian ink.
10. Vegetables and fruit (i.e. "Still Life").

Old traditions may well have influenced this table of values; the importance attached to religious subjects and to pictures of strangers may reflect the interests of early T'ang times. Of course, chance must have played a good part in the collection, much of which was inherited, but the numbers of the pictures mentioned as by particular artists gives an impression of the spirit behind the collection with sober clarity, qualities which one always expects and generally finds in China. One might make a statistical analysis the basis of a sociological study of taste at K'ai-feng and elsewere about the year 1120. What the Emperor actually collected shows a different appreciation of values from the classical categories. "Flowers and Birds" come easily top with 2,786 examples by as few as 46 painters; next come "Taoist and Buddhist Themes" with 1,179 works by 49 artists; then "Landscapes" with 1,108 pictures by 41 masters; but all the other categories trail far behind. Of the "Flower and Bird" painters Huang Ch'üan comes top with 349, next comes his son, Huang Chü-ts'ai, the first director of the K'ai-feng academy, with 332. Among "Landscape" painters Li Ch'eng takes first place with 159 pictures. But we have too vague a notion of what all these names imply for it to be worth while carrying the investigation further.

However this Emperor, who was both an outstanding painter, albeit rather one-sided, and a most fastidious aesthete, was certainly able to establish a school. The Academy was there at hand as a channel for his activity; through it he offered prizes for set themes from poetry and other

competitions, and distributed honours and distinctions. There is an emphatic contrast between Hui-tsung's behaviour and that of Ming-huang. "His Radiant Majesty" was a man sound and wise, fundamentally tolerant and disinterested in his love of art, so that his benevolence in bestowing honours went far beyond the limitations of one man's private judgement. Whereas Hui-tsung was a highly gifted man who set himself strict and demanding aesthetic standards, and directed art down fine, poetical and charming paths and not, blessedly, into a mere dull fairway. His achievement deserves our admiration, and not the mockery which greets Ch'ien-lung's attempt to do the same.

A nephew of Hui-tsung succeeded in escaping from the Kin over the Yangtse, and, as the Emperor Kao-tsung, founding the Southern Sung dynasty. Kao-tsung too had some gift for painting and encouraged others. Some members of the former Academy in K'ai-feng escaped south with him, and he was soon able to open a new Academy at Hangchou, his *Hangchou* capital. In these richer, happier and less threatened surroundings lovely new flowers bloomed. It is to Japan that we owe almost all the fine Southern Sung pictures which have survived. The safest passage from Japan landed at Ning-po, the port of Hangchou, which was linked to the capital by a fortified canal. When the Academy moved there, Hangchou became all the more attractive to the Japanese, especially to the Buddhist monks and priests who loved to come and study in China. In Hangchou and the nearby "Eye of Heaven Mountains" (*T'ien-mu* or, in Japanese, *Temmoku*) in the 12th century the meditative school of Buddhism was evolving new thoughts. We have not enough detailed information about the people then and there to be able to say positively that the shift to this scenery was at the back of the development of Ch'an Buddhism. But it cannot have been a matter of chance that in the year 1191 the celebrated Eisai, the founder of the Ch'an (in Japanese "Zen") school returned to his homeland. Japanese monks long continued to come on pilgrimage or to study, and brought home Chinese works of art from Hangchou and the district round. By the 14th and 15th centuries the Shoguns too, who ruled at Kyoto in the name of the Emperors, began to take an interest in such things. The Shoguns at that time were convinced disciples of Zen and sought for pictures, lacquer and ceramics in China with zeal and discrimination. They paid great sums to add works to their collection, which were then reverently preserved in Japan, and have survived the earthquakes and revolutions there better than similar works in China.

Among other things which we owe to their zeal is the little Indian ink painting of a winter landscape, in which a herdsman rides home on his water-buf- PLATE ON PAGE 179

185

falo, carrying on a stick the pheasant he has caught in the fields. A little colour, on the bird's feathers only, makes a scarcely perceptible counterpoint to the fine and delicate harmonies of the Indian ink. The picture is by Li Ti who was first a leading member of the K'ai-feng Academy, and then *Indian ink painting* helped to found that of Hangchou. The poetry of the picture, the economical means with which the spirit of the winter landscape has been evoked, speaks for itself. Perhaps the design is more firmly anchored in its frame than is the case with, say, Hui-tsung's "Parrot", but fundamentally they are alike; in this picture too the thrift and loneliness of the subject matter, and the asymmetry of the composition, mean more than they seem to say. About the year 1200 Ma Yüan and Hsia Kuei, both famous as landscape painters, brought this style to perfection, and the former was given the nickname of "One-corner Ma", which throws a lightning flash of illumination on what his contemporaries were looking for and found in this style. The name is based on an allusion to a saying of Confucius, which holds the whole of this aesthetic doctrine in a nutshell: "If a man won't try, I will not teach him; if a man makes no effort, I will not help him. I show one corner, and if a man cannot find the other three, I am not going to repeat myself." (Lun-yü VII,8).

It is significant that the Pi-yen-lu, one of the most important of Ch'an Buddhist writings, the first edition of which was dedicated to the Emperor Hui-tsung, says on the first page " ... to see horns behind a hedge, and know at once that they are buffalo's; in one corner to make the nature of the other three clear ... that is like daily bread for the disciple of Ch'an." This example illuminates the fruitful exchange of thought between Buddhism and Confucianism which was then taking place. A little problem of art history, which has been posed recently, will perhaps lead us to an understanding of the essential spirit of the "one-corner" style. There exists a companion piece to Li Ti's picture, showing a herdsman with a hare, and the two together would make a perfect dyptich. Japanese authorities now doubt the authenticity of the companion piece, and think it is Japanese work; in that case it might equally well be either an excellent *"One-corner" style* copy of a formerly existing work, or a 15th century invention to complete the open composition of the lovely picture and hold it together as a dyptich. The whole spirit of Southern Sung painting, the whole con-

← Kuan-yin, the Bodhisattva who 'hears the cries of men', and comes to help them. On her head is an image of Amida Buddha whom Kuan-yin incarnates on earth. *Art Institute, Chicago (painted wooden sculpture, 6 foot 2 inches high)* ception of painting which evolved in Hui-tsung's reign, is put to the test by the question, "Was there a companion piece? Need there have been one? Does not Li Ti's lovely picture stand alone, and is it not better so standing?" It is quite possible that the companion piece might one day be recognised as the true original. The posing of such questions teaches us to understand the nature of an art which says little, but leads the beholder on to think and feel with the painter, and which actually wishes to turn him into artist so that he can supply from his own intuition all that is not there.

The "one-corner" style is only one aspect of Southern Sung painting and of the activity of the Academy. The figure pictures, especially when they were long scrolls, could not be so epigrammatic as the landscapes or flower pictures. We are told that Hui-tsung and his successors had an equal fondness for figure subjects, and perhaps sometimes preferred them. We *Figure painting* are acquainted with a number of excellent works, but we cannot place them in their correct century, let alone decade, so we cannot use them to illustrate the spirit of successive ages. In China, as elsewhere, there are favourite themes, which are often painted and taken up again from age to age. It is altogether wrong and stupid to say, as is often said, that Chinese painting repeats itself, and that this tendency is especially pronounced in the so called "late period", which is supposed to be from about 1200 A.D. onwards. The fact is that we have more pictures surviving from the 12th century onwards, and that the Chinese had the same tendency to paint landscapes and figure subjects which resemble one another, as the Europeans in the case of Madonnas and Martyrdoms. A cultivated Chinese gentleman once left the Brera in Milan in a state of fury; such a surfeit of martyrs' agonies stuck in his throat, and for all his goodwill he no longer had the strength to look there for the spirit of the art of the Renaissance or the Baroque. So the first things we should ask about Chinese pictures are whether they are well painted, and whether they are true art, and not shut the door of appreciation in our own faces by noting that this or that theme has been previously treated by another master. Our reward for lingering is the ever fuller appreciation of, say, Ch'ien Hsüan as one of the greatest painters of China and the world. This conviction will become firmer the more we learn to distinguish originals from copies in the excessive mass of work attributed to him, and to see when he is following earlier masters, and when he is giving his own ideas concrete expression.

FRONTISPIECE The picture of Yang Kuei-fei mounting a horse, now in the Freer Gallery in Washington, must be reckoned a masterpiece, and is certainly one of the

188

Vase. Light pottery covered with a dark slip out of which a pattern of peonies has been left standing; a transparent green glaze has then been applied. From the Tz'u-chou kiln in Hopei. 12th-13th century. *Musée Guimet, Paris (7 inches high)*

preparation, and it says a lot for the Sung spirit of humanity that Kuan-yin was one of their favourite themes, and that they took as their patroness the incarnation of Mercy. Among the many painted wood statues, rightly or wrongly described as Sung, the one in the Art Institute of Chicago is among the best. For all its dignity this is a gentle and kindly presence; there is naive delight in natural grace and at the same time fine plastic quality in this work which hardly claimed to be more than a good piece of craftsmanship; this figure may stand as a memorial to the Sung spirit.

Sung ceramics Sung ceramics are so well known and loved by every amateur and collector, many of whom regard them as the zenith of Chinese pottery, that it is

Gold brocade with medallions of dragons and tendrils of a climbing plant. Such brocades were much admired in Europe from the 13th century onwards, and had a great influence on the development of textiles. Beginning of the 14th century. *Museum of Arts and Crafts, Hamburg.*

impossible to deal with them fully here. Interesting researches are in progress in an effort to identify the products of individual imperial kilns and to establish what types of utensils might have been ordered for the palace by Hui-tsung and his successors. Meanwhile, even the ordinary vessels for everyday use have such unquestioned aesthetic quality that nearly all of them would serve as models to help any potter of taste to solve the invariable problems of his craft. One single vase among so many must here represent Sung achievement. The shape is well adapted for use, clearly but not sharply articulated; the outline is gentle but sure. The clay has baked to a pale reddish colour; over this there is a slip of dark brown verging to black. Much of this slip has been scraped away to leave a free and flowing pattern of peonies. It was only after that, that the greenish glaze was applied and the pot put in the kiln. Could simple means be used to greater effect? This pot was "mass produced" but yet it is an unmistakeably individual work, and the nameless craftsman rivalled the painters and calligraphers. Never before, even in China, had pottery, made for use, restricted in its means, and without a painter's help in its decoration, shown such clear marks of personality with all the strength and weakness of simple humanity. PLATE ON PAGE 189

Though we know that Sung lacquer work was highly prized, none characteristic of the period between 750 and 1300 has been found. But we can gain an impression of the brocades and silks. These are found more in Europe, especially in church treasuries, than in China itself. Chinese brocades worked wonders in mediaeval Europe; soon after Marco Polo's return, the cities of Northern Italy began to seek out these stuffs and copy their designs. The brocades of Lucca owed their reputation to their imitation of the Chinese. The Hamburg Museum of Arts and Crafts possesses a Chinese gold brocade probably dating from the early 14th century. *Brocade*

PLATE ON PAGE 192

Its design was one current in China at that time; twelve-petalled medallions with dragons writhing inside them on a background of honeysuckle pattern. The influence of these brocades radiated out into other fields of art. We find patterns taken from them on the gold background of our gothic altarpieces, and they are evidence for the widespread inter-relationships of art forms, which is characteristic of world history from about the year 1200. Since the Crusades and the appearance of the Mongols brought Europe into fresh contact with the Near and Far East, her culture began to widen and she was at pains to catch up with the others at an ever increasing rate in each succeeding century. After some time China began to fall back in the race, but she never stood still and her civilisation never grew old or rigid. Its life continued and it made progress, albeit at a gentler pace. The Chinese spanned abysses and reached new heights like other peoples. Only the tempo was calmer and more restrained, perhaps also more natural and better suited to the sense of humanity which was the great strength of the epoch of the Sung Academy. At that time, they made no advances in the technical apparatus of painting, but great painters, artists and emperors united in friendly and peaceful emulation.

Gatehouse tower at the entrance of the "Ch'ang-ling" tomb enclosure of the Emperor Yung-lo, 1403-1424, the builder of the Great Wall and of the temple of Heaven. Tombs of the Ming emperors to the north of Peking.

195

A new conception comes in with the Mongols who, calling themselves the Yüan dynasty, had ruled the north since 1271, and the whole of China from 1278. It was a conception with which they dug their own grave; nationalism. The Mongols thought of China just as a part, albeit the best part, of their world empire. The layout of the city of Peking on a grander scale than was naturally required, shows this. No one would have minded the Mongols giving up the profession of arms and turning into pensionaries of the state. But they started the mad practice of basing their privileges on racial laws, and these they made increasingly oppressive in proportion to the growing resistance to their power. The Chinese could not bear to be treated as second class citizens in their own land, and it is understandable that in fighting back they used Beelzebub to turn out the Devil.

Ming dynasty   The Chinese considered the Mongols as foreigners and, more than in fact they were, barbarians. The idea of national liberation gained increasing force in the course of the rebellions which kept on breaking out, now here now there, from about 1330. In the course of time Chu Yüan-chang (1328—1398) came to be the leader of these unorganised revolts. This poor peasant boy from Anhui had lost his parents in a plague when he was quite young; he found asylum in a monastery, and then, being strong and well-built, he joined one of the peasant armies; he gained promotion and made the simple, but not obvious, decision to stop plundering and burning. By this means he brought the gentry over to his side, and was able to count on the advice of able members of this class. He then consolidated his position in central China. His slogan, to drive the Mongols out, attracted ever larger forces to his side, and when his object had been accomplished, Chu Yüan-chang ascended the throne in 1368 as founder of the Ming dynasty. He ruled as Emperor Hung-wu in Nanking for a generation. From this time onwards the emperors never changed the reign name which they adopted on ascending the throne.

No one did more to secure the position of the Ming dynasty than his son Yung-lo (1403—1424) who was equally energetic and able. He governed Peking, and while there learnt that the son of his elder brother who had died young, had been made emperor at Nanking. Three years later he set aside this nephew and ascended the throne himself. He immediately made Peking his capital, but Nanking in the rich rice district was at the same time recognised as second capital and kept its importance for the arts, literature especially. Yung-lo discovered that the Mongols ruling in western Asia had not forgotten China or given her up. The great Timur Lenk, known to Europe as Tamurlane, planned to conquer China from his headquarters at Samarkand. This new "scourge of God" who laid Delhi waste in 1398, pillaged Syria and Asia Minor, and piled high his pyramids of skulls along the Volga, luckily died in 1405. Yung-lo was then at pains to turn the Great Wall, until that time only an earthern rampart, into the great stone structure which still survives. He won great fame as a builder; the Temple of Heaven in Peking dates from his time, though it has often been renewed, and his tomb enclosure to the north of the capital is one of the finest monuments of Chinese architecture. He once more established the city with all the magnificence proper to an imperial residence, so that it should not be inferior to the former Khan-Balik. This will throw a side light on his way of doing things. Yung-lo learnt that the Japanese valued and paid high prices for lacquer work, especially the cut-lacquer of the masters Chang Ch'eng and Yang Mao

"Hermit in a Chasm of the Forest" by Wang Meng, one of the "Four Great Masters" of the Yüan dynasty, the painters of solitude and peace. *Art Institute, Chicago (on paper 6 foot 8 inches by 2 foot 1 inch)*

who had their workshop in the Chia-hsing district not far from Hangchou, and he gave orders for these masters to be brought to Peking. That was not possible as they were already dead, but their successors opened the lacquer section of the imperial workshop, and a genuine piece of lacquer with Yung-lo's mark scratched on it even now fetches a specially high price. This Emperor was succeeded by his son who was gifted for the arts. He took the reign name of Hsüan-te and there is significance in this choice. Of the many reign names of the Sung Emperor Hui-tsung that of Hsüan-ho came to stand for the zenith of his aesthetic achievement. The famous catalogue of his collection of paintings with its division into categories was called Hsüan-ho hua-p'u. So the reign name Hsüan-te (1426–1435) indicated that the Emperor intended Peking to rival the Hangchou of Hui-tsung's time as a city of the Muses. He himself painted well; he summoned painters to the court from Chekiang, for Hangchou is in Chekiang and the tradition of the Sung Academy had stronger vitality there. There were marked refinements at that time, perhaps over-refinements, in the art of bronze casting. A Hsüan-te inscription is still regarded as the mark par excellence on a bronze bowl or other object; there are so many of them that we are left in doubt as to whether any particular specimen is genuine. Much the same is true in the case of cloisonné or enamel work for which the reign mark of Ching-t'ai (1450–56) still has the same prestige. Hsüan-te set such high standards for lacquer workers that the latter, to save their heads, were forced to buy up objects of the previous reign of Yung-lo and alter the reign marks. There were later Ming emperors, who often came to the throne very young, who painted a little and attracted painters to their court; the chief of these were Hung-chih (1488–1505) and Cheng-te (1506–21); the poet-emperor Chia-ching (1522–62) introduced new types of ornament, and the young T'ien-ch'i (1621–27) took pleasure in working as a cabinet maker and lacquer master, and his reputation in this field compares with that of Hui-tsung in painting, but only two certain works of his are known.

Nationalism What lies behind all this? The Ming dynasty had come to the throne promising to drive the foreigners out, and bring a truly Chinese constitution back into operation. They were true to this promise, and have always been considered as the most Chinese of the dynasties in this millenium; and the image of China, which the world still accepts, is largely the creation of the Ming dynasty. This general tendency was carried further by the Ming philosophers who consciously returned to the Neo-confucianism of the Sung, and particularly to the 12th century philosopher Chu Hsi who was the Thomas Aquinas of that movement. But they

198

did not confine themselves to that. They carried on a continual discussion with Buddhist thinkers, and developed what is called the Doctrine of Intuition, which was most fully developed by Wang Yang-ming (1472–1528), perhaps the greatest of Chinese philosophers in the strict sense of the word.

The Ming age was also the great time of the middle classes. In the "forbidden city" in the middle of Peking the emperors themselves lived and guarded their privacy in the same way as the most important of the citizens, and in so doing lost contact far too much with their subjects. It is typical of the social conditions of the time that the novel and the drama, both means of expression which in form and subject matter were essentially middle class, came to flower under the Ming. Moreover the land was now exclusively ruled by civil servants; power was never delegated to generals, as had been done so often and with such disastrous results in later T'ang times, when the generals had acted as viceroys and very often had no better means than arms to support their authority. It would certainly be going too far to describe Ming rule as democratic, but certain features which are often connected with democracy, influenced the politics and economy of that age; there were lobbies, corruption and pressure groups, which finally got out of hand at the court of Peking. The palace eunuchs played an important part in later Ming times; in earlier days they had generally been mere hangmen, but later they were often highly educated and able men. The "dance round the golden calf" was such that members of the gentry of their own free will became eunuchs, so as to get their own hands, and those of their supporters in the lobby, on the gold. No sufficiently objective history of the end of the Ming dynasty has yet been written, but presumably its fall was due to the hopelessly selfish behaviour of factions. In the end there was no class left to oppose the warring cliques with good sense, moderation and energy. So eventually the day came when the factions again began to forward their pretensions by force of arms. Once that point was reached, there was an end of patriotic feeling. There was always one faction or another that was ready to call in the help of powerful barbarians, thinking perhaps that they could have the better of them later, rather than come to terms with their rivals. That is how the Manchus, a people of Tungus stock, were summoned into the land. The Mongols, who had never forgotten Jenghis Khan and Kublai, joined up with them. The Mongols handed over the great seal of the Yüan dynasty, which they had kept all this time, to the Manchus. After a long and often hard-fought struggle the latter ascended the throne of Peking as the Ch'ing dynasty. The Manchus had adopted the name of Ch'ing in 1616 before they had

Bourgeois quality

Manchus

199

Gentleman of high rank looking at a waterfa[ll]
in Lu-shan. By Wen Cheng-ming, 1470-1599,
Eastern Art, Cologne (Fan painting o[n

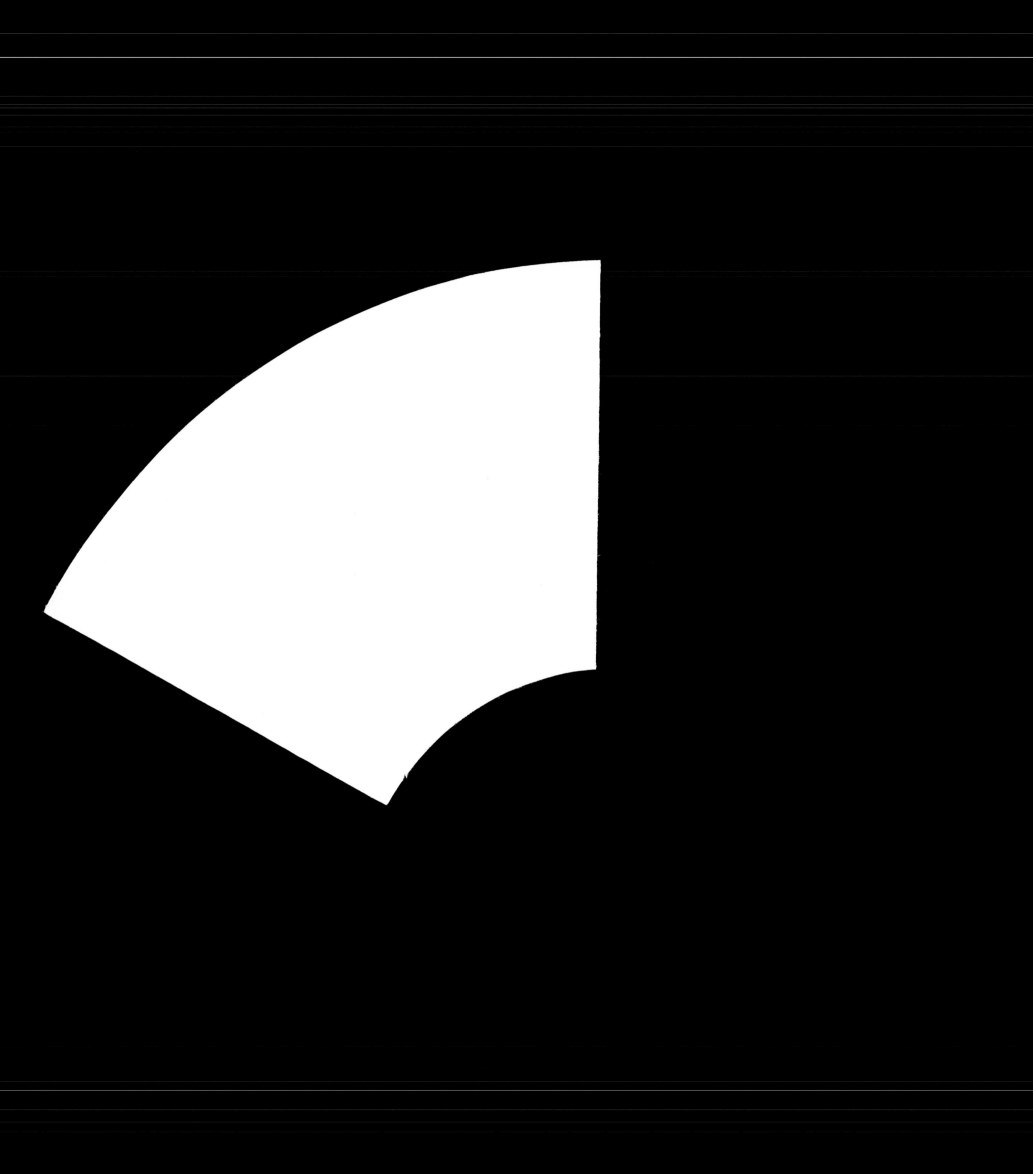

ure echoes Li T'ai-po's poem about a waterfall
is followers such as Ch'ien Ku. *Museum of Far*
rinkled with gold dust; 7 inches by 21)

mastered the whole of China. While the conquest was still in progress, they set a child on the throne of Peking as their first emperor; the child was gifted, and unusual in that he could prove to the Chinese that the Manchus were just as capable of profiting by education as themselves. This puppet on the throne was of more use in impressing the educated classes, than in fighting or political activity. The Banner-bearers of the Privy Council, in which there were no more eunuchs, saw to that, while the first Emperor, Shun-chih, won a deserved reputation as a painter and was brought up entirely in accordance with Chinese tradition. After his early death in 1662, he was followed on the throne by his son, K'ang-hsi, who was also very young and subject to a regency. In the sixty years of his reign K'ang-hsi not only proved himself one of the greatest emperors in China and the whole world, but also a really outstanding example of an

Round wooden box with a black lacquer ground, lacquer painting and inlays of mother-of-pearl. The decoration is a variation on the "Eastern Fence" motif. Hsüan-te reign mark, 1426-1435. *Museum of Fine Arts, Boston (3 by 8 inches in diameter)*

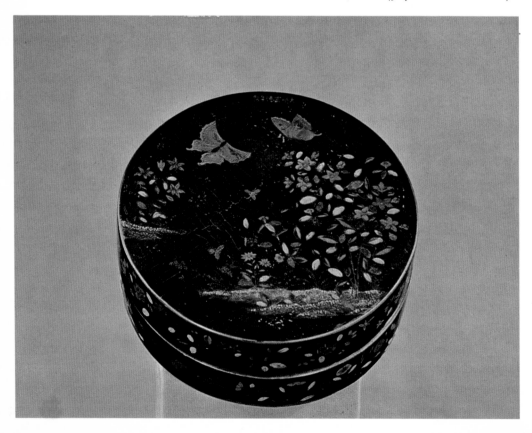

enlightened monarch. His life was lived in hard times, and it needed all K'ang-hsi's strength of character, ability, modesty and benevolence to master his fate. Naturally only a small faction could be counted as friends of the Manchus. Their social position in China was almost exactly the same as that of the Mongols. They were the backbone of the privileged military caste, though there were also Chinese army corps, and they enjoyed generous pensions from the state, but apart from the army, learning and art, no profession was open to them. In two respects they went beyond the Yüan regulations. For a long time they were forbidden to marry Chinese women, and, when it was permitted, could only have them as secondary wives. In addition they compelled the Chinese to adopt a foreign fashion, which was just the opposite of what had happened 800 years before, and by forcing them to wear pigtails imposed a visible sign of their subjection. This law must have hurt and strengthened Chinese feelings of patriotism, which had been awakened by the Mongols and intensified by the Manchus, but of course such patriotism was very different from the nationalism which swept over the world in the 19th century. Naturally in such circumstances the resistance to K'ang-hsi tended to stiffen, and it says much for that great man that arms were not the only means he used to overcome it. While he was defeating his last formidable adversary in the west, in Ssech'uan, K'ang-hsi promulgated a decree setting forth under 16 headings the basic principles of his government, so that everyone could understand them. His first principle is reverence *(hsiao)*. This "Sacred Edict" of 1671, which was to be read every week in all Chinese schools, and which has been translated by F. W. Baller, had an epoch-making influence In the first place it marked the turning point, after decades of fighting, towards a peace which soon was pretty well established; that fact by itself might be taken as an historical accident. Then it is purely Confucian in essence, and in many respects it was for the first time through this edict that Confucianism became the basis of Chinese political thought. As a result of this, although certain of its conceptions continued to have some influence, the Neoconfucianism of Sung times in fact leaves the stage, and so does the philosophy of intuition of the Confucian Wang Yang-ming, which for all its onesidedness was still the best expression of the Ming spirit. In the life of the spirit, the great event of the Ming epoch was the appearance of a middle class which knew its own worth, and which finds its purest aesthetic expression in the works of Ni Tsan from 1341 onwards. Its other great achievement was to work out a new, and at the same time old and elaborate system of political thought, which was made law by the Sacred Edict of 1671.

Ni Tsan (1301—1374) was not alone in his distaste for the naked power which seemed to be ruling the world, though he was the best and most uncompromising fighter for the new conception. Ni Tsan also composed sensitive lyric poems, while his three contemporaries who helped him to create the new style, were all painters; Huang Kung-wang (1269—1354), Wu Chen (1280—1354) and Wang Meng (1308—85); to these must be added their many friends and disciples. They are called "The Four Great Masters of the Yüan Dynasty", and are still considered to be among the greatest of Chinese painters. Before examining their work it seems permissible to

Porcelain jar with decoration in cobalt blue under the glaze and enamel colours over it, representing fishes and waterplants. On the base is a blue reign mark of Chia-ching, 1522-66. *Museum of Far Eastern Art, Cologne (13 inches high)*

ask what they still considered worthy to be expressed, since the emperor and the world no longer meant anything to them, and they had no conception of a good God in whom they could put their trust. In China only one answer is possible; nature as she manifests herself in landscape. The way in which they conceived landscape is the clearest hallmark of the new style. It was different from the traditional style which had been current for many hundreds of years, and different too from that of Li Ti who, 200 years before, had been the friend of Hui-tsung and Kao-tsung. Now the landscapes are empty, without sign of man or the works of men. Ni Tsan loves to put huts in his pictures, but they are always empty and emphasise the impression of loneliness. Never have so many pure landscapes without any extraneous incident been painted as in China after 1341, and there is little reason to believe them when these modest, hermitlike spirits make out that they are following the example of the masters of the 10th and 11th centuries. There is also no trace at all of the asymmetry of the "one-corner" style which had inspired the composition of many beautiful landscapes about the year 1300. Instead of the carefully chosen and suggestive detail, they are at pains to build up a firm and self-sufficient composition, which can be extended in any direction and leads out into the unlimited. The tension in a Sung landscape between the significant corner and the background often veiled in fine mist, a tension which never makes the composition fall apart, is here relaxed and made subordinate to a higher integration. Moreover, the atmosphere which modified the visibility of everything in a landscape, now no longer plays a part. One could not say that there is no air in this style, but it is transparent, cool and clear, without any of those washes of concealing mist which express and suggest so many subjective feelings. The use of colour is also different; broad, finely *Brushwork* graded washes of Indian ink and the brilliance of bright colours are alike avoided; it is essentially brush painting, making use of the most sensitive lines and dabs of paint completed with a most sparing addition of light colour washes. These washes are almost exclusively of a delicate reddish brown or bluey grey, corresponding to Goethe's symbolism of colours, according to which red and blue are the emblems of the self-reliant, free spirit. Among those great artists Wang Meng is the easiest to understand, PLATE ON PAGE 197 and the one most ready to compromise. He is the least strict about banishing humanity from his landscapes, but his hermits and their huts, his grand gentlemen who have withdrawn to the mountains and valleys, transparently reflect the thoughts and wishes of himself and his friends. The Emperors Yung-lo and Hsüan-te restored the people's faith in the *Buildings* government. Yung-lo commissioned outstanding buildings which put new

205

life into traditional forms. The imperial tombs to the north of Peking are all magnificent in the scale on which they have been planned, but it is his tomb which has the most assured and best proportions. No over-refinement has been allowed to detract from the sound feeling for architectural con-

PLATE ON PAGE 195 struction. It is not ashamed of the massive power of great blocks, broad walls and clear lines. It is possible that the gatehouse tower of the tomb may have suggested the building of the Great Wall. The new regime is careful to preserve this monument and to renew its colours. It has also had no compunction in opening up the vaulted tomb of the Emperor Wan-li and putting its treasures on view, and we find that there is less strength and balance in them than we had expected.

The young Hsüan-te wished to become a new Hui-tsung. He painted flowers and, more especially, cats with care and some success, but he seems in all probability to have lacked an assured independence of judgement. The following anecdote about the painter Tai Wen-chin throws a sidelight on his court. He came from Chekiang, and was later esteemed the head of the Chekiang school which had always specialised in landscapes with figures, keeping as loyal as possible to the traditions of the Southern Sung school. A comment intended as praise of Tai Wen-chin said that he understood Ma Yüan and Hsia Kuei so well that, when his pictures were hung next to theirs, no one could tell which was which. And yet Tai Wen-chin was sacrificed through a transparent intrigue of his rivals.

Under Hsüan-te the "one-corner" style of the Southern Sung made its return by way of Japan, and took root in a most unexpected branch of art, namaly lacquerwork. Only a few examples of this category of art so characteristic of the Far East have so far been discovered or published and, while we hope to know more later, at present no full survey of the subject is possible. It is at least clear that the Japanese showed a special talent in this field from the very beginning, having endless patience, sensitivity to the tips of their fingers and a sixth sense for the possibilities of craftsmanship. The Chinese discovered in about the year 1400 that the princely collectors of Japan were enthusiastic for the cut-lacquer which they had never prized so greatly themselves. At the same time, they discovered the work of Japanese lacquer masters. For the Japanese, having learnt the art from China some hundreds of years before, had undoubtedly improved it. Although just at that time the coastal provinces of China were having endless trouble from Japanese pirates, they were objective enough to recognise without reserve that in this field the pupil had surpassed the master. One result

Lacquer of this was that a well-known lacquer master in Nanking, Yang Hsün, sent some of his craftsmen to Japan to learn the technique of gold lacquer

206

painting, and the sprinkling of gold dust. They did this so well that, we are told, their Japanese fellow craftsmen "bit their fingers in jealousy". However Yang Hsün would hardly have merited a mention in the story of Chinese art, if he had stuck to lacquer work only and not made his name as a painter too. Besides cut-lacquer, the fashion for inlaying simple round

Wooden dish with painted lacquer background and the picture of a peony and a poem inlaid in mother-of-pearl. 17th century. *Dr. Kurt Herberts, Wuppertal. (1¾ inches by 14 inches in diameter)*

207

boxes, bowls and plates with cut-out patterns of silver, mother-of-pearl and gold, reached the high standard formerly attained by the Han. Of course shapes and ways of expression had changed; these shapes, plain and simple in outline, were often based on flowers, and flowers are frequent

PLATE ON PAGE 202 as ornament. One of the several lovely round boxes in the Boston Museum is decorated with beds of autumn flowers, a few red chrysanthemums among them, on a black background; a couple of butterflies flutter over the flowers. Now butterflies, in China, count as birds, so it is easy to see the reference to T'ao Yüan-ming's "Eastern Fence" poem (see page 97), and the feeling is that of the "one-corner" style.

Thus from the beginning of the 15th century there were two developments in opposite directions; the independent followers of the Four Masters of the Yüan dynasty, who were resolved to have no contact with the court, and the Emperors who, from Hsüan-te onwards, looked for the co-operation of artists, especially painters, and who therefore very naturally tried to revive the Southern Sung tradition. Each party had its supporters; then about the year 1500 a fusion took place which enriched them both, and led to a new flowering. By and large it is fair to say that round the year 1500 painting and the applied arts, especially porcelain, had never been more "Chinese", nor had shape, technique, purport and content ever been in more lively or harmonious free relationship with one another. "The Four Great Masters of the Ming Dynasty" mark the zenith of that proud hour; Shen Chou (1427–1509), T'ang Yin (1470–1524), Wen Cheng-ming (1470–1599) and Ch'iu Ying (about 1500–50). Like their contemporaries in Europe, Leonardo, Michelangelo, Raphael and Titian, they stand for one of the high points in the art of the world. All the Four Masters were natives of Suchou or lived there. Shen Chou never had an official position; Wen Cheng-ming did have one; T'ang Yin was an official for a short time only; Ch'iu Ying never. The first three were typical members of the class of gentry, but the last came from a poor family and first earned his living as a lacquer painter; his striking talent for painting induced T'ang Yin to instruct and help him. Many of their pictures survive, not all were published. There is passion and greatness in them, but nothing aggressive.

The school of Suchou, generally called the Wu school after the surrounding countryside, long set the standard for style, and was the finest expression in painting of the Ming spirit. Wen Cheng-ming lived to great old age and had a powerful influence on younger painters, so there is some doubt PLATE ON PAGE 200 whether the fan picture in the Museum of Far Eastern Art in Cologne is painted by him or one of his followers, Ch'ien Ku. The seal may have

208

been added to the picture later, and not be genuine. But the picture is certainly of that period and in his spirit. The hallmark of his style is that Southern Sung themes are represented in the manner of the four Yüan masters. A gentleman of high rank, accompanied by his boy, has gone into the loneliness of the mountains and sits down on a jutting rock to look at a waterfall. One cannot be sure that the figure is intended for Li T'ai-po, but there is certainly a reminiscence of his poem about the waterfall in Lu-shan. There is the same stylised felicity in the scene and the figure itself as in a Sung picture, say the "Herdsman" of Li Ti. Here too, wide surfaces are left empty, but they are not veiled in mist nor held together by the tension dear to Sung painters; rather are they firmly welded together in a harmonious composition after the manner of the Yüan masters. The subsidiary arts again come into prominence in the reign of the Emperor Chia-ching who came to the throne in 1522. It is easy to recognise the lacquer of this time and the porcelain of which so much has been preserved by the shapes which are elongated, and often sophisticated, but not lacking in spirit. A new element, whose importance should not be exaggerated, *Contact with Europe* comes into play; in 1517 the Portuguese first landed in Canton and in 1557 they obtained the concession of Macao which they still possess. This was the beginning of direct commercial contact with Europe and allowed the admired pottery and porcelain, which before could only be seen and acquired in the Near East, to come direct from China. It is interesting to note the way in which the Europeans paid for these imports, not with exports of their own, which would not have been likely to impress the Chinese, but with the produce of the European colonies in Asia, especially food and spices. But one thing the Chinese did immediately get the Portuguese to show them, and had learnt it by 1519; how to make fire arms. Cannon and hand grenades had long been known in China, but they had not discovered this more skilful use of powder. The West too had known about porcelain for a long time, and since the 13th century it had been exported in considerable quantities to the Near East; the porcelain with patterns in cobalt blue under the glaze especially pleased the customers. From the 14th century there had been thousands of kilns in the potteries centred around Ching-te-chen, producing porcelain for the home market and for export. In Europe these vessels were taken as models and the Delft "onion pattern" is nothing but a misunderstood imitation of the Chinese PLATE ON PAGE 204 "peach and pomegranate". New patterns came in under Chia-ching, and though none of them were specially designed to please European taste, the abstract beauty of their shapes and the brilliance of their enamel colours now as always delight every sensitive eye.

209

"The three peaks of the mountain range" by Shih[...]
phy opposite from an album with twelve views o[...]
Far Eastern Art, Cologne

210

...30 to about 1707). Illustration and page of calligra-
...fou mountains in South-East China. *Museum of*
...er; 9¾ inches by 6½ inches)*

211

Chrysanthemums and a pair of butterflies, a variation on the theme of T'ao Yüan-ming's "Eastern Fence" poem. Colour print from a wooden block printed in Suchou about the year 1685. It is one of the so-called "Kaempfer" prints, the earliest known prints in colour from wood blocks, which a doctor called E. Kaempfer brought back to Europe in 1692. *Museum of Arts and Crafts, Hamburg (12 by 14½ inches)*

X THE AGE OF POLITICAL THOUGHT

It is easy to promulgate principles of morality, but hard to observe them. The Emperor K'ang-hsi deserves the credit for doing that. In 1671 he did not simply promulgate his Sacred Edict as a manifesto of the basic principles of his policy, a thing which had often been done in China before, but actually carried it into practice. He forced others to follow his own good example in taking his principles seriously, and thus won the respect of his people. The 16 principles of the edict were distilled from those parts of the teaching of Confucius which provided guidance for the conduct of the ordinary man. It has often been said, and perhaps it is not overstating the case, that the undiluted doctrine of Confucius had a wider influence over Chinese thought under the Manchus than at any other time in history. In every respect K'ang-hsi was disinterested, unprejudiced and energetic in his efforts to heal the wounds of close on fifty years of war. *K'ang-hsi* His very strenuous efforts to put the economy on a sound basis, entitle him to rank as one of the first advocates of mercantilism, an economic doctrine which, after his death, spread over the whole civilised world. In 1644 Ching-te-chen, the great centre of porcelain manufacture, had been almost entirely destroyed, and the Japanese had seen their chance to make porcelain in the Chinese manner and export it to Europe. As soon as he could, K'ang-hsi ordered the rebuilding of Ching-te-chen, and he sent a specially selected official of high rank there as director of production. Likewise in 1677 he forbade the use of his reign mark, as had before been the custom. He knew that the times were uncertain, and his object was to avoid a break in production, and to save the customers from danger; any day an opposition party might be breaking into people's houses, and breaking everything stamped with the name of the hated foreigner. His motives were utilitarian, but they prove that he was both extremely perceptive and modest in that he did not believe in the magic of a name, and saw the connection between new name and new reality. This law must later have fallen silently into oblivion, for to this day K'ang-hsi porcelain ranks as the best ever made.

During K'ang-hsi's 60 year reign (1662–1722), and perhaps partly due to his policy, there was a quite unprecedented increase in the population. This introduced a serious new element into Chinese history, something with the force of a natural catastrophe, which has placed a heavy and inescapable task on every subsequent government of China down to the

Porcelain plate with a design of scattered flowers. Underglaze decoration in cobalt blue with enamel colours over the glaze and also dry 'iron red' which had to be baked separately in a less hot kiln. An example of the classical age of porcelain. On the base there is a reign mark of K'ang-hsi enclosed in a double ring, 1662-1722. *Museum of Far Eastern Art, Cologne (8 inches in diameter)*

216

present day. One hardly knows how much faith to put in Chinese statistics, but there is no doubt of the gigantic size of the new problem. In 1578 the registered number of inhabitants was about 60 million, an increase of about 10 million over the number in the reign of Ch'in Shih-huang-ti 1,800 years before. The registered area of the ploughland to nourish them was about 3 million acres which, taking into account the very intensive methods of cultivation employed in China, methods which could hardly be improved by mechanisation, may be supposed normal and sufficient. By 1710 the population had doubled, reaching 120 million, and went on increasing continually, while the cultivable area did not increase and in- deed decreased somewhat during the years of unrest; in the years that followed there was no increase in available supplies of food proportionate to the rise in population. We do not know the reasons for this sudden, phenomenal multiplication of the population. Peace, industry and hygiene, the classical reasons given for the increase of population in Europe in the 18th and 19th centuries, do not apply in 17th century China. It might be worth enquiring whether a change in the social position of women could have been at the back of it, fewer female babies being exposed, and respect for human life, that of women particularly, having increased in the 17th century. The writings of Li Li-weng (1611–80), some of which have been translated by Eberhard, provide a hint in this direction. He was certainly not concerned with equality of rights in the modern sense of the term, and he may not have been the first to write about the question, but he is certainly the best known of those who discussed the position of women and he earned many reproaches for doing so. Anyone who is pri- marily interested in the spiritual aspects of history, is perhaps too much attracted by the idea that his humanity is the result and expression of the spirit of Ming times; and that the great Emperor K'ang-hsi, with his exem- plary practical sense, unhesitatingly took over and developed this spiritual inheritance.

Increase in population

This phenomenon of the rapid increase in population since K'ang-hsi explains the importance attached from that time to the correlation be- tween political thought and the population. It was no longer possible to step aside seeking a self-sufficient life outside society, leaving everything to Nature and letting things grow as they would. Without a properly functioning government, whatever form it might take, the vast millions of China stood then and ever since face to face with the primitive danger of naked starvation. We may well ask how far Confucian political thought showed itself capable of coming to grips with this new task. This should help us to understand the last three hundred years of Chinese history and

the thought of those who took the lead therein. We may take one saying of Confucius (Lun-yü XII 7) as giving the heart of the matter; his disciple Tzu-kung had asked K'ung-tse about the nature of government and the order of importance of its tasks: "The Master said: 'Enough food, enough weapons, and the people's trust' *(Hsin,* truth and faith). Tzu-kung asked: 'When one cannot have everything and must give one up, which of the three should go first?'. The Master: 'Weapons'. Tzu-kung: 'But if one still cannot have the remaining two, which of them should go first?' The Master: 'Food; since we must all die one day. But if the people has no more confidence *(Hsin),* it can no longer stand' ".

Nowadays it is certainly easier to understand and take into account the interconnections between population, cultivable area, civilisation and spirit, and to heap reproaches and insults on the men of earlier ages who did not do so. No doubt there were many Confucianists before Li Hung-chang who so interpreted this sentence in the Lun-yü that they felt they could look down on the military, who bothered very little about feeding other people and overlooked the duty which K'ung-tse included in his answer about the connection between morality and food; indeed, there are other places in which he had often enough expressed himself on the interrelation between rights and duties. The gentry who were mostly Confucians, so little understood the new tasks that they themselves largely became impoverished during the 18th century. One other point must be noted; for a hundred years the West upset and hindered the development of China; its mercantilism was short-sighted, unchristian and selfish. The Emperor Ch'ien-lung's behaviour looks different when seen from this point of view.

K'ang-hsi was succeeded by his able son, Yung-cheng, who was certainly *Ch'ien-lung* rough and uncultivated, but substantially helped to make the dynasty's position firm. When he died young, his twenty-five-year-old son Ch'ien-lung came to the throne in 1736; sixty years later he voluntarily abdicated from a sense of piety to his grandfather's memory. Ch'ien-lung was born in the purple and everything seemed to go well with him. His tastes ran to poetry — he made a collection of 34,000 poems — painting, calligraphy, the collection of pictures and bronzes, building, horses and hunting. The Empire was in such good state when he ascended the throne that to begin with he hardly had to raise taxes. Then he conceived the desire to add the trophies of victory to his other collections. He did not indeed lead the

← "Studio in an Autumn Wood" by the monk Shang-jui dated 1729. The inscription says that the picture was painted in the style of T'ang Yin, one of the Four Great Masters of the Ming dynasty, 1470-1524. *Museum for Far Eastern Art, Cologne. (On paper 2 ft 7 inches by 1 ft 8 inches)*

armies himself, as his grandfather had done; that was the business of his generals. They were continually victorious and added to the empire all those outlying countries with which K'ang-hsi had had hard fights, and established the boundaries of China as they are today. The wars, conducted over huge distances and across great deserts, brought ruin to the finances, and that, in conjunction with the famine due to the increase in population, led to revolts; but yet China today owes to Ch'ien-lung all those lands which modern techniques may be able to make fruitful, and which may possibly be able to feed a population greater than the present 600 million. Ch'ien-lung treated the revolts against his successful and brilliant government with scorn. He too, as a good Confucianist of the 18th century, could only understand the saying in the Lun-yü in a one-sided way and attributed all that went wrong to the decline in morals. For that reason he appointed an Inquisition in 1773; that was just a hundred years after his grandfather's Sacred Edict and eighty years after his Edict of Toleration; he appointed a learned commission to catalogue and censor all the books in the imperial library. This catalogue which was concluded in 1782, was an immense philological and "moral-theological" achievement which no sinologue in the world can afford to neglect.

It includes all the officially permitted literature of the age, but makes us curious to know what was sacrificed to the censor's scissors, and why; for that would give us a sure basis for appreciating the spirit of the age, though it might often prove hardly possible to understand it. We are all indebted to L.C. Goodrich for his researches into this Inquisition, which was not only literary. The year 1773 marks the peripeteia in the life of the Emperor and the life of the Manchu dynasty. In 1793 the first important embassy, from England under Lord Macartney, came to establish diplomatic relations with Ch'ien-lung. We know from detailed records of the Embassy that everyone was impressed with the personal dignity of the eighty-two-year old Emperor, although he turned down all their requests. After that, Europe soon turned to the use of force, and it is very sad to record how the extremely kind and well-intentioned Emperor Tao-kuang (1821—50) had to pay for all the deficiencies which might have been avoided by timely reforms directing China's progress into new paths. After the Opium War of 1842 he was forced to sign the Treaty of Nanking, which gave the foreigners extra-territorial rights in China. After 1843, what had till then been the unimportant country town of Shanghai, swelled to a population of a million and became the greatest port in the Far East. Almost immediately after Tao-kuang's death, a dangerous revolt broke out in central China with the object of driving out the Manchus who were clearly no

longer able to control the situation. This rising, known as the T'ai-p'ing rebellion, lasted fourteen years and led to appalling destruction. The whole of Nanking and half Suchou were razed to the ground. Finally the rebellion was suppressed with the aid of a European expeditionary force. The Europeans were then only too glad to help the Manchu Emperors as a guarantee of Chinese impotence. Among other mad acts of the soldiery was the destruction of the Summer Palace, Yüan-ming-yüan, not far from Peking, which had been built a hundred years earlier by the French Jesuit Fathers for Ch'ien-lung in imitation of Versailles, a monument to the cosmopolitan spirit such as could not have been conceived before the 18th century.

The tragic story of China between 1842 and 1949, a cautionary tale of folly, selfishness and hypocrisy, is fresh in all our memories. Once again, the cleverest politicians felt, as they had felt before at the end of the Han and T'ang dynasties, that their hour had come to prove themselves saviours of the Empire. These were the generals who so gladly confused the last resort of politics with the first, and who paid very little attention to their first duty of seeing that the people were fed. So a new regime which saw this duty as the most imporant, was naturally successful, although its methods may have been hard. This regime moreover had hardly been in power for seven years when in 1956 it surprised even its friends with a programme one part of which had this very Chinese political conception: "Let there be flowers of every kind, and let all schools of thought wrestle with one another". How fast and how far this programme can be put into practice remains to be seen. But China would not be China if she did not use her greatest capital asset, the intelligence which she has cultivated for thousands of years, and if she does not recognise the claims of the spirit, whatsoever the form of society may be.

Naturally, the quantity of works of art preserved become much greater as we get nearer to the present time. Many books have been written about the Chinese ceramics of the last centuries alone, but only about ceramics. It is a great advance that we are now beginning to realise what the Japanese had known all along, that the 17th century was one of the greatest and most fruitful periods of Chinese painting. The painting of the 18th century has been neglected as 'late' and the painting of the 19th century has only attracted the attention of a few who realise that delightful surprises are hidden there. The impression is very understandable that it is not worth bothering about the most recent phases of Chinese art, since the sculpture, bronze, jade and lacquer of the 18th century so easily substitute quantity for quality and try, by piling on colours, inlays and

Porcelain vase of the type known as 'Graviata', with sprays engraved under the red background. On the base a blue reign mark of Ch'ien-lung, 1736-1796. *Museum of Far Eastern Art, Cologne (11 inches high)*

mixed techniques to drown the hopeless vacillations of uncertain taste. The T'ai-p'ing rebellion destroyed the last lacquer workshops which were mostly situated on the lower Yangtse and carried on the tradition of cut-lacquer. From then onwards the great Chinese talent for crafts- *Copies and fakes* manship seems to have been almost exclusively employed in making copies and fakes, though one must admit that their achievements in this line are altogether astonishing. We can however, hardly blame the crafts- men, since people only asked for "old" things, including pictures, and paid ever higher prices for them. No one was ever ready to appreciate it, if anyone did do something new. The developments of the last three hundred years are not very attractive and have not been satisfactorily studied. Here there is only room for a general sketch and a few characteristic illustrations. The Emperors K'ang-hsi was more interested in science than in art. He studied mathematics and natural history for hours on end with the learn- ed fathers whom the Jesuits sent to China. Father Verbiest for instance designed the instruments for an observatory for him in 1670, and had to make cannon too. The Emperor's practical bent also took in every sort of artistic craftsmanship, and his strong, sensible character made itself felt there also. As he would not allow the use of his reign name on the marks, most of the porcelain copied early Ming models, and vases were made on which the marks of Hsüan-te, Cheng-te etc were carefully reproduced, and if one only considers material and technique, they were superior to the originals. The same thing was happening in the lacquer workshops, so it is possible that we may one day discover that the very best plates and dishes with Yung-lo and Hsüan-te marks came from K'ang-hsi's workshops. The Emperor also commissioned the work of painters and colour print engravers, mostly to provide illustrations of his travels, or for books about agriculture or the cultivation of silk-worms. Wang Yüan-ch'i (1642—1715), a notable painter and man of learning, was summoned to Peking to become Censor and Chancellor of the Han-lin Academy; the Emperor entrusted him with the supervision of many scientific and artistic enter- prises, and with the education of his Manchu courtiers. The Emperor's own calligraphy commands respect; it too is an expression of his unclouded and assured personality. Occasionally he would honour the painters of his closer entourage with short inscriptions; most of these painters were Manchus of rank and high dignitaries such as Ho I and T'ang-tai who had studied with the Privy Councillor Wang Yüan-ch'i. T'ang-tai also gave lectures at court about painting and aesthetics, and these lectures have a particular interest for us as a case of a man of foreign origin who, with some success, penetrated the inner sanctum of Chinese aesthetic theory. We have to thank R. Goepper for a translation of this revealing book. However the greatest masters in the land were, for the most part, *Colour prints* reserved in their attitude to the court and remained loyal to the ideal of the independent artist.

Perhaps there have never been such lovely coloured woodcuts printed in China as those of the seventeenth century and in the reign of K'ang-hsi, and it may be that the reason why they are so good is that were made to serve a purpose, and not as ends in themselves. The colour prints had to reproduce paintings and also to provide simple suggestions of current motifs for the many practitioners and amateurs of painting. From about the year 1600 they were for the most part printed in Nanking. The notable man of letters Li Li-weng to whose book about women we have already referred (see page 204) took pleasure in printing a series of colour prints in his tiny garden in Nanking, which was "as large as a grain of mustard-seed", in the year 1679. He called them "The painting book of the mustard-seed garden" and these Chinese colourprints became famous throughout the world. There were also some sheets printed in Suchou about 1685 that were the first to reach Europe by a remarkably roundabout way. The German doctor E. Kaempfer who had accompanied a Dutch Embassy to Japan, acquired two dozen of these sheets there and brought them home in 1692. At the time they did not arouse any interest, but in the end the greater part of them reached the British Museum. These are undoubtedly first prints with their colour perfectly fresh; their delicate tones delight every lover of graphic art. The subjects remain in the framework of the known tradition; the sheet in the Hamburg Museum for arts and crafts, for instance, shows chrysanthemums and a pair of butterflies so that it clearly refers to the "Eastern Fence" poem of T'ao Yüan-ming who was PLATE ON PAGE 214 also called T'ao Ch'ien. To make this clear, a two-line poem is printed too:

Do not strive to rival the high renown of T'ao Ch'ien.
The Eastern Fence keeps you safe from the raw autumn wind.

Every successful piece of porcelain made in K'ang-hsi's reign is worthy to count as the high point of Chinese ceramics and of porcelain in general. PLATE ON PAGE 216 The plate in our illustration is a good example of the care taken in applying the colour. There are a great variety of casually scattered flowers. The blue is painted with cobalt under the glaze; the yellow, green and manganese are enamel colours baked on top of the glaze, and the iron red has been added in a separate final process, for up to the end of K'ang-hsi's reign no way had been found of making a red enamel. In the reign of his successor this was achieved by an alloy of gold.

Covered vase of bronze decorated with **many-coloured** layers of lacquer in which jewel-like landscape **scenes** have been cut. Ch'ien-lung reign mark on the base, 1736-1796. *Museum of Far Eastern Art, Cologne (11½ inches high)*

Yung-cheng did also appoint some artists as court painters as a mark of esteem, but he did not concern himself further with their work or their experiments, leaving them a completely free hand. This freedom was just what was needed for the arts, and those years before Ch'ien-lung started dictating his wishes, were a time of calm creative activity in painting. It is significant that many painters looked back for inspiration to T'ang Yin, the most sympathetic of the four Ming classical masters, and they found his quality of inner contentment congenial and aspired to attain it.

PLATE ON PAGE 218 Such a picture as Shang-jui's landscape, painted in 1729, probably gives a very accurate rendering of the composition of a picture by T'ang Yin, but the broader treatment of colour would prevent its ever being confused with the original. The motif of the gentleman of high rank who has retreated to a lonely hut to read his books, is a variation on an old and often painted theme, but if one compares such a picture with one by Wang Meng or PLATE ON PAGES 197 AND 200 Wen Cheng-ming, one feels the calm relaxed handling and the fond dwelling on every detail which prove that Shang-jui, a Buddhist monk withdrawn from the world, was a true painter. Such a feeling was characteristic of many of his contemporaries.

Ch'ien-lung was many-sided and impatient, and his ever changing desires left his entourage breathless. He fancied himself as a poet and spoilt many pictures by his mania for enriching them with inscriptions; one finds, for instance, twenty-one poems on a single picture by Tung Ch'i-ch'ang in his collection. The Emperor's own painting is passable, but he was no Hui-tsung. However, his collection of pictures and bronzes was much more extensive than that of his forerunner. It would seem that anyone who wished to ingratiate himself with the Emperor had only to bring a couple of picture scrolls along. They were uncritically accepted and immediately stamped with the imperial seal. No less than 195 different seals of this Emperor are known. Ch'ien-lung showed an exaggerated curiosity for technical tricks, not in painting alone, but for such things as clocks and fountains. The Jesuits had sent Castiglione, a painter of some distinction, to Peking where he became the Chinese Privy Councillor Lang Shih-ning. The Emperor expected him to produce overnight everything, including pictures of himself and of his horses. When these pictures, mostly in decidedly Rococo style, were ready, the Emperor would agree with his adviser on aesthetics, Tsou I-kuei, that they were works of very passable

Chung K'uei, the Driver-out of demons, by Chang Ta-ch'ien. The picture was painted in 1930 and has elements of a self-portrait. For a translation of the poem, see page 229. *Copy in a private collection. (On paper; 4 ft 11 inches by 23 inches)* →

226

craftsmanship but the heaviness of their shadows and the failure in "brushwork" did not entitle them to be classed as works of art. His desultory attitude to painting may not have done much harm, for most of the best painters of the 18th century kept increasingly away from the court and its passion for experiment. But the constant search for innovation and elaboration was dangerous for craftsmanship. Porcelain vases and other things of Ch'ien-lung's reign may generally have preserved unexceptionable shapes and have kept their gay colours and technical refinements within certain limits. But when one looks at such a specimen as the vase illustrated

PLATE ON PAGE 222 on page 235 on which flowers have been very painstakingly engraved under the glaze against a background of one colour, one begins to feel that one step more, and technical dexterity and handling would submerge the aesthetic intention. The products of the imperial lacquer works were also many-coloured and come close to the line which separates an *objet d'art* from a work of art. It was now the fashion to apply three layers of differ-

PLATE ON PAGE 225 ently coloured lacquer on top of one another and to carve therein jewel-like landscapes or battle-scenes. The scenes are now often framed in adaptations of European Rococo ornament, and inlays of coloured stones as well as mother-of-pearl are often used. But though the craftsmanship is undoubtedly sound, neither of these expedients add anything of deep aesthetic value.

Art at Ch'ien-lung's court was "nouveau riche" rather than enriched, and in this very different from that of Ming-huang or Hui-tsung. The sure taste of sound craftsmanship was brought perilously in question. Such tendencies got increasingly out of hand as the political and economic situation went from bad to worse after 1800, and the great of the land tried to hide their aesthetic poverty by sham grandeur and ostentation. Great quantities of porcelain were still produced at Ching-te-chen in the 19th and 20th centuries, but specimens that give undoubted pleasure became now as much the exception as they had once been the rule in the reign of K'ang-hsi. After 1800, painters were almost alone in maintaining the dignity of Chinese art. At first, even their best pictures had no greater merits than delicacy and sophistication. But after 1852, and more strongly after about 1880, there is a true sense of deep personal feeling. Their style is connected with that of the "individualists" of the 17th century, who had then recently been rediscovered. This painting is clearly an expression of disgust against the humiliations and cruelties of the surrounding world and the senselessly reactionary regime of the Empress Tz'u-hsi (1835–1908), a second Wu-hou.

Recent painting The reforms in education and examinations which were finally forced

228

through in 1905, made a break in a 2,000 year old cultural ideal, and marked the transition to the specialised modern world. The painters too became specialists, who no longer painted for pleasure or renown but in order to get paid. There are of course still lovers of the traditional form of painting, even under the completely new regime which is rightly proud of the old tradition and encourages painters in the "national style", even though it does also encourage other ways of painting more suitable for the masses. In 1930, for the first time China sent works by contemporary painters to Europe, indicating that she was prepared to take her place in the peaceful rivalries of the international world of art. Further exhibitions followed. In that same year 1930 a young man of talent painted Chung K'uei, the Driver-out of Demons, a subject which long ago brought fame to Wu Tao-tse. This painter, Chang Ta-ch'ien, (born in 1899) is the youngest of the Four Great Masters of the 20th century, if one may call them so. The others were Wu Ch'ang-chih (1844–1927), Ch'i Pai-shih (1863–1957) and Hsü Pei-hung (1894–1953). At the time of the exhibition he was only thirty years old, and it is very characteristic of China that Chang Ta-ch'ien had to pretend to be ten years older for his pictures to be thought worth show-PLATE ON PAGE 227 ing. It is also characteristic of China that excellent copies of his Chung K'uei were immediately made and became the beacon-light of a new conception. There are elements of a self-portrait in this Chung K'uei, and, something almost unknown in China before, there are one or two shadows and a clearly three-dimensional composition, both fruitful lessons from the modern world. But his concentration on the essential point, his bold shorthand, economy of means, and sure calligraphy are unchangeably Chinese. Chang Ta-ch'ien has forged a new link in the millenial history of an old tradition.

Perhaps the painter himself did not realise how far the simple, gay, four-line poem, which he wrote on the picture, carries a meaning far beyond its immediate context, and as far as words can do so, captures the essence of all Chinese art and civilisation:

> *Children see him, children laugh;*
> *Demons see him, demons fly;*
> *No man can paint the sage's portrait;*
> *But with the man of learning one can catch the devil.*

APPENDICES

TABLE OF THE MOST IMPORTANT PEOPLE AND EVENTS IN ART HISTORY

C = capital, F = family; -1524- means first, or last, certain date

2500	Neolithic culture:	Painted pottery: Yangshao-Panpo	
		Painted band pottery: Kansu	
2000		Rope- and mat-pottery: Hsiao-t'un	
		„ „ „ „ : S. E. China	
		Red pottery: Shansi	
		Black pottery: Lungshan	
		(Duration still uncertain)	
1800	HSIA dynasty; Shansi, still legendary		
1600	SHANG dynasty c. 1600-1027		
1500	*C:* Ao/Cheng-chou		
1300	*C:* "Yin"/Anyang		
1000	CHOU dynasty		Bronze and towns
	1027-250	Chou-kung c. 1020	Invention of writing
	C: P'ang near	Wu-wang	
	Ch'ang-an	c. 1027-1020	Royal inscriptions on sacred bronzes
		Ch'eng-wang	
		c. 1020-1000	
		K'ang-wang	
		c. 1000-980	
		Chao-wang	
		c. 980-964	
		Mu-wang c. 964-927	
		Kung-wang	Height of Chou power
		c. 927-912	
900			Peoples of steppe press southwards
		Li-wang 873-841	841 beginning of fixed chronology
800		Hsüan-wang 827-782	
		Yu-wang 781-772	
	C: Loyang (Lo-i) 770		704 Ch'u kingdom
700	Ch'un-ch'iu 722-484, time of the "Spring and Autumn Annals"	THE FIVE 'HEGEMONIES'	
		Huan of Ch'i 680-643	680-669 Aasarhaddon, treaty with Scythian king Partatua
		Wen of Chin 632-628	
		Hsiang of Sung 667-628	616 Medes drive the Scythians out of Persia (Ziwiye)
		Mu of Cin 627-620	
600		Chuang of Ch'u 613-590	606 Destruction of Niniveh

232

DYNASTIES	RULERS	THINKERS A. POETS	EVENTS	
Chan-kuo 481-205 Time of the 'Warring States'	Ho-lü of Wu 514-496			*500*
	Fu Ch'ai of Wu 496-473	K'ung-tse c. 500-480	486 Death of Buddha	
		Mo Ti c. 480-400 Meng-tse 372-289 Chuang-tse c. 370-300	c. 484-425 Herodotus	*400*
		Yang Chu 4th century	c. 346 Sarmatians cross the Don	
	Wei-wang of Ch'i 378-333	Lao-tse 4th century		
	Hsüan-wang of Ch'i 332-314	Shang Yang c. 360	336-323 Alexander the Great	
		Tsou Yen c. 330		
		Chü Yüan c. 300	c. 300 Kurgans at Pazyryk	*300*
		Hsün-tse c. 305-235	247 BC.-226 A.D. Parthian kingdom	
CH'IN dynasty 246-206 *C:* Hsien-yang near Ch'ang-an	Shih-huang-ti 246-210	Lü Pu-wei till 235	221 Unified State	
		Han Fei till 233	'Great Wall' rampart	
		Li Sse till 209/8		
HAN dynasty 206 B.C.-220 A.D. 'Western' Han, *C:* Ch'ang-an, till 25 A.D. *F:* Liu	Kao-tsu 202-195	Chia I 204-168	176 Mao-tun, khan of the Huns	*200*
	Wen-ti 195-157	Liu An till 122 Huai-nan-tse	163 Reign names, 'nien-hao', introduced	
	Wu-ti 140-87	Sse-ma Ch'ien c. 145-80	138-126 Chang Ch'ien's expedition to the Oxus	*100*
		Liu Hsin till 23	114 Silk road open till c. 120 A.D.	
		Liu Hsiang 77 B.C.-6 A.D.	108 Conquest of North Korea, *C:* Lolang	
	Wang Mang 6-25	Yang Hsiung 55 B.C.-18 A.D.	27 B.C.-14 A.D. Augustus	*0*
'Eastern' Han 25-220 A.D.		Wang Ch'ung 27-97		
C: Loyang	Ming-ti 58-75 Chang-ti 76-88	Pan Ku 32-92 Chang Heng 78-139	166 Syrian merchants at Loyang: Oc-eo find	*100*
		Cheng Hsüan 127-200	169 Huns cross the Volga	

DYNASTIES		RULERS	THINKERS a. POETS
200	LIU-CH'AO 220-589 the 6 dynasties of NANKING San-kuo, the 3 kingd.		
	Wu, C: NANKING 220-280	FOUNDERS: Sun Ch'uan 181-252	
	Shu, C: Ch'engtu 220-261	Liu Pei till 223	
	Wei, C: Loyang 220-265	Ts'ao Ts'ao 155-220	Ts'ao Chih 192-232
	Chin 265-420 F: Sse-ma, C: Loyang		Hsi K'ang 223-268
	'Western' Chin 265-316	Chao-Shih-lo 274-305	Lu Chi 261-303
300	'Eastern' Chin 317-420, C: NANKING	NORTH CHINA: Wei dynasty 386-550 T'o-pa peoples	Wei Shao c. 320 Hsieh An 320-385 Wang Hsi-chih 321-379 Pao-p'o-tse 4th century
		'North.' Wei 386-535 C: Ta-t'ung, till 452	T'ao Yüan-ming 365-427 Hsieh Ling-yün 385-433
400	'Liu'-Sung 420-477		Wei T'ai-wu 424-452	Pao Chao 421-465
	F: Liu, C: NANKING	C: Loyang, 452-535		Shen Yo 441-518 Hsieh T'iao 464-499
	Ch'i 479-501 F: Hsiao, C: NANKING		Fan Chen c. 450-515 Chang Hung c. 500
500			Hsieh Ho c. 500
	Liang 502-555	PARTITION:	Liang Wu-ti 502-549	
	F: Hsiao, C: NANKING	'Western' Wei 535-57 C: Ch'ang-an	Ch'i Wen hsüan 550-559	Hsiao I 506-554 Hsü Ling 507-583
		'Eastern' Wei 535-550 C: K'ai-feng	Ch'en Hou chu 583-589 (lived 553-604)	Yü Hsin 513-581 Yao Tsui c. 550-570
	Ch'en 557-589	'Northern' Chou 557-581		
	F: Ch'en, C: NANKING	C: Ch'ang-an 'Northern' Ch'i 550-577 C: Yeh (near Anyang)		
	SUI 589-618 F: Yang, C: Loyang, till 605		Wen-ti 589-605	

234

BUDDHISTS	PAINTERS	EVENTS	
			200
		226 East Roman merchants in Nanking	
Mou Yung c. 200	Ts'ao Pu-hsing c. 240	266-642 Sassanian rulers in Persia	
		272 Death of Mani	
		c. 200-427 C. of the Kokuryo nr T'ung-Kou; frescoes	
	Chin Ming-ti 299-335		300
		313 Korea free	
Tao-an 312-385		325 Entry into Buddhist mon.allowed	
Hui-yüan 334-416	Wang Hsi-chih 321-379	338 Oldest known Chinese bronze Buddha	
Tao-sheng c. 360-434	Tai K'uei till 395		
Seng-chou 441-484	Ku k'ai-chih c. 344-406	399-413 Fa-hsien in India	
	Tsung Ping 375-443	427 Pyöng-yang C. of Kokuryo	400
		428 1st embassy to Ceylon	
Hui-kuan till c. 443/7		446-452 Persecution of Buddhists in Wei	
	Ku Chün-chih c. 460	447 Advance of Wei to the West	
Tamo c. 460-520		451 Defeat of Attila	
Seng-chou 480-560	Lu T'an-wei c. 440-500	455 1st Sassanian embassy to China	
Hui-chiao 497-554	Chang Seng-yu c. 500-550	453-559 Tomb animals near Nanking	500
	Liang Yüan-ti 508-555	c. 470 Colossal Buddha at Yünkang	
		c. 530 Pagoda on the Sung-shan	
		530 Wen-hsüan anthology	
		551 Silkworms to Byzantium	
Ch-k'ai 531-597		556 Edition of classics in Ch'i	
Seng-ts'an c. 530-606		560 Persecution of Buddhists in Chou	
		c. 570 Reliefs on 'Ts'ao' tomb	

	DYNASTIES		RULERS	THINKERS a. POETS
600	*C:* Ch'ang-an from 605 T'ANG 618-906		Yang-ti 605-618	Sui Yang-ti 571-618 Li Chi 594-669
	F: Li, *C:* Ch'ang-an		T'ai-tsung 627-649 Kao-tsung 650-683 Wu-hou, lived 625-705	Yang Ch'iung, till 692 Meng Hao-jan 689-740 Wang Wei 699-759
700			Ming-huang 713-756 K'ai-yüan 713-741 T'ien-pao 742-756 Su-tsung 756-762	Li T'ai-po 701-762 Tu Fu 712-770 Lu Yü, till 804 Han Yü 768-824 Liu Tsung-yüan 773-819
800			Hui-tsung 874-889	Po Chü-i 772-846 Yüan Chen 779-831 Li Ho 790-816 Tu Mu 803-852 Li Shang-yin 813-858
900	WU-TAI 907-960 the five dynasties of north China: Hou-liang 907-823 *C:* K'ai-feng Hou-T'ang 923-936 *C:* Loyang Hou-Chin 936-947 *C:* Loyang Hou-Han 947-951 *C:* K'ai-feng Hou-Chou 951-960 *C:* K'ai-feng	NORTH CHINA: Liao (Ch'i-tan) 907-1125 *C:* Lin-huang SOUTH CHINA: Nan-T'ang 937-975 *C:* Nanking & other places	Li Yü 960-975	Li Fang 924-955 Li Yü 937-978 Lin Pu 967-1028

236

PAINTERS	BUDDHISTS	EVENTS	
Han-shan 577-654	Chan Tzu-ch'ien c. 580-620	552-621 Shotoku regent of Japan	600
Tao-hsüan 595-667		606-647 Harsha Gupta emperor at Kanauj	
Hsüan-tsang 602-664		630-645 Hsüan-tsang in India	
Hung-jen 601-674	Yen Li-pen, till 673	622 Hegira	
Shan-tao 612-681	Wei-ch'ih I-seng c. 690	642 Omar conquers Persia	
		645 Taikwa reform in Japan	
		668 Chinese master Korea	
		673-5 Colossal Buddha at Lungmen	
Hui-neng 638-713	Li Ssu-hsün 651-716	710-794 Nara capital of Japan	
Hsüan-chüeh 665-713	Li Chao-tao c. 670-730	725-1911 Han-lin Academy	700
Shen-hsiu 668-760		724-748 Shomu-tenno (died 756)	
I-hsing 683-727	Ts'ao Pa c. 720	756 Shosoin at Nara	
Chien-chen 688-763 (Kanshin)	Ch'en Hung 726	718-756 Yang Kuei-fei	
	Wu Tao-tse c. 690-760	751 Battle of Samarkand	
Ma-tsu, till 788	Wang Wei 699-759	781 Nestorian stele	
Hui-kuo 746-805	Chang Hsüan c. 750		
	Han Kan c. 750	768-814 Charlemagne	800
Hui-hai 749-814		786-809 Harun al Rashid	
Tsung-mi 780-841	Chou Fang c. 780-810	774-835 Kobo-daishi, at Ch'ang-an in 803	
Huang-po, till 850	Pien Luan c. 800	838-883 Palace of Samarra, excavations	
Lin-chi, till 867	Li Chen c. 800	843/5 Great persecution of Buddhists	
	Kuan-hsiu 832-912	847 Chang Yen-yuan's history of painting	
	Sun Wei c. 880	879 Massacre at Canton	
Tung-shan 807-869		880-884 Emperor and painters at Ch'eng-tu	
Hsüan-sha 831-908		845-903 Michizane, Chancellor of Japan	
	Ching Hao c. 900		
	Kuan T'ung c. 907-923		900
Pu-tai, till 916			
	Li Ch'eng c. 916-967		
Yün-men, till 966	Ku Hung-chung c. 943-960		
	Huang Ch'üan c. 900-965	918 Tomb of Wang Chien	
	Hsu Hsi c. 961-975	923-933 Kiang-ning pagoda, reliefs	
	Chou Wen-chü c. 961-975		

DYNASTIES AND EMPERORS	POETS AND WRITERS	PAINTERS	EVENTS
SUNG dyn. 960-1279 'Norther' Sung, *F*. Chao, *C*. K'ai-feng, till 1126		Tung Yüan c. 970 Chü jan c. 980	
T'ai-tsu 960-975		Huang Chü-ts'ai 933-c. 1000	Academy in K'ai-feng
T'ai-tsung 975-998	Hsüeh-tou 980-1052	Fan K'uan 950-1026	
1000	Fan Chung-yen 989-1052	Yen Wen-kuei 967-1044	
Chen-tsung 998-1022		Kao K'o-ming c. 1008-1053	
	Ou-yang Hsiu 1007-1072	Hsü Tao-ning c. 1000-1050	
Hsi-Hsia dynasty 1032-1223, *C*. Ning-hsia	Chou Tun-i 1017-1073	Liao Hsing-tsung 1016-1055	1031 Ch'ing-ling frescoes
	Wang An-shih 1021-1073	Kuo Hsi c. 1020-1090	
Jen-tsung 1023-1085	Shen Kua 1030-1093		
	Su Tung-p'o 1036-1101	Su Tung-p'o 1036-1101 Li Lung-mien 1049-1106	1087 'Western Garden'
	Huang Shan-ku 1045-1105	Mi Fu 1052-1107	
Shen-tsung 1063-1085	Ch'ao Pu-chih 1053-1109	Wang Shen -1087-	1096-99 1st Crusade
1100	Yüan-wu 1063-1135	Li T'ang c. 1050-1130	1099 et seq. Frescoes at Pai-sha
Hui-tsung 1101-1126	Li Ch'ing-chao 1081-1141	Hui-tsung 1082-1126	1108 Flooding of Chu-lu-hsien; finds
'Hsüan-ho' 1119-1125		Li An-chung c. 1090-1160	
'Souther' Sung, *C*. Hang-chou 1126-1379		Li Ti 12th cent.	110 Death of Li Chieh, architect
	Cheng Ch'iao 1104-1162	Su Han-ch'en -1125-62-	
Kao-tsung 1127-1163	Yang Wan-li 1124-1206	Chao Po-chü 1120-1182	
Chin dynasty 1125-1239	Lu Yu 1125-1210	Yen Tz'u-p'ing c. 1160	
KIN, *C*. K'ai-feng		Ma Ho-chih c. 1130-1180	
Hsiao-tsung 1163-1189	Chu Hsi 1130-1200	Liang K'ai c. 1140-1210	1191 Eisai introduces Zen into Japan

238

DYNASTIES AND EMPERORS	POETS AND WRITERS	PAINTERS	EVENTS	
Kuang-tsung 1190-1195		Ma Yuan c. 1150-1230		
Chin Chang-tsung 1190-1208		Hsia Kuei c. 1200-1233		*1200*
Ning-tsung 1195-1225		Ch'en Chü-chung c. 1205	1206-27 Jenghis Khan	
		Li Sung-nien c. 1180-1220	1215-50 Emperor Frederick 11	
Li-tsung 1225-1264		Li Sung c. 1160-1240	1233 Ch'i-hsi-tsien palace	
	Hui-k'ai 1185-1260	Ma Lin c. 1190-1260	1241 Battle of Liegnitz	
Tu-tsung 1265-1278	Chou Mi 1232-1308 Wen T'ien-hsiang 1236-1283	Mu-shi c. 1220-1290 Ch'ien Hsüan 1235-c. 1300		
YÜAN dynastiy 1278-1368 Mongols, C: Peking Kublai born 1260, 1248-1294	Chao Meng-fu 1254-1322	Li K'an 1245-1320 Kao K'o-kung 1248-1310 Chao Meng-fu 1254-1322	1254-1323 Marco Polo	
	Yang Tsai 1271-1323	Huang Kung-wang 1269-1354	1263-1323 Ming-pen, abbot of T'ien- mu-shan	*1300*
Jen-tsung 1311-1320	Ma Tuan-lin 1275-1322 Yang Yü 1285-1361	Ts'ao Chih-po 1272-1355 Wu Chen 1280-1354 Sheng Mou -1313-1362-		
MING dynasty 1368-1644 F: Chu, C: Nanking, till 1409	Ni Tsan 1301-1374 Sung Lien 1310-1381 Yang Chi c. 1373	Ni Tsan 1301-1374 Wang Meng c. 1308-1385 Hsü Pen -1345-1397-	1303-77 Ibn Batuta c. 1380 Chang Ch'eng, lacquer-painter	
Hung-wu 1368-1398	Ts'ao Tsung-i c. 1320-1410	Wang Mien 1355-1407		
Chien-wen 1398-1402 Yung-lo 1403-1424 C: Peking 1409-1644	Chang Yü 1333-1385 Kao Ch'i 1336-1376 Fang Hsiao-ju 1357-1402	Wang Fu 1362-1416 Hsia Ch'ang 1388-1470 Tu Ch'iung 1396-1476	1405 Death of Tamurlane Great Wall, Temple of Heaven and other buildings	*1400*
Hsüan-te 1426-1435		Hsüan-te 1398-1435 Pien Wen-chin -1413-28- Tai Wen-chin -1430-50-		
Cheng-t'ung 1436-1449		Liu Chüeh 1410-1472	c. 1440 Yang Hsün, lacquer-painter	

239

DYNASTIES AND EMPERORS	POETS AND WRITERS	PAINTERS	EVENTS
		Yao Shou 1423-95	
Ching-t'ai 1450-56	Shen Chou 1427-1509	Shen Chou 1427-1509	Cloisonné in fashion
T'ien-shun 1457-64		Shih Chung 1437-1517	
Ch'eng-hua 1465-87		Kuo Hsü 1456-1526-	1468/9 Sesshu in China
		Wu Wei 1458-1508	
Hung-chih 1488-1505		Chang Lu c.1464-1538	
		Chiang Sung c. 1500	
		Lü Chi c. 1500	
_1500_		Lin Liang c. 1500	
		Hsü Lin c. 1514	
			1471-1528 Dürer
Cheng-te 1506-21	T'ang Yin 1470-1524	T'ang Yin 1470-1524	1483-1520 Raphael
	Wang Yang-ming 1472-1528	Wen Cheng-ming 1470-1559	1517 Portuguese land at Canton
		Hsieh Shih-ch'en 1487-1559-	1519-56 Emperor Charles V
	Li Meng-yang 1472-1529	Lu Chih 1495-1576	1534 Jesuit order founded
Chia-ching 1522-66	Ho Ching-ming 1484-1522	Ch'iu Ying c. 1500-1550	1506-52 Francis Xavier, in Japan in 1549
	Wu Ch'eng-en c. 1501-1580	Wang Ku-hsiang 1501-1568	
	Chia-ching 1507-1566	Ch'ien Ku 1508-1579-	
	Li P'an-lung 1514-1570		
	Hsü Wei 1521-93	Hsü Wei 1521-93	
		Sung Hsü 1523-1605-	
	Wang Shih-chen 1526-93	Hsiang Yüan-pien 1525-1602-	
Lung-ch'ing 1567-72	Li Chih 1527-1602	Sun K'o-hung 1532-1610	c. 1570 Huang Ch'eng, lacquer painter
		Ch'en Chia-yen 1539-1625	
		Mi Wan-chung till 1628	
		Chang Fu 1546-1631-	
		Mo Shih-lung 1567-1601-	
_1600_ Wan-li 1573-1619	T'ang Hsien-tzu 1556-1617	Tung Ch'i-ch'ang 1555-1636	1552-1610 Ricci
		Ch'en Chi-ju 1558-1639	
		Li Jih-hua 1565-1635	
		Tseng Ch'ing 1568-1650	
		Yüan Shang-t'ung 1570-1661	

240

DYNASTIES AND EMPERORS	POETS AND WRITERS	PAINTERS	EVENTS
T'ien-ch'i 1621-27		Chang Hung 1580-1660	'Lacquer emperor' T'ien-ch'i
Ch'ung-chen 1628-43		Lan Ying 1585-1659-	-1621- Shao K'o-wang, lacquer-painter
	Chin Sheng-t'an till 1661	Yün Hsiang 1586-1655	
		Wang To 1592-1652	
		Ts'ui Tzu-chung c. 1595-1644	1591-1666 A. Schall
CH'ING dynasty 1644-1911		Wang Shih-min 1582-1680	1592-1673 Yin-yüan, in Japan in 1654
Manchu, C: Peking		Yang Wen-ts'ung 1597-1645	
		Wang Chien 1598-1677	
Shun-chih 1644-62		Shao Mi -1626-62-	1633 Paintingbook of 'The Hall of the ten bamboos'
		Ch'en Hung-shou 1599-1652	
K'ang-hsi 1662-1722	Wu Wei-yeh 1609-1671	Fu Shan 1602-83 Ch'eng Cheng-k'uei 1603-76-	
	Li Li-weng 1611-1679-	Ch'eng Sui 1610-93-	
	Chou Liang-kung 1612-72	Hung-jen 1610-63 Ch'a Shih-piao 1615-98	
	Ku Yen-wu 1613-82	Kung Hsien 1616/7-89 Shih-ch'i 1617 to b. 1680 Mei Ch'ing 1623-97 Pa-ta shan-jen 1626-1705- Shih-t'ao 1630-1707- Wu Li 1631-1718	
		Wang Hui 1632-1717	1671 Sacred Edict
		Wang Wu 1632-90	1679 Paintingbook of *1700* the 'Mustard-seed garden' 1683 Ts'ang Yin-hsüan, director of Ching-te-chen 1689 Treaty of Nertschinsk
	Wang Shih-chen 1634-1711	Yün Shou-p'ing 1633-90	
	P'u Sung-ling 1640-1715	Wang Yüan-ch'i 1642-1715	1692 Edict of Toleration
		Huang Ting 1660-1736 T'ang-tai c. 1660-1749- Kao Ch'i-p'ei 1662-1734	

DYNASTIES AND EMPERORS	POETS AND WRITERS	PAINTERS	EVENTS
Yung-cheng 1723-36		Shang-jui -1704-29-	
		Chiang T'ing-hsi 1669-1732	
		Chu Lun-han 1680-1760	
		Shen Ch'üan 1681-1759-	
		Hua Yen 1682-1756-	
		Chang Tsung-ts'ang 1686-1756	
Ch'ien-lung 1736-96		Tsou I-kuei 1686-1772	1688-1768 Castiglione (Lang Shih-ning), painter
		Huang Shen 1687-1756-	
		Chin Nung 1687-1764	
		Li Shan -1711-56-	
	Cheng Pan-ch'iao 1693-1765	Cheng Hsieh 1693-1765	1736-c. 53 T'ang Ying, director of Ching-te-chen
		Yüan Yao -1742-68-	
	Wu Ching-tzu 1701-54	Tung Pang-ta 1699-1769	1740-7 Summer Palace, Yüan-ming-yüan, built
	Yüan Mei 1716-98	Ch'ien-lung 1711-99	
	Ts'ao Hsieh-ch'in c. 1719-63	Ch'ien Wei-ch'eng 1720-72	
	Tai Chen 1723-77	Wang Ch'en 1720-97	1793 Macartney in Jehol
		Lo P'ing 1733-99	
		Fang Hsün 1736-99	
		P'an Kung-shou 1741-94	
		Hsi Kang 1746-1803	
Chia-ch'ing 1796-1820		Chai Ta-k'un -1773-1804	
		Wang Hsüeh-hao 1754-1804	
1800	Shen Fu 1763-1808-	Chu Ang-chih c. 1760-1840	
	Chang Wen-t'ao 1764-1814	Ch'ien Tu 1763-1884	
	Juan Yüan 1764-1849	Kai Ch'i 1774-1829	
		Huang Chün 1775-1850	
	T'u Cho 1781-1828	T'u Cho 1781-1878	
Tao-kuang 1821-50		Chang Hsiang-ho 1785-1862	1840/2 Opium war
		Ch'eng T'ing-lu 1797-1857	

242

EMPERORS AND GOVERNMENTS	POETS AND WRITERS	PAINTERS	EVENTS	
Hsien-feng 1851-61	Ho Shao-chi 1800-74	Tai Hsi 1801-60	1850-64 T'ai-ping rebellion	
		Fei Tan-hsü 1802-1850	1857-60 Lorcha war; Summer Palace, Yüan-ming-yüan, destroyed	
		Ch'in Ping-wen 1803-73		
		T'ang Lu-ming 1804-74		
	Tseng Kuo-fan 1811-72	Wu Yün 1811-83		
		Chang Chih-wan 1811-97		
		Jen Hsiung 1820-60		
	Li Hung Chang 1820-1901	Hu Yüan 1823-86		
		P'eng Yü-lin 1824-90		
		Ch'in Tzu-yung 1825-84		
		Hsü-ku 1825-96		
T'ung-chih 1861-75		Chao Chih-ch'ien 1829-84		
		Chü Lien 1829-1904		
Tz'u-hsi, lived 1835-1908		Ku Yun 1835-96	1891 Trans-Siberian railway begun	
		Wu Ta-ch'eng 1835-1902	1894-5 Japanese war	
Kuang-hsu 1875-1908		Wu T'ao 1840-95		
		Jen Po-nien 1840-96		
Hsüan-ts'ung 1908-1911		Wu Ch'ang-shih 1844-1927	1900-1 Boxer rising	*1900*
		Lu Kuei 1851-1920	1904/5 Russo-Japanese war	
			1905 Abolition of class. examinations	
MIN-KUO, republic sincel 1912, C: Peking	K'ang Yu-wei 1856-1928	Lin Shu 1852-1924	1911 Abolition of the Han-lin	
		Ni Pao-t'ien 1855-1919		
		Ts'eng Hsi 1861-1930		
		Ch'i Pai-shih 1863-1957		
		Huang Pin hung 1864-1955	1917 Entry into world war	
	Sun Yat-sen 1866-1925	Li Mei-an 1866-1920		
	Lo Chen-yü 1866-1940	Wang I-t'ing 1867-1938		
	Ts'ai Yuan-p'ei 1867-1940	Wang Lo-nien 1870-1925		
	Liang Ch'i-ch'ao 1873-1929	Ch'en Heng-ko 1875-1923		

POETS AND WRITERS	PAINTERS	EVENTS
Wang Kuo-wei 1877-1927	Chin Ch'eng 1876-1926	1922 Excavations at Yangshao
	Ch'en Pan-t'ing b. 1876	
Lu Hsün 1881-1936	Kao Chien-fu 1880-1952	
	Yeh Kung-cho, born 1880	1930 Lüttich exhibition
	Ch'en Shu-jen, born 1884	
	Chang Yü-kuang, born 1885	
	P'u Ju, born 1887	
C: Nanking 1937-37 Ch'iang Kai-shek born 1888	Kao Ch'i-feng 1888-1933	
	Yü Fei-an, born 1889	
Hu Shih born 1891	Hu Pei-heng, born 1892	
Kuo Mo-jo born 1891	Hsü Pei-hung 1894-1953	1933 Paris exhibition
Mao Tse-tung born 1893	Huang Shao-chiang c. 1895-c. 1940	
Lin Yü-t'ang born 1895	Liu Hai-su, born 1894	1943 Berlin exhibition
	Ch'en Chih-fu, born 1896	
	P'an T'ien-shou, b. 1897	
Mao Tun born 1898	Lin Feng-mien, b. 1898	
	Chang Ta-ch'ien, born 1899	1937-45 Japanese invasion
	Chang Shu-ch'i, b. 1900	
	Chao Shao-ang, b. 1904	
	Wang Hsüeh-t'ao, born 1904	
	Chiang Chao-ho, born 1904	1949 People's Republic
	Wu Ching-t'ing, b. 1904	
Ting Ling born 1906	Fu Pao-shih, born 1905	
	Li K'o-jan, born 1907	1956 'Hundred Flowers' progr.
	Yeh Ch'ien-yü, born 1907	
	Wu Tso-jen, born 1908	
	Hsieh Shi-liu, born 1908	
	T'ang Yün, born 1910	
	Chan An-chih, born 1910	
	Li Hsiung-ts'ai, b. 1915	
	Chao Wu-chi, born 1920 (Zou Wou-ki)	
	Tseng Yu-ho, born 1923	
	Fang Tseng-hsien, born 1931	

BIBLIOGRAPHY

Those works especially have been selected which have bibliographies useful for further study, and recent books and those cited in the text.

W. R. B. Acker, Some T'ang and Pre-T'ang texts on Chinese Painting. Leiden 1954

F. W. Baller, The Sacred Edict. Shanghai 1917

S. Beale, Buddhist records of the Western World (Hsüan-tsang). London 1906

J. and A. H. Burling, Chinese art. 3rd Edition. New York 1955 (Bibl.)

Cheng Te-k'un, Archaeology in China. Vol. I Cambridge 1959 (Bibl.)

Cheng Te-k'un, The Ya Lü-kuei. OA 1956, p. 9 ff

Cheng Te-k'un, Ch'ih-yu, the God of War in Han Art. OA 1958, p. 45 ff

W. Cohn, Chinese Painting. 2 Ed. London 1951 (Bibl.)

E. Consten, Das Alte China. Stuttgart 1958. (Lit.)

G. Debon and W. Speiser, Chinesische Geisteswelt. Baden-Baden 1957 (Bibl.)

T. Dexel, Die Formen chinesischer Keramik. Tübingen 1955 (Lit.)

H. Dumoulin, Zen. Bern 1959 (Bibl.)

A. and W. Eberhard, Die Mode der Han- und Chin-Zeit. Antwerp 1946

W. Eberhard, Chinas Geschichte. Berne 1948

W. Eberhard, Li Li-weng. Die volkommene Frau. OZ 1939/40

W. Eberhard, Das Tobareich in Nordchina. Leiden 1949

V. Elisseeff, Preface, Tchang Ta-ts'ien. Paris 1956

E. Erkes, Zu Ch'ü Yüan's T'ien-wen. MS 1941

M. Feddersen, Chinesisches Kunstgewerbe. 2nd Edition. Brunswick 1955 (Bibl.)

E. Feifel - K. Nagasawa, Geschichte der chinesischen Literatur. Peking 1945

O. Fischer, Die Kunst Indiens, Chinas und Japans. Berlin 1928 (Lit.)

O. Franke, Geschichte des Chinesischen Reiches. I - V. Berlin 1930-52 (Lit.)

A. Godard, Le tresor de Ziwiye. Harlem 1950

R. H. Goepper, T'ang-tai (Museum für Völkerkunde) Munich 1956

G. S. G. M. Gompertz, Chinese Celadon Wares. London 1958 (Lit.)

L. C. Goodrich, The literary Inquisition of Ch'ien-lung. Baltimore 1935

B. Gray and J. B. Vincent, Buddhist Cave Painting at Tun Huang. London 1959

B. Gyllensvärd, T'ang Gold and Silver. BMFEA 1957. S. 1—230.

C. Hentze, Le symbolisme des oiseaux dans la Chine ancienne. Sinologica, Basle 1957 and 58 (Lit.)

A. Herrmann, Historical and Commercial Atlas of China. Cambridge Mass. 1935

A. Hoffmann, Die Lieder des Li Yü. Cologne 1950

W. B. Honey, The Ceramic Art of China and other Countries of the Far East. London 1945 (Bibl.)

Hsü Po, Pai-sha sung-mu (Sung tombs in Pai-sha, Honan, with frescoes). Pekin 1957
Hui-hsien fa-chüeh pao-kao (Report of Excavations at Hui-shien). Vol. I. Pekin 1956

H. Ikeuchi, T'ung-kou (Frescoes). Tokyo 1938

K. Jettmar, The Altai before the Turks. BMFEA 1951, S. 135—223 (Bibl.)

A. Jakubovskij and M. M. Djakonov, Zivopis drevnego Pjandzikenta (Painting in ancient Piandjikent), Moscow 1954 (Lit.)

B. Karlgren, Yin and Chou in Chinese Bronzes BMFEA 1937 et seq. (Bibl.)

B. Karlgren, A Catalogue of the Chinese Bronzes in the Alfred F. Pillsbury Collection, Minneapolis. London 1952 (Bibl.)

E. S. Kirby, Wirtschafts- und Sozialgeschichte Chinas. Munich 1955 (Lit.)

S. V. Kiselev, Drevnjaja Istorija Juznoj Sibiri (Ancient History of Southern Siberia) Moscow 1951 (Lit.)

H. Köster, Symbolik des chinesischen Universismus. Stuttgart 1958 (Lit.)

F. Koyama - D. Seckel, Keramic des Orients. Würzburg 1959 (Bibl.)

O. Kümmel, Die Kunst Chinas, Japans und Koreas. Wildpark-Potsdam 1929 (Bibl.)

O. Kümmel, Biographien in Thieme-Beckers Künstlerlexikon. (Bibl.)

H. Kuntze-Shroff, Leben und Dichtungen des Ni Tsan. (Diss. Cologne) Bombay 1959

K. S. Latourette, The Chinese; their History and Culture. 3rd Edition. New York 1956 (Bibl.)

Li Chi, The beginnings of Chinese Civilisation. Seattle 1957

D. Lion-Goldschmidt, Les poteries et porcelaines chinoises. Paris 1957 (Bibl.)

M. Loehr, Chinese Bronze Age Weapons. London 1956 (Bibl.)

H. Lützeler, Weltgeschichte der Kunst. Gütersloh 1959 (Bibl.)

E. Minns, The Art of the Northern Nomads. (British Academy) London 1942 (Bibl.)

S. Mizuno, Chinese Stone Sculpture. Tokyo 1950 (Bibl.)

A. Moortgat, Tammuz; der Unsterblichkeitsglaube in der Altorientalischen Kunst. Berlin 1949

J. A. Pope, Chinese Porcelain from the Ardebil Shrine. Washington 1956 (Lit.)

S. Reinach, La représentation du galop. Paris 1925

T. T. Rice, Die Skythen. Cologne 1957 (Lit.)

S. Rokkaku, Toyo shikko-shi (Account of Far East Lacquer Painting) Tokyo 1932

S. I. Rudenko, Kultura naselenija gornogo Altaja v Skifskoe vremja (Civilisation in the Atai mountains in Scythian times) Moscow 1953

A. Salmony, Archaic Chinese Jades from the Edward and Louise B. Sonnenschein Collection.

G. F. Sayer, T'ao Ya, or Pottery Refinements. London 1959

D. Seckel, Buddhistische Kunst Ostasiens. Stuttgart 1957 (Bibl.)
Sekai bijutsu zenshu (World history of Art; China: Vols. 2, 7, 8, 14, 20) Tokyo 1950—52 (Bibl.)
Sekai Toji zenshu (Ceramic Art of the World; China: Vols. 9—12, contributions by F. Koyama and others) Tokyo 1955

T. Shabad, Chinas neues Gesicht. Berlin 1957

Shang Ch'ien-tsu, Ch' ang-sha ch'u-t'u Ch'u ch'i

ch'i t'u-lu (lacquer of the Ch'u kingdom dug up in Ch'ang-sha) Shanghai 1955
Shou-hsien Ts'ai-hou-mu ch'u-t'u i-wu (Tomb of Marquis Ts'ai in Shou-hsien, 5th century B.C.) Peking 1956

L. Sickman - A. Soper, The Art and Architecture of China. Harmondsworth 1956 (Lit.)

O. Siren, Kinas Konst under tre Artusenden. Stockholm 1942 (Lit.)

O. Siren, Chinese Painting. London 1956—58 (Bibl.)

W. Speiser, Die Kunst Ostasiens. Berlin 1946

W. Speiser, Vorderasiatische Kunst. Berlin 1952 (Lit.)

W. Speiser, Meisterwerke chinesischer Malerei. Berlin 1958 (Bibl.)

W. Speiser, Chinesische und japanische Malerei. Berlin 1959 (Lit.)

M. Sullivan, Chinese Art in the Twentieth Century. London 1959 (Lit.)

K. M. Swoboda, In den Jahren 1950—1956 erschienene Werke zur Kunst Ostasiens. Kunstgeschichtliche Anzeigen. Graz-Vienna 1957.

J. Tamura and Y. Kobayashi, Tombs and Mural Paintings of Ch'ing-ling. Kyoto 1953

N. N. Terechova. Pogrebal'nye konstruckcii epochi Chan v Kitae (Construction of the Han tombs in China). Sovetskaja Archeologija 1959, Vo. 3

A. Waley, Wu Ch'eng-en; Monkey's Pilgrimage. Zürich 1947. Wang-tu han-mu pi-hua (Wall painting in Han tombs in Wang-tu) Peking 1955

M. Weber, Konfuzianismus und Taoismus. Gesammelte Aufsätze zur Religionssoziologie. I,S. pp. 276—536. Tübingen 1920 (Lit.)

W. Willetts, Chinese Art. Harmondsworth 1958 (Lit.)

Yang Yu-hsun, La Calligraphie Chinoise. Paris 1937

E. v. Zach, Die chinesische Anthologie. Cambridge, Mass. 1958

E. Zürcher, The Buddhist Conquest of China.

PERIODICALS AND ABBREVIATIONS

AA   Artibus Asiae. Leipzig; Ascona, 1925 ff.

AAs   Arts Asiatiques. Paris, 1954 ff.

ACASA   Archives of the Chinese Art Society of America. New York, 1945 ff.

AM   Asia Major. Leipzig; London, 1924 ff.

AO   Ars Orientalis. Washington, 1954 ff.

BEA   Bulletin of Eastern Art. Tokyo, 1940–43.

BK   Bijutsu Kenkyu. Tokyo, 1932 ff.

BMFEA   Bulletin of the Museum of Far Eastern Antiquities. Stockholm, 1929 ff.

CP   China Pictorial. Peking, 1954 ff.

FECB   Far Eastern Ceramic Bulletin. Cambridge, Mass., 1948 ff.

HJAS   Harvard Journal of Asiatic Studies, Cambridge, Mass., 1948 ff.

Hōun. Tokyo, 1932 ff.

ILN   Illustrated London News. London, 1842 ff.

JOS   Journal of Oriental Studies. Honkong, 1954 ff.

Kokka. Tokyo, 1888 ff.

KKHP   K'ao-ku hsüeh-pao. Peking, 1946 ff.

KKTH   K'ao-ku t'ung-hsün; seit 1959 K'ao-ku (Archäologie) Peking, 1955 ff.

MN   Monumenta Nipponica. Tokyo, 1938 ff.

MS   Monumenta Serica. Peiping; Tokyo, 1935 ff.

OA   Oriental Art. London, 1948 ff.

OE   Oriens Extremus. Hamburg, 1954 ff.

OZ   Ostasiatische Zeitschrift. Berlin, 1912–1943.

PC   People's China. Peking, 1950 ff.

RAA   Revue des arts asiatiques. Paris, 1924–1942.

TOCS   Transactions of the Oriental Ceramic Society. London, 1921 ff.

Tōji (Keramik). Tokyo, 1929 ff.

Wen-wu (Kultur); früher: Wen-wu ts'an-k'ao tsu-liao. Peking, 1950 ff.

YB   Yamato Bunka. Osaka, 1951 ff.

GLOSSARY OF THE MORE IMPORTANT TECHNICAL TERMS

Amida
Popular Japanese form of the Sanskrit word Amithāba, one of the great Buddhas called "the Buddha of measureless light". He reigns in "the paradise of the west", the "pure land" (ch'ing t'u), where of his grace he teaches the faithful about Nirvana.

Ao
Capital in middle Shang times, about 1500-1300 B.C., near Cheng-chou, the modern capital of the province of Honan. Excavations are in progress.

Bodhidharma
Chinese Tamo, Japanese Daruma, son of a prince from Ceylon who came to China in about 500 A.D. as a missionary of the Yoga School, and is revered as the first patriarch of the Meditative School.

Bodhisattva
Chinese P'u-sa, Japanese Bosatsu, the "one who has insight" in the sense of the Buddhist Nirvana. Either a man ready to become Buddha who voluntarily remains in this existence on earth, or the incarnation of a Buddha on earth; for instance Kuan-yin, Japanese Kwannon, as the incarnation of the Buddha Amida. Usually represented in princely garments in contrast to the simplicity of the Buddha of "enlightenment".

Buddha
Anyone who has become "enlightened" by insight into the unreality of all existence, this being in Buddhist conception the final state of all being. The historical Gautama Buddha, who died in 486 B.C. is only one of many Buddhas, and the first to appear in our world cycle.

Chin-ts'un
"Gold town' near Loyang, the capital of the Chou dynasty from 770-250 B.C. In this neighbourhood, and that of nearby Ch'ing-chou, the cemeteries of the capital have yielded magnificent finds.
Lit.: W. Ch. White. Tombs of Old Lo-yang. Shanghai 1934. B. Karlgren. Notes on a Kin-ts'un Album, BMFEA 1938, S. 65-81.

Cicada
This is often a mistranslation for "cricket".

Crickets, in this differing from cicadas, lay their eggs in the earth, live as larvae in the earth and, according to Dr. Krieger's observations, generally bore their way backwards up to the surface, and turn into insects. In China, for three thousand years, they have been the symbol of the cycle of life, death and resurrection.

Chronology
The way of reckoning by reign names (*nien-hao*) was introduced in 163 B.C. and from the Ming dynasty onwards no change was made in the reign name during an emperor's rule. Besides this, there is the way of reckoning by 60 cyclic signs which are continually repeated, and so have no precise meaning without some further datum such as the *nien-hao*.

"Eastern Fence"
The most famous of T'ao Yüan-ming's (see page 109 drinking songs. The "Eastern Fence" motif is popular in the art and crafts of the Far East; chrysanthemums are the most important element and there is often also a bamboo paling and perhaps a couple of birds or butterflies.

"Eight views"
The views are those of the rivers Hsiao and Hsiang which flow into Tung-t'ing lake in Hunan. Ever since the 11th century they have provided classical themes for landscape painters; mountain village in light mist; returning sailing boat with distant shore; autumn moon over Tung-t'ing lake; rainy night on the Hsiao and Hsiang; evening bells of a distant temple; sunset over a fishing village; the flight of wild geese over flat sandbanks; snow at evening over the river.

Iconography
Kohn and Feddersen give the best Bibliography.

Individualists
Group of painters born between 1610 and 1630 whose lives were shaped by the experience of the revolution of 1644. The expression dates back to the writings of Shih-t'ao, one of the best of these painters. The first mention in European literature is by Teng Ku in O.Z. 1931, p. 162.

248

Kharezm
The table land between Persia and the Aral sea. Excavations at Toprak-Kala and other places.
Lit.: S. P. Tolstov, Auf den Spuren der Altchoresmischen Kultur. Berlin 1953.

Kokuryō
North Korean dynasty founded in the 1st century B.C.; from 200 to 427 A.D. centred on the middle Yalu (excavations at T'ung-kou) and from 427-688 A.D. on the modern Pyöngyang.

Kuan-yin
Japanese Kwannon, translation of the Sanskrit Avalokitesvara, the Bodhisattva who "listens to the cries of men". Considered to be the incarnation of Amida Buddha, whose image appears as an emblem in the ornament of the hair. Frequently, but not always, represented as a woman.

Lohan
Japanese Rakan, Sanskrit Rahat. A man who has gained insight into Nirvana by his own, usually ascetic, efforts. Lohans begin to be portrayed in China at the beginning of the 9th century.

Lo-lang
Opposite Pyöngyang in Korea, headquarters of Chinese power from 108 B.C. to 313 A.D. Fruitful excavations still in progress; the Pompeii of China.

Lotus
Symbol of Buddhism: as its flowers unfold in stainless purity out of the slime of the pond, so may creation rise from the "dust of the world" to an insight into the pure non-existence of Nirvana.

Loyang
One of the most important of the ancient capitals and art centres. In older maps it is generally called Honan-fu, the capital of the province of Honan.

Lu-shan
A little range of high hills in central China, north west of Poyang lake. Famed for its waterfall, Li T'ai-po's poem, and the many famous men, including Tao Yüan-ming and Chou Tun-i, who lived there as hermits.

Makimono
Japanese expression for handscroll, Chinese *ch'üan*, often many yards of silk or paper joined together for pictures and text. It could be unrolled from one hand to another like a Roman "volumen".

Meditative school
Chinese *Ch'an*, Japanese *Zen*. A Buddhist school developed in China in the 6th century which provided many themes for painters.

Ming-t'ang
"Hall of light" apparently a royal hall of audience which was probably also used for ancestor worship and was introduced by the Chou about 1000 B.C. We have no certain information about their construction or significance.

Names
In China, the family name comes first and is as a rule monosyllabic. But there are dissyllabic family names such as Sse-ma and Ou-yang. Anybody could add as many "brush" (*hao*) names as he liked, for instance "T'ao Ch'ien" is, T'ao Yüan-ming. The Emperors were given names after death symbolising their qualities and achievements. Thus the Emperor Hsüan-Tsung was given the name of Ming-huang "Radiant Majesty".

Pagoda
Chinese *T'a*. This tower-shaped form of building was developed in China to take the place of the Indian *Stupa* as a Buddhist reliquary or tomb monument.

Pai-sha
Place some hundred miles southwest of Loyang, in which frescoed tombs dating from 1099 A.D. onwards, have recently been discovered.

Pan-po
More correctly Pan-p'o, place four miles East of Hsian-fu. This is the most important Neolithic settlement yet found, probably dating from the second half of the 3rd millenium B.C. It has been covered with a glass roof and turned into a museum.

Pazyryk
Place in the Altai mountains where tumuli (kurgans) dating from about 300 B.C. have been discovered. Eight of them have so far been excavated.
Lit.: S. I. Rudenko and T. T. Rice.

Southern School of painting
An invention of Tung Ch'i-ch'ang and his circle, who traced their aesthetic descent back into the 8th century.

Sutra

Chinese *Ching*, the books of Buddhist doctrine.

T'ao-t'ieh

This word, which is first found in the 4th century B.C. can neither be explained nor given an etymological derivation. It seems to comprise all the symbols of the earth demon of Shang times, consisting of snakes, tigers, buffallo's and ram's horns, cowrie-shells, elephants etc, often abbreviated into a mask.

Temmoku

Popular Japanese expression for *T'ien-mu*, the "eye of heaven" mountain not far from Hangchou. A beloved place of pilgrimage for Japanese Zen monks. The word then came to mean a type of Sung ceramics which are still regarded as the most suitable for the tea ceremony, which is a Zen development.

Wu school

School of painting named after the ancient district around Suchou. The Four Great Masters of the Ming dynasty and their successors, who wished to keep their independence from the Imperial court in Peking, worked there about the year 1500.

Yin

Late phase of the Shang dynasty, from about 1300 to 1027 B.C. The town and district round the modern Anyang were then called Yin.

Yin-yang

The ideogram in Shang inscriptions signifies darkness and light. It expressed the polarity between the dark, restful, female substance and the bright, moving, male spirit. The *Yin-yang* school of speculative philosophy has a wide following, and the symbol of a circle divided into light and dark halves is a common art motif.

Zen

Popular Japanese form of the Chinese *Ch'an* denoting the meditative school of Buddhism.

INDEX

254